The *Art* of Educational Leadership

Balancing Performance and Accountability

Fenwick W. English

The University of North Carolina at Chapel Hill

SAGE Publications
Los Angeles • London • New Delhi • Singapore

For information:

Sage Publications, Inc.
2455 Teller Road
Thousand Oaks, California 91320
E-mail: order@sagepub.com

Sage Publications Ltd.
1 Oliver's Yard
55 City Road
London EC1Y 1SP
United Kingdom

Sage Publications India Pvt. Ltd.
B 1/I 1 Mohan Cooperative Industrial Area
Mathura Road, New Delhi 110 044
India

Sage Publications Asia-Pacific Pte. Ltd.
33 Pekin Street #02-01
Far East Square
Singapore 048763

Printed in the United States of America

Library of Congress Cataloging-in-Publication Data

English, Fenwick W.
The art of educational leadership: Balancing performance and accountability/Fenwick W. English.
    p. cm.
Includes bibliographical references and index.
ISBN 978-1-4129-5741-0 (cloth)
ISBN 978-0-7619-2811-9 (pbk.)
   1. Educational leadership—United States.
  2. School management and organization—United States. I. Title.

LB2805.E638 2008
371.2—dc22   2007014720

This book is printed on acid-free paper.

07   08   09   10   11   10 9 8 7 6 5 4 3 2 1

Acquisitions Editor:	Diane McDaniel
Editorial Assistant:	Ashley Plummer
Production Editor:	Diane S. Foster
Copy Editor:	Tina Hardy
Typesetter:	C&M Digitals (P) Ltd.
Proofreader:	Emily Rose
Cover Designer:	Candice Harman
Marketing Manager:	Nichole M. Angress

The *Art* of Educational Leadership

Larry E. Frase (1945–2005)

This volume is dedicated to the memory of friendship, professional work tasks shared, and a zest for life of my times with Larry Eugene Frase. Larry came into my life at Arizona State University in 1970 where we were doctoral students together. He was the youngest doctorate awarded at that time, at the tender age of 26. He was idealistic, energetic, focused, and open to new ideas and practices. I soon learned he had a wonderful sense of humor and we struck up a long-lasting friendship and professional relationship over the next 30-plus years. I followed his career as he became an assistant superintendent on Long Island and later superintendent in the Catalina Foothills of Tucson. Later, he joined the faculty of the College of Education at San Diego State University in California where he attained the rank of full professor in 1 year's time. He wrote prodigiously and read extensively. He was a dedicated teacher. He brought not only a sense of realism from the field into his classroom and scholarship, but a deep love for profound ideas. One of his beloved research areas was with the concept of flow and he developed a friendship with Mihaly Csikszentmihalyi, its creator. He reported that research at the University Council for Educational Administration and the American Education Research Association.

My wife and I traveled with Larry and his lovely wife, Maria, in Prague and the Danube River, Portugal and the Douro River, and New Zealand. There were stops along the way for local cheese and wine and to learn about the countryside, the people, and what was important to them. Larry was always a student and he enjoyed lively conversation, libation, and good times. Those are already sorely missed. Such friends do not come along in very great numbers in a person's existence. I feel fortunate to have spent some time on this road called life with Larry Eugene Frase. I am the richer for it. He leaves behind friends everywhere, grateful students, and a loving wife who miss his presence more than they can express. I think Larry would have liked this book. He's certainly in it in many ways.

Contents

Preface ❖

This volume argues that for educational leadership as a field of professional studies to advance intellectually and practically in the 21st century, a better balance between the science and art of leading must emerge. Science alone will not improve practice unless and until it is also concerned with "artful performance." That involves reconnecting to the humanities (drama, literature, history, philosophy) in order to reconsider what Eugenie Samier (2005) has so poignantly described as "individual agency" (p. 24). Unless people matter, leaders can't matter, at least leaders that are human. So I reject Lakomski's (2005) assertion that notions of leadership are mostly "folk psychology" (p. 73) and are not real. While I agree that leadership is socially constructed and linguistically dependent within a culture, I think history will show that leaders matter a lot. The idea that leadership just can't be defined adequately and so doubts are raised about it existing at all (although admitting it is a construct) is because notions of leadership cannot be objectively examined outside of the perspectives in which they function. There's no way we can stand outside a social construct without being contained within it. Definitions end up being synonyms and correlative instead of predictive and "objective." This is the heart of Jacques Derrida's (1967) concept of *différance*. As part of the volume's position that reconnecting to the humanities instead of continuing to be dependent on the social sciences, particularly management science, is critical to restoring a capacity to lead morally, the re-insertion of forms of life writing as viable texts in the preparation of educational leaders is advocated and illustrated. The last topic of the book is a foray into the debate regarding national leadership standards and a deconstruction of some of the proposals being advanced from various perspectives. Current national standards are lopsidedly pushing an agenda that is reductionistic and paradoxically antipractice because it is devoid of any indications of artful performance. Instead, the national standards are replete with the jargon of total quality management and the gospel of efficiency, a familiar and unproductive vein that has been overmined for many years and offers very little promise for improving the practice of educational leadership

How to Use This Book

The professor and student who are going to use this book as part of a formal graduate preparation program may proceed along two lines. The first is the keeping of a personal journal of reflective writing. Critical practice involves learning how to engage in serious and sustained examination of practices and the underlying assumptions and theories that support them. The questions at the end of each chapter are designed as a jumping off point to begin this process. Students should not be constrained by them, however. There are many questions that could be asked at the end of every chapter. A good exemplar of a personal journal and critical practice is Deborah Meier's (1995) *The Power of Their Ideas: Lessons for America From a Small School in Harlem.*

The inclusion of definitions of terms of key concepts will serve as a way to clarify what is meant in class and in personal discussions. There are 102 such definitions included in the volume.

Finally, this volume makes use of films/video as classroom pedagogical tools. I have used all of them in my graduate classes in educational leadership at the University of Kentucky, Iowa State University, and currently at the University of North Carolina at Chapel Hill. The use of film is a powerful way to teach leadership. It is unsurpassed as a vehicle to illustrate the interaction between context, culture, decisions, and outcomes. While one can read about leadership theory in written texts, film involves more than cognition because it also brings into immediate play the psychology of leadership and the connection between emotion, drama, and decision-related situational content (see English & Steffy, 1997, pp. 107–108; Trier, 2001). While traditional written texts can present or discuss nearly all of the elements contained in film, the written form requires linearity (left to right on horizontal lines) and hence sequence in such a presentation. The "discourse of print media" (see Cotter, 2003) contains its own logic embedded in linguistic conventions. Although film is also sequential and linear in a different way than written text, it is able to show situations at many levels simultaneously and engage the student in a wider range of intellectual/emotional responses. This distinctive aspect of film means that it is a "supersaturated form(s) of information and present(s) [both] further opportunity and difficulty in analysis" (Collier & Collier, 1986, p. 176).

The use of film in teaching educational leadership offers a healthy counterbalance to the dominant traditions of viewing leadership exclusively via the social sciences. For professors who are not adequately schooled in the humanities, there may be some reluctance to venture into this alternative perspective. But I maintain that discussions regarding morality, social justice, and equity cannot be adequately taught or learned without involving the emotional side of human existence. And the social science approach works to systematically eliminate human emotion as an inherently unpredictable and destabilizing influence in understanding human interaction. It is often something to be eliminated in research designs approaching leadership because of its difficulty in being measured and its elusive nature in creating subjectivities hard to control. Yet, how can social movement be understood unless one comes to grips with the human emotion that is necessary to sustain it? Social movements may be born in libraries (I think here of Marx toiling away on *Capital* in the reading room of the British Museum; see Wheen, 1999, p. 166), but they are implemented in the day-to-day interactions of humans in the streets and arenas of power far removed from reading rooms and academia. Written text alone, whether books or case studies, is not adequate to teach leadership. The use of film offers the opportunity of emotional context. It adds the power to leadership preparation, which is the crucible of learning about leading in context.

I offer here the Ghandian notion of *ahimsa,* the kind of creative power that leads to constructive and nonaggressive action, which leads to social change. Gandhi called it "soul force" because

. . . it is independent of pecuniary or material assistance, usable by all men, women and children, applicable to all human relationships. It is to violence and to all tyranny and injustice what light is to darkness, one of the world's great principles which no power on earth can wipe out. (Iyer, 1973, p. 184)

Clemens and Wolff (1999) said it best: " . . . leadership is not solely about practice and technique. It also depends on the much more complex qualities of insight, compassion, moral perception, values, and emotional balance"(p. xv). If we are serious about teaching morality, social justice, and equity in a program preparing educational leaders, we must augment our teaching with pedagogical approaches that include human emotion as an integral part of the equation of changing schools within the existing social order. I proffer film as one such pedagogy to accomplish that purpose.

It is my hope and my intent to redirect the teaching of educational leadership by regrounding it on different axes. The social sciences have all but petered out in telling us anything new or different about leadership. Leadership studies must move beyond the sciences and recognize that effective leading is about drama and performance— artistry! Artistry involves the whole human, not simply the head, but the heart. Human action contains vision, emotion, and belief embodied in artful performance. So let us begin the journey.

Fenwick W. English
R. Wendell Eaves Senior Distinguished Professor of Educational Leadership
School of Education
The University of North Carolina at Chapel Hill

References

Clemens, J., & Wolff, M. (1999). *Movies to manage by: Lessons in leadership from great films.* Chicago: NTC/ Contemporary Publishing Group.

Collier, J., & Collier, M. (1986). *Visual anthropology: Photography as a method.* Albuquerque: University of New Mexico Press.

Cotter, C. (2003). Discourse and media. In D. Sciffrin, D. Tannen, & H. Hamilton (Eds.), *The handbook of discourse analysis* (pp. 416–436). Malden, MA: Blackwell.

Derrida, J. (1967). *Of grammatology* (G. C. Spivak, Trans.). Baltimore: Johns Hopkins University Press.

English, F., & Steffy, B. (1997, February). Using film to teach leadership in educational administration. *Educational Administration Quarterly, 33*(1), 107–115.

Iyer, R. (1973). *The moral and political thought of Mahatma Gandhi.* New York: Oxford University Press.

Lakomski, G. (2005). *Managing without leadership: Towards a theory of organizational functioning.* Amsterdam: Elsevier.

Meier, D. (1995). *The power of their ideas: Lessons for America from a small school in Harlem.* Boston: Beacon.

Samier, E. (2005). Toward public administration as a humanities discipline: A humanistic manifesto. *Haluskultuur, 6,* 6–59.

Trier, J. (2001). The cinematic representation of the personal and professional lives of teachers. *Teacher Education Quarterly, 28*(3), 127–142.

Wheen, F. (1999). *Karl Marx: A life.* New York: Norton.

Acknowledgments ❖

If there is a starting point for this book, it perhaps began with a paper I gave at Division A of the American Educational Research Association (AERA) in Atlanta, Georgia, in 1993. There, for the first time, I was able to break up the landscape of educational administration into typologies and begin the process of examining the field by stepping outside it. For me, the intellectual geography began to become differentiated in a more novel way than I had previously been able to conceptualize it. The rupture, if it can be called that, was prompted by a lot of reading in poststructuralism and postmodernism. One year later, my book, *Theory in Educational Administration,* published by HarperCollins and now out of print, was released.

Much of this book is firmly rooted in that work, with some sections repeated in various chapters where I believed them to remain relevant to the discussion at hand. Chapter 7 is largely drawn from a piece titled "Understanding Leadership in Education: Life Writing and Its Possibilities," which was published in 2006 in a special issue of the *British Journal of Educational Administration and History* edited by Peter Ribbins. Chapter 8 was largely, but not exclusively, drawn from an invited lecture I gave at the National Council of Professors of Educational Administration (NCPEA) Summit Meeting in Washington, DC, in 2005 titled "Educational Leadership for Sale: Social Justice, the ISLLC Standards, and the Corporate Assault on Public Schools."

This piece was subsequently condensed and reworked and a smaller section was published in the August 2006 *Educational Administration Quarterly* titled "The Unintended Consequences of a Standardized Knowledge Base in Advancing Educational Leadership Preparation." Other selected sections came from my article titled "Cookie-Cutter Leaders for Cookie-Cutter Schools: The Teleology of Standardization and the De-Legitimization of the University in Educational Leadership Preparation," which appeared in *Leadership and Policy Analysis* of March 2003.

Figure 3.4 is used with permission of Rowman and Littlefield and appeared in my chapter in the 2002 NCPEA Yearbook titled "The Fateful Turn: Understanding the Discursive Practice of Educational Administration," edited by George Perreault and Fred C. Lunenburg.

The section on film discussed in the Preface was part of an earlier paper given at the 2004 University Council of Educational Administration (UCEA) Conference in Kansas City titled "Developing Contextual and Theoretical Understanding of Leadership Through Film: Inserting the Emotional Component of Leadership Context to Prepare Future Educational Administrators to Be Active for Social Justice and Equity in the Schools."

I am extremely fortunate to have the privilege of knowing so many colleagues at different universities who have enriched my life with their friendship and conversation over many years at UCEA, AERA, and NCPEA. Many will never know how they have influenced me, if only to give me pause to reconsider a position I had taken or to offer support at times when my perspective was at odds with the mainstream. Dissent always has a price and those special colleagues who took time to offer their moral support, even when they did not agree with me, are indeed precious. I want to thank all of my colleagues at the University of North Carolina (UNC) at Chapel Hill who have had to put up with me in so many faculty meetings and office conversations: Catherine Marshall, Kathleen Brown, Frank Brown, Linda Tillman, Bill Malloy, Stan Schainker, Neil Shipman, and Jim Veitch. I think our program at UNC–Chapel Hill is so very special in the way that so much diversity remains productive and positive. I also want to thank two deans who supported and encouraged me at Chapel Hill whom I also consider colleagues: Madeleine Grumet and Tom James.

At the national level I have to acknowledge all of my colleagues who also listened to my sometimes impassioned voice who served on the UCEA Executive Committee over many years, beginning with the executive director, Michelle Young. Michelle's leadership and her unusual sensitivity to dissent are especially appreciated by this author.

My Executive Committee colleagues have provided me with some of the most intense and far-reaching discussions about important issues in the field: Gail Furman, Maria Luisa Gonzalez, Gary Crow, Fran Kochan, Margaret Grogan, Steve Jacobson, Jay Scribner, Richard Andrews, George Petersen, Michael Dantley, Jim Scheurich, James Korschoreck, Alan Shoho, and Fergus O'Sullivan. Other professional colleagues whose friendship and support have been critical to me were Charles Russo, Ira Bogotch, Joann Klinker, Catherine Lugg, Juanita Garcia, Ted Creighton, Duncan Waite, Jeff Brooks, Floyd Beachum, Martha McCarthy, Carol Mullen, Judy Alston, Gary Anderson, Rose Papalewis, John Hoyle, Joann Barbour, Carolyn Downey, William Kritsonis, William Poston, Jr., Helen Sobehart, Connie Moss, Bob Furman, Rick McCowan, John Schuh, Walt Gmelch, Jerry Gilley, Carolyn Shields, Donald Hackman, Eugenie Samier, Peter Ribbins, Jackie Blount, Cheryl Bolton, and Khaula Murtadha.

There are so many more that have touched me through the years that there is not space to list them all. My apologies if any not cited feel slighted in anyway. I acknowledge my many doctoral students over the years who have taught me so much while I was mentoring them: Stan Landis, Fred McCoy, Karen Casto, Jerry Sasson, Jay Kemen, Martha McClure, Sandy Kestner, Craig Nikolai, Linda Chappel, Lorraine Tuck, Sherry Stout Stewart, Urmila Deva Dasi, John Heath, Mark Minskey, Anita Alpenfels, Frank Creech, Fara Zimmerman, Parry Graham, and John Tharp.

At last I offer a note to my colleague, wife, and very gentle critic, Betty Steffy. Her sense of balance, good humor, professionalism, and common sense have been important in providing me the anchor and a safe harbor from which to venture forth from time to time and do battle for change.

The Leadership Challenge

This chapter deals with the most famous dichotomies that have historically been part of the field of educational leadership, such as whether leadership is a science or an art, or whether there is a difference between leadership and management. It focuses on leadership as performance because practice is the art of leadership. It presents brief portraits of four leaders who began inauspiciously but acquired the habits and skills of leadership over time, stressing that even while leadership may be distributed over more than one person in an organization, the criticality of individual "human agency" cannot be underrated in importance in preparing for leadership roles in schools.

Leadership is both a science and an art. The science is easier to teach and to measure. It's the stuff in graduate school lectures, textbooks, most research papers, and the state's competency exam to be passed for licensure. The art of leadership, however, involves performance. It is anchored in practice. It has to be modeled, observed, and carefully constructed, and it must pass the test of credibility in real schooling situations.

This book is about the art of leadership. The art of leadership is anchored to the central moral questions of life around which your very being is enveloped. First and foremost it's about you, who you are, what you value, matters of means and ends, and what you believe to be good and true. Indeed the "art" has been called by Fullan (2002) "the spiritual domain" or "the spiritual voice" by Dantley and Rogers (2001). Your relationship with others is critical. For example, are teachers, students, and schools means to your ends? Or, are you the means to their ends? Are all of you means to society's ends? And who determines what those ends might be?

In a study of an empowering elementary school principal, Keyes, Hanley-Maxwell, and Capper (1999) examined the life of an educational leader who indicated she was a "spiritual leader" (p. 222). First, the principal exclaimed, "Spirituality has nothing to do with organized religion" (p. 222). Rather, it consists of "what people believe about the human spirit and the kinds of values that they have for people" (p. 222). This elementary principal affirmed that her spirituality was about her ability to render decisions about a human being's individual dignity and value.

These issues are not the stuff of stodgy philosophers wandering the ancient streets of Athens as sometimes represented in the dreaded philosophy/foundational courses so abhorred by the practical types who want to engineer better education and "get on" with improving schools. Rather, all human interactions, large and small, are embedded in networks of narratives and values, some of which are conscious and many of which are not. Transactions in these human networks have been called "social capital," and in one study by Flora Ida Ortiz (2001) of three Latina superintendents, they were important factors in determining "the success of superintendents and school districts" (p. 82).

The first question to be broached in a study of the art of educational leadership, which is also the most important and enduring, is about you and it's about your being a leader. Do you really have what it takes to do this job? Let's try and give some perspective to this central question.

Leaders and Leadership Are Universal in the Human Experience

Humans are social creatures. They band together, form networks, and engage in communal activities for survival, procreation, and recreation. Commonalties in language, beliefs, and customs produce culture that is the cradle of tribes, societies, and nations. Throughout the ages some humans step forward with their peers while others do not. Some humans command respect because they possess unusual physical or mental abilities or insight, demonstrate prowess with finding food, engage in common defense against danger, demonstrate language facility or thought, heal the sick, or perform religious rituals deemed essential to align themselves with the gods or God. This ubiquitous and nearly universal process is part and parcel of all human socialization, whether in primitive or advanced societies.

The great community organizer and public radical of the 20th century, Saul Alinsky (1909–1972), understood that for the people to build an organization that could accomplish something, the organizers had to find out who were the community's true leaders. Alinsky (1969) called these persons "native" or "indigenous leaders" (p. 64). They were the actual representatives of the people. Alinsky sharply disagreed that "indigenous leaders" were those usually found in the local Rotary Club or Chamber of Commerce. "Real community leaders" were of the people and these were not the ones to get selected by "conventional social do-gooders" (p. 67). In contrast to a local business person, every community had "many little natural leaders who possess a following of twenty or thirty people" (p. 72). These little "natural leaders" may not be "complete leaders," because their leadership depended on how their individual skills were apprised by those who looked up to them. These "partial leaders" are in all communities. They are everywhere as they always have been throughout the ages. Alinsky used this analysis to debunk the common myth that there was no leadership in the rank and file.

If you think about "partial leadership," it is likely that you have experienced at least some form of it in your life. Somewhere in your past people looked to you for what you thought or did. It may have been narrowly expressed, but undoubtedly you noticed it.

If it had not been a positive experience in some way, you would most likely not be pursuing school leadership now.

Partial leadership roles must be perceived as sensitive to gender, culture, and community. For example, Collins (1990) proffers that one of the cultural expectations working within the African American community is that there are "othermothers." These are women "who assist blood mothers by sharing mothering responsibilities," and that this tradition has "been central to the institution of black motherhood" (p. 119). This strong orientation to sharing in the job of raising children is a "natural" place to demonstrate one's "partial leadership" abilities (see the following biographical portrait on Ida Wells-Barnett for an example of an African American woman who moved from partial leadership as a schoolteacher protesting the conditions in which Negro children were being educated in Memphis, Tennessee, to a national leader in the antilynching movement in the United States). Murtadha and Larson (1999) posit that "the leadership narratives of African-American women are strikingly rooted in anti-institutionalism, rational resistance, and sense of urgency, and deep spirituality" (p. 4).

BIOGRAPHY BOX 1.1

Ida Wells-Barnett (1862–1931)

"Iola" Protests Against Lynching; Fired for Criticizing the Inadequacies of Negro Schools in Memphis

She was a fiery and feisty opponent of the inadequate education for Negroes and founded societies opposed to lynching. The daughter of slave parents, Ida grew up in Holly Springs, Mississippi. While the end of the Civil War brought freedom, she lost much of her family to a yellow fever epidemic. At the age of 14, she became the family's breadwinner by lying about her age (she claimed she was 18) and becoming a schoolteacher at the salary of 25 dollars per month. She pursued her education at Fisk University. Like Mohandas Gandhi in South Africa, Ms. Wells-Barnett was forcibly removed from the white-only section on a train. The incident occurred on the Chesapeake and Ohio Railroad. However, unlike Gandhi, Ms. Wells-Barnett sued the railroad and won her case, only to have the decision of the circuit court reversed by the Tennessee Supreme Court in 1887.

Ms. Wells-Barnett wrote under the pen name "Iola" and worked for better schools for Negro children. Because of her criticism of the inadequacies Negro children were suffering, she lost her job as a schoolteacher in Memphis when the school board did not renew her contract in 1891.

In 1892, an incident occurred that changed her life. Three men, who were friends of hers, were lynched in Memphis. She took to the press to denounce the increased competition and was murdered for this reason. The newspaper offices were subsequently destroyed by angry white mobs.

(Continued)

(Continued)

> Ms. Wells-Barnett began a journey of protesting against lynching in Eastern cities, founding antilynching societies and lecturing in Great Britain against racial segregation. She married an African American attorney in Chicago in 1895 and wrote *A Red Record,* a history of 3 years of lynching in the South.
>
> She was a member of a group that met with President McKinley to protest the lynching of a Negro postmaster in South Carolina in 1898. After the race riots in East Saint Louis in 1918, Ms. Wells-Barnett traveled there and assisted Negro victims of the mobs in finding legal aid. Shortly thereafter, she tried to warn the people of Chicago of incendiary conditions in a letter to the *Chicago Tribune* that went unheeded. Within weeks a disastrous race riot occurred.
>
> She was a colleague of W. E. B. De Bois and was a participant in the founding of the National Association for the Advancement of Colored People (NAACP) in 1910. She worked tirelessly for women to acquire the right to vote. This courageous, outspoken daughter of slave parents did not attain world acclaim as in the case of Gandhi or Churchill, but her leadership grew from conviction and her efforts brought about gradual improvements. Her path reveals a move from partial leadership to that of complete leader. In the end, Ms. Wells-Barnett was even disappointed in the NAACP because she believed it was not assertive enough on issues impacting the Negro people (Flexner, 1971, pp. 565–567).

Pursuing Graduate Study to Become the "Complete Leader"

There is a difference in the indigenous "partial leadership" roles in everyday communal life and the role of a school administrator in a formal organization such as a school or school district. In the position of a school principal or superintendent, you have to become the "complete leader," at least insofar as the activities of schools and districts interface with the larger communities in which they are located. As illustrated in Figure 1.1, becoming a "complete leader" results from formal academic study, an internship in a real educational setting to enable you to try out new skills in an actual school or district, and your own continued personal and professional growth. This process is dynamic and unique to every student.

The road to becoming a "complete leader" in an educational organization is the prime purpose of your graduate course of studies. Becoming a complete leader involves a study of what is believed to be the "field," that is, the boundaries in which professional practice is defined and carried out (see Murphy, 2006). Formal academic study should also involve an internship experience. In this experience, you will be placed in a school or school district and be mentored by a seasoned school administrator. Many university programs structure this experience so that the full breadth of school administration is encountered. In this way, the candidate gets to try out the skills and knowledge acquired in the university classroom. Becoming a complete leader means acquiring the skills of leading teachers, parents, students, and other educators toward goals that are important to accomplish. In this process, a leader constructs his or her "self" as a public

❖ **Figure 1.1**   From Partial Leader to Complete Leader in Educational
           Administration

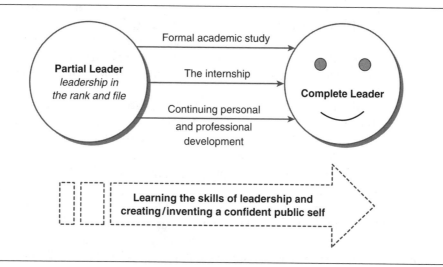

persona, something that all leaders do with great care. Sometimes this has been called
"the mask of command" (Keegan, 1987). It isn't a mask for a party where a person is
hiding behind a fake image. Rather, the "mask of command" represents that part of a
leader he or she chooses to make public. All leaders have a private self that they choose
not to share for a variety of reasons. What is shared or not is determined by the leader
and the situation. Constructing a mask is about presenting the "real you" but not necessarily "all of the real you" in the act of leading people. There is nothing phony about
it because what you choose to show is real.

Leadership Is an Art Because It
Involves a Purposive Construction of Self

Leadership is involved with the construction of a public self, which includes a public
face. In this respect it isn't "natural" although it may appear to be so to others and to
observers. The exposure of that face to a group of people is a form of an exhibition.
This public exhibition moves into a performance when it is employed as a means to
persuade others of the value of a belief and/or action directed toward some kind of
goal. A goal is simply a desired state of affairs. Your physician, minister, yoga teacher,
or tennis coach have all constructed a public face in which they have attempted to
influence you. When physicians used to make house calls, how well a doctor "performed" on a visit to a sick patient was referred to as his or her "bedside manner." Some
doctors were much better at it than others (Klass, 1987). Since performance involves
the interaction of your public face with others, it is a form of acting.

We rarely think of ourselves as actors in teaching, counseling, or coaching, but we
are performing within a role that is prescribed by our culture and by the agencies/
organizations for which we work. A job description or a job advertisement is simply

the delineation of a role. Whereas an actor "plays" a role and pretends to have the background and skills necessary to do it, our roles involve the acquisition of specific values, skills, and experiences and are sketched out in career ladders within the agencies and organizations where we work. But we engage in a public performance, not before theater audiences, but before our colleagues, parents, students, and citizens. But make no mistake about it, we are performing. Our performance involves "the art" of leadership, so leadership can be described in application as "artful performance" (Maxcy, 1995, p. 169).

As Elliot Eisner (2003) of Stanford University was describing the purpose of education, he was also describing what leaders do when he said, "The ultimate aim of education is to enable individuals to become the architects of their own education and through that process to continually reinvent themselves" (p. B4). As we shall see as we examine the lives of leaders, the process of being a leader involves a consistent reinvention of self, especially in the wake of major defeats. Politicians are perhaps the best models in this respect. Think of Richard Nixon, who spent a life reinventing himself. Even after Watergate and his resignation as President, he reinvented himself as an elder statesman. Jimmy Carter did the same thing after enjoying a rather mediocre tenure as President. He reinvented himself and won the Noble Peace Prize in the process. Eisner comments further about the importance of the arts:

> The arts are among the resources through which individuals recreate themselves. The work of art is a process that culminates in a new art form. That art form is the re-creation of the individual . . . the arts contribute to the development of human consciousness. . . . (p. B4)

On the matter of whether leaders are born or "made," perhaps it is most accurate to say that leaders have to be born like everyone else, but everything after birth is cultural and interactive (or "made"). Portraits of leaders from biographies, autobiographies, diaries, journals, and other sources reveal that leaders engage in a purposive construction of self, that is, they actively engage in creating the persona they want to become and what they perceive potential followers want and need them to be. The evidence also suggests that when a particular persona (or "mask") is no longer effective or accepted, they engage in altering their persona to comply with the new requirements, dynamics, and situations involved with leadership (see Barber, 1985; Caro, 2002; Deal & Peterson, 1994; Gardner, 1995; Keegan, 1987).

The process of engaging in self-construction casts a shadow on the idea that somehow great leaders were born with a peculiar genetic makeup that "automatically" propelled them into the forefront of their followers. While there is some scattered evidence that combinations of genes may produce what has been termed "social potency" (Simonton, 1994, p. 17), it is not nearly as simple or linear as early geneticists such as Francis Galton believed (Simonton, p. 18). In fact, modern day studies of chromosomal interactions reveal a complex swapping of genetic material that defies the idea of men and women representing separate and one-dimensional lineages in which two distinct "lines" are mixed in sexual reproduction. What nature apparently does is link "random fusion with scrambled fission" so that every new human being "reflects a novel combination of sexless chromosomes and genes" so that "All the sons and daughters of the next generation have mixtures of chromosomes that previously inhabited male or female bodies" (Dover, 2002, p. 28).

To reinforce the idea that context or environment plays the greatest role in producing leaders instead of genetic determinism, we need only examine the inauspicious beginnings of some notable leaders of the past.

BIOGRAPHY BOX 1.2

Mohandas Gandhi (1869–1948)

Afraid of the Dark, Petrified of Public Speaking to the Liberator of His Country and the Conscience of the World

The towering but frail figure of Mohandas Gandhi (1869–1948) twice defeated the British Empire in South Africa and India. He walked into the teeth of military strength with nothing but a dhoti and a shawl, humility and supreme moral conviction. Louis Fischer, Gandhi's biographer (1950), reports that the Mahatma was a mediocre student, ignored penmanship, and had trouble learning his times tables. Once for classroom misbehavior he was administered corporal punishment and because of the shame "wept piteously"(p. 19). Gandhi considered himself a coward. He imagined ghosts and serpents in the evening, was afraid to go outdoors, and had to have a light on in his room at night.

While in England for the study of law, Gandhi was terrified of public speaking. He could not speak informally and when expected to do so, he wrote out his remarks and had someone else read them for him. For his fear of speaking publicly, Gandhi was "a complete failure as a lawyer . . . he could not utter a word during a ten-dollar case in court" (Fischer, 1950, p. 38).

How then did this rickity and fearful little man become the mighty leader of a huge country like India? Gandhi invented himself. He created a persona based on action, which steadily fed his self-confidence. "Gandhi advanced to greatness by doing," says Fischer (1950, p. 29). Gandhi's struggles to come to terms with himself and to work against social injustice, prejudice, and oppression are now legendary. One of his countrymen in South Africa commented that "Gandhi has in him the marvelous spiritual power to turn ordinary men around him into heroes and martyrs," and in his presence one "is ashamed to do anything unworthy" (Fischer, p. 108).

For students who believe that age may be an obstacle to becoming a leader, one must remember that Gandhi stayed in South Africa 20 years. He did not return to India to lead that nation toward independence until he was 45. The transformation of Gandhi is described by his biographer in this way: "It is not that he turned failure into success. Using the clay that was there he turned himself into another person. His was a remarkable case of second birth in one lifetime" (Fischer, 1950, p. 40).

BIOGRAPHY BOX 1.3
Winston Churchill (1874–1965)

Placed in Classes for Dullards,
Twice Flunking Public Examination for
a Military Career He Became the
Indomitable and Immovable Object to Nazi Legions

Then take the case of one of Gandhi's contemporaries, a colossal figure on the world stage, Winston Churchill (1874–1965). Churchill, like Gandhi, was a poor student in school. In fact, he was placed in a remedial class "for dullards" where he spent three school sessions (Keegan, 2002, p. 26). He could scarcely do work in math and he despised foreign languages. He twice failed the examination to embark on a military career. Finally, in desperation, his parents hired a tutor and he attended a "cram school" that gave him rote lessons on the topic of the exam and he qualified (barely) for the cavalry, the lowest branch of military service in England at the time.

Neither Churchill nor Gandhi were athletically robust. Neither would or could be called "brawny" or rugged physical specimens of manhood, yet both possessed exceptionally strong wills and great inner strength, although neither could be termed an "intellectual" by any account. They wrote and spoke prodigiously, and both left an indelible mark on their countries and the world as incomparable leaders of great integrity and moral purpose.

BIOGRAPHY BOX 1.4
Mary Harris (1837–1930)

From Widowed, Poor, Elderly, and Irish to the
Most Dangerous Woman in America

Mary Harris (1837–1930) was born in Cork, Ireland, the second child of Richard and Ellen Harris. She lived in the crowded quarters of the poor in Cork, choked with animals and humans alike traversing narrow, sewage-strewn streets. When the famous Irish potato famine came to Cork as it did to much of the rest of Ireland, within 5 years over 1 million people perished from starvation and 2 million left Ireland, among them Mary's father and brother. Later Mary and her mother left for Canada. It was in Toronto that Mary received her elementary education, later becoming a schoolteacher in Monroe, Michigan, at the age of 23.

Mary Harris later moved to Chicago and took up dress-making. A short time later she migrated to Memphis, Tennessee, where she took up teaching again and married in 1861. Her husband, George Jones, worked as an iron molder and was a staunch member of the Iron Molders Union. George Jones was part of the growing American labor movement, reading widely in labor literature and undoubtedly discussing the issues with his wife, Mary Jones. Their family soon consisted of four children and they lived in a section of Memphis that bordered a bayou, a place perfect for the reproduction of mosquitoes.

Mary Jones's life was soon to experience an epic tragedy. A yellow fever epidemic swept Memphis and carried away her husband and all of her children. She tended to them as they perished. Mary Jones's biographer, Elliott Gorn (2001), commented that yellow fever was a particularly gruesome way to die. The victims bled from the nose, mouth, and uterus. As the body hemorrhaged, they vomited black blood. In the final stages, the disease brought about liver failure and delirium. It must have been devastating to Mary as she watched her husband and all four of her children perish in this indescribable agony. Yet from this crucible came a towering figure, a fiery spirit, a sharp tongue often filled with obscenities and invective, and an uncompromising leader and moral voice in the American labor movement. In time, "Mother Jones," as she came to be called, was labeled the most dangerous woman in America by the masters of management and some government officials. In this transition from a real mother to the "Mother" of an entire movement, she had reinvented herself as many great leaders do.

Her speeches were oratorical performances combining charming and powerful stories, interlaced with religious themes and metaphors about doing "God's work," and given in a musical cadence with an Irish brogue and nonverbal gestures tightly interwoven and wrapped around her audience's reactions. By any account they were also highly emotional. Gorn (2001) says her speeches were combinations of scolding, coaxing, comforting, uplifting, moralizing, cursing, fulminating, and weeping and that they were examples of righteousness in labor's cause, a great moral principle founded on turning over long grievances of the miners against the injustices they had all experienced (pp. 175–180).

Mother Jones could not be intimidated, bought off, or frightened. The Pinkertons, a detective agency often used for union busting by management, described her as a "vulgar, heartless, vicious creature, with a fiery temper and a cold-blooded brutality rare even in the slums" (Gorn, 2001, p. 108). Lawrence Lynch, a newspaper writer sympathetic to management, wrote the following of Mother Jones:

> She is the woman most loved by the miners and most feared by the operators . . . She knows no fear and is as much at home in jail as on the platform. In either situation she wields a greater power over the miners than does any other agitator. (Gorn, 2001, p. 181)

A miner in West Virginia who became an official in the United Mine Workers commented that Mother Jones "could permeate a group of strikers with more fight than could any living human being. She fired them with enthusiasm . . . burned them with criticism, then cried with them . . . The miners loved, worshipped, and adored her. . . ." (p. 181).

(Continued)

(Continued)

> Mother Jones lived on the road for 30 years. "My address is like my shoes; it travels with me wherever I go," she observed (Gorn, 2001, p. 4). She gave herself to labor's cause from coal mining towns in West Virginia and Pennsylvania to the copper mines in Montana and the silver mines in Colorado. It was said of her, "While others of her generation shrank from the issues of the day, Mother Jones was consumed with them. But who she became was inseparable from who she had been. Tragedy freed her for a life of commitment" (Gorn, p. 55).

The Importance of Individual Agency

There is much discussion today about "distributed leadership," that is, where certain leadership functions are clustered into a variety of persons and not just one person is referred to as "the leader" (Lakomski, 2005; Smylie, Conley, & Marks, 2002, pp. 172–177). There are even certain places experimenting with "leaderless schools." Actually, this is somewhat of a misnomer since what comprises leadership has simply been restructured into more than one person or role in a school. As Bottery (2004) points out, one of the advantages of the idea of distributed leadership is that it prevents "leadership from being seen as some kind of insulated personal quality" and expands the idea that leadership involves "an interdependence between the individual and the environment (which includes other actors) . . ." (p. 23). Other critics or perspectives regarding leadership indicate that for schools to become more effective, ideas regarding leadership have to become "de-romanticized" (Elmore, 2000). If by this is meant that leaders are not the superheroes of comics or film, we would concur.

We agree with Bottery (2004) that leadership has to be about not only the leader but the important interactions with others. However, there is no mistaking the fundamental notion that the individual human being, driven by commitment, ideals, a mission, or a cause, can make a huge difference. People who are passionate about ideas represent the concept of "individual agency," the sole human being inspired to go forth in search of a better future (see Samier, 2005). Leaders such as Ida Wells-Barnett, Mohandas Gandhi, or Mother Jones are examples of moral leaders whose mission became righting terrible socioeconomic wrongs in working for social justice. When leadership is vested in one person called the leader, or in education, a school principal or superintendent, the potential for releasing individual moral agency is always present. The power to inspire, or model a new response by example, is the wellspring of a leader whose authority has been called "charismatic" (Weber, 1968, p. 215). The dynamism of a leader who has such charisma is bestowed on him or her by his or her followers. It refers to his or her social status (Smith, 1998) and so leadership is constructed and is not some sort of supernatural endowment. Leadership is a human construct. It is always human. Its strengths and its weaknesses reveal its essential humanity. As such, leadership can be good or evil. The power to lead is independent from the cause or motivation of the leader. Followers can be inspired to engage in horrific acts. Brutal dictators who dot the historical landscape over the centuries are testimony to the "dark side" of leadership.

Leadership Is an Acquired Set of Habits and Skills

Leaders learn how to be leaders. Leadership is an acquired habit. It fits in nicely with the human socialization process. For example, Angela Mondou, a self-described "21-year-old party animal," joined the Canadian armed services. After being denied access to becoming a pilot because of her sex, she went through 18 months of intensive training in logistics, and "Whammo, at 22, I found myself in charge of a team of 80 people" (Pitts, 2002, p. B3). Mondou was dropped into Croatia as part of a Canadian peacekeeping group involved with reconnaissance. She coordinated the movements of 1,200 troops and their supplies, transporting them with over 50 trains. She made on-the-spot decisions when she "couldn't even get information on what tracks had been blown up" (Pitts, p. B3). Promoted to captain, she decided to enter a career in business. Looking back on her growth and promotion in the military, she reflected as follows: "Can you learn leadership skills or are they innate? I honestly believe you can learn this stuff" (Pitts, p. B3). Goleman, Boyatzis, and McKee (2002) assert that the 18 specific competencies that comprise the 4 domains of emotional intelligence are learned abilities.

Why Academic Study?

Kurt Lewin (1890–1947), a legendary social psychologist who became famous for creating the idea of "life space" and mapping such spaces using mathematical topology, once remarked that "nothing is as practical as a good theory" (Simonton, 1994, p. 128). Theory has many functions, but one important one is to provide meaning to any set of actions and to establish boundaries for which actions are appropriate and which are not.

Educational leadership is also governed by theories. Famed international management guru W. Edwards Deming (1986) explained that "experience alone, without theory, teaches management nothing about what to do to improve quality and competitive position, nor how to do it . . . Experience will answer a question, and a question comes from theory" (p. 19).

Figure 1.2 indicates the relationship between theories in use and how the "knowledge base" of the field is defined by those theories. The knowledge base rests on a set of critical assumptions called a *foundational epistemology* (meaning a set of primary beliefs about the nature of truth and knowledge and how they are defined; see Creswell, 2003, pp. 4–23). For the most part, it is this knowledge base that has come to define the content of most state licensure tests that you must pass to engage in the practice of public school administration in the United States (see also Donmoyer, Imber, & Scheurich, 1995). The beliefs that support the knowledge base were created and instituted within a specific point in time and indeed have their own story of development (Murphy, 2005). The juncture in time when the "field" of educational administration was constructed and allegedly became a "science" is called the *point of scientificity* (see Foucault, 1972, p. 58; English, 2002).

The POS (point of scientificity) is a special kind of demarcation. It signals that apex in time where educational administration became "scientific" and began to assume the virtues of professional practice based on research instead of rules of thumb

❖ **Figure 1.2**   The Relationship Between Theories in Use and a Field of Practice in Educational Administration

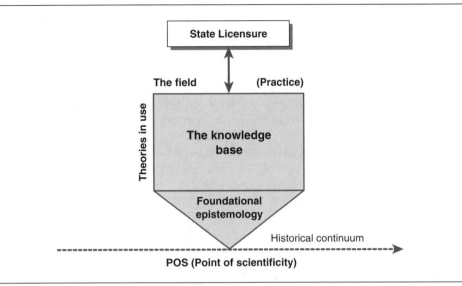

or what has been called "craft knowledge" (Blumberg, 1989). The quest for such a science of administration represents a long line of thinkers and a desire to advance and enhance the status of educational administration as a profession over more than a century (see Culbertson, 1988; Donmoyer, 1999). Whether educational administration is a profession based on science is a theme that will be taken up again in this book. The purpose of graduate study is to be introduced to the science and art of educational leadership. Most graduate students have come from a background of classroom teaching and observed school administrators doing a variety of tasks, some mundane and others much larger. Very few understand the theories in use that govern any administrator's actions. It is the purpose of this book to attempt to provide you with insights into the theories in use in educational leadership.

Is There a Difference Between Leadership and Management?

Much of the core of most graduate programs is concerned about categorizing schools as one type of human organization. It should not be surprising then that the theoretical base of most graduate degrees comes from ideas about organizations and how they are effective or ineffective (see Ogawa, 2005). This body of knowledge is usually called *organizational theory* and it has its conceptual roots in sociology (see Becker & Neuhauser, 1975; Blau & Scott, 1962; Hall, 1972; Krupp, 1961; Likert, 1967; March & Simon, 1958; Mintzberg, 1979; Perrow, 1986; Presthus, 1962; Senge, 1990; Thompson, 1967) and later social and behavioral psychology (see Argyris, 1962; Duke, 1998; Golembiewski, 1972; Katz & Kahn, 1966; Lippitt, 1982; McGregor, 1960; Ogawa & Bossert, 1995; Simon, 1945; Zaleznik, 1966).

❖ **Figure 1.3** On the Dimensions Connecting Management and Leadership

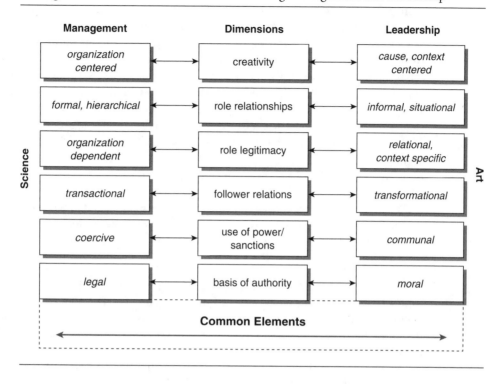

Understandably, the focus in organizational theory is on the characteristics of organizations and determining their impact on humans and the purposes for which the organization has been formed. The essence of management is about what people in positions of authority and responsibility do in organizations. Managers perform their duties in organizations and therefore their first loyalty is to the maintenance or continuation of that organization for it is the organization that provides the role they occupy. For this reason, managers are bound to their organizations and are usually conservative in their outlook and may view change with great suspicion (see Bennis, 1989, p. 25; Dunham, 1964, p. 22; Fullan, 2001, pp. 31–34).

Social and behavioral psychology is centered on how individuals and their behaviors do or do not make a difference to notions of organizational effectiveness. Much of the very popular readings in business literature are focused on how leaders can make a difference for and within their organizations (Fullan, 2002; Senge, 1990).

Figure 1.3 highlights the difference between leadership and management. Both management and leadership rest on a common set of attributes and dispositions as it pertains to individuals. However, Kotter (1990) proffered that management was about making the current organization function better compared to leaders who were out to engage in changing the organization (p. 6). From this perspective, managers are simply leaders who choose to work inside organizations and accept the boundaries, conventions, rules, and relationships within them. Warren Bennis (1989) framed Kotter's distinction more pejoratively when he remarked that "leaders master the context and managers succumb to it" (p. 44). By this he meant that managers do not generally question some things about organizations, while leaders may engage in the process of intensive examination of purposes, procedures, and organizational borders. Leaders may work outside organizations and may not need them. Their leadership may lead to the establishment of an organization to carry on their purposes as in the case of the leadership of Martin Luther King, Jr., and the Southern Christian Leadership Conference.

Leaders may also retain their skepticism about organizations and especially the state. The exemplar here is Mahatma Gandhi, who distrusted the ever increasing power of the state, pointing out that it was a "soulless machine" (Iyer, 1973, p. 254). Gandhi argued that the moral authority of the citizen came first and the state's authority second (Iyer, p. 256). Furthermore, he held the following:

> . . . every ideology that pretends that it must not be put in doubt in the interests of society or civilization or something else, becomes the natural basis for dogmatism or fanaticism. In Socratic terms all logos must be submitted by its author or follower to critical examination. . . . (Iyer, 1973, p. 249)

Gandhi thought that it would be cowardly to blame the administrators of an unjust system because they were "creatures of circumstance" and were engulfed in the evils of an unjust system. If such a system were unjust it would be an evil to propagate it and to obey its rules. It became the test of a "good man" to resist such an evil system (Iyer, 1973, p. 257).

Gandhi then laid the groundwork for differentiating between leadership and management. Leaders, said Gandhi, must exhibit "courage, endurance, fearlessness, and above all self sacrifice" (Iyer, 1973, p. 138). On the other hand, noted the Mahatma, in an organization, "leaders are elected . . . for convenience of work, not for extraordinary merit" (Iyer, p. 138). Such persons are simply "first among equals" and are no better than the weakest among them. He concluded that "a leader is useless when he acts against the promptings of his conscience" (Iyer, p. 139). Let us examine more closely the dimensions that separate leadership and management.

The Basis of Authority

Working within an organization today usually means that it contains some or all of the characteristics of a bureaucracy. For example, bureaucracies contain defined roles arranged in a hierarchical relationship of superior to subordinate called "the chain of command" as well as job descriptions that are contained and reflect organizational rules with specialization attached to those roles. The separate roles enable the organization to provide differing pay scales or compensation schemes that reflect this difference called "the division of labor."

Bureaucracies also contain forms of advancement by merit, although merit may be defined differently in them. Bureaucracies are also known for their impersonality and a reliance on written records that are used to document transactions and decisions (see Silver, 1983, pp. 73–94). The root of the authority of the bureaucracy is the law. Legal authority is the basis of power. Bureaucracies contain a predetermined and official jurisdictional area ordered by rules, activities are fixed within a governance structure, and the authority to give commands or orders is based on a delimited use of coercive means located within specific roles of the organization (see Gerth & Mills, 1970, p. 196). The "bottom line" is that bureaucracies are marked by legal power, stable structures, and routine operations. Bureaucracies have become an almost universal organizational structure in the world, from Beijing, China, and Tokyo, Japan, to Johannesburg, South Africa, Berlin, Germany, Buenos Aires, Argentina, and Ottawa, Canada.

The Use of Power and Sanctions

"Coercive power" in Figure 1.3 refers to the ability of certain officers within an organization to issue orders, directives, or "commands" that must be obeyed. Formal organizations are centered in legal, coercive power. Schools and school districts are one kind of formal organization. While their social function may differ, their foundational orientation is ribbed around these two dimensions. Contrast these qualities with a nonorganization or a different type of organization in which the leader bases his or her authority on moral conviction and a cause, such as Gandhi's leadership in the movement in South Africa and India to secure independence from Great Britain, or Martin Luther King, Jr.'s, leadership in the American Civil Rights Movement. In those cases, the focus of leadership is communal, centered on a cause and fueled by an idea that binds the participants together.

One of the dimensions of leadership is to provide the focus for the cause, explaining its meaning and persuading followers of the need for cohesion and commitment toward its realization. The use of power in a communal approach is based on cohesion to the moral cause, and the leader uses all the powers of persuasion to maintain constancy over time. Instead of the power to compel response by coercive means, a leader within a communal approach uses shame and moral outrage. In this respect, the use of persuasion resembles what has been called "servant leadership" (see Greenleaf, 1977; Sergiovanni, 1992).

Follower Relations and Interactions

A manager in a bureaucracy has the means of compelling obedience by legal, coercive power. The relationship to followers is *transactional,* that is, "you do this for me, and I will do this for you," not the least of which is to keep employing the person in his or her current position. Working in a hierarchy reinforces the superior/subordinate nexus of transactional relationships (see Burns, 1978, pp. 417–418). *Transformational* interactions involve the leader and followers in a relationship that is more equalitarian, in which followers are uplifted, and there is within the relationship an exchange that becomes dynamic and intensely interactive (see Duncan & Seguin, 2002). Both leader and followers are empowered by each other. Great causes are propelled by transformational patterns of interactions between leaders and followers, from Gandhi's immortal salt march against British rule in India, Martin Luther King, Jr.'s ringing sermons in the Birmingham Bus Boycott in Alabama, or Mother Jones's rodomontade to ensure worker allegiance and solidarity supporting a strike by the United Mine Workers.

Role Legitimacy and Relationships

The legitimacy of a role within a bureaucracy rests on a legal foundation. Roles are established within a pattern of ascending authority and responsibility (called "line" responsibility) or by specialization and expertise in support of line authority (called "staff" responsibility). By contrast, role legitimacy in politics, labor, or religion, which is more cause centered and volatile, is relational and context specific. Leaders arise in contestations over causes. They may occupy roles for short times, but it is not uncommon for them to be replaced or even the roles to be abolished.

Creativity

Sometimes called "thinking out of the box," creativity represents one of the hallmarks of greatness in leaders. For example, Simonton (1994) argues that creativity is a neglected realm of understanding leadership because "a leader is that group member whose influence on group attitudes, performance, or decision making greatly exceeds that of the average member of the group" (p. 411). Managers are already "in the box," as it is represented by the boundaries, rules, and customs of the organization in which they occupy a role. Leaders in a cause-driven and defined movement are required to be creative on a much more demanding basis. They have no boundaries except those that add to the power of their momentum toward realizing the aims of the cause. Since they have no formal organization, their leadership involves creating and sustaining a vision that is compelling and clear, and they continue to build coalitions of support around it to attain it. Managers, on the other hand, bound as they are by context in creating their visions, have to ensure that such visions are compatible with the broad functions for which the organization was created. Visions are defined and confined to those products or services that enhance the organization.

Creativity for organizations enhances the organization. Creativity for leaders outside organizations enhances the cause for which they toil. Creativity for leaders has been described in the works of Edward De Bono (1980). De Bono criticizes "yes–no" systems of thought as dealing with fixed ideas and old truths, and having 'no creative ability whatsoever'" (p. 30). The problem with "yes–no" systems (know as "logic") is that they produce "box definitions" (p. 31) and frameworks, called by De Bono "concept packages" that are self-justifying. Such frameworks become obstacles to change. Thomas Kuhn (1996) called them "paradigms" (p. 10). When a leader exhibits creativity, he or she has learned how to think outside the "box definitions" because "neither logic nor computers produce right answers; they only produce answers consistent with the initial concept package" (De Bono, 1980, p. 50). Fullan (2002) also notes that one of the five "action-and-mind sets" that effective leaders possess is they have a proclivity to make sense of often chaotic situations. This capacity involves creativity (p. 2).

Because management has roots in sociology and social psychology, it lays claim to being scientific. Leadership, however, remains first and foremost an art. An art involves formal training but contains elements that some may label *subjectivity* but that may also contain universal themes. To gain an insight as to what is art, perhaps we can learn something from one of the greatest sculptors in the world, Auguste Rodin (1840–1917). In describing art, Rodin indicated that "art is contemplation . . . It is the joy of the intellect which sees clearly into the Universe . . . [it] is the most sublime mission of man, since it is the expression of thought seeking to understand the world and to make it understood (Gsell, 1983, p. 1.) Rodin spoke of expressing the spiritual state of his subjects and the world in which they lived (Gsell, p. 11). He spoke of looking deeply into things. Mediocre artists simply reproduced an exterior. Rodin searched for the spirit that was underneath. "I see all the truth and not only that of the outside," remarked Rodin (Gsell, p. 11). Rodin penetrated his subjects for something called *character* and it was this ingredient that provided his works with power. "There is nothing ugly in art except that which is without character, that is to say, that which offers no outer or inner truth" (Gsell, p. 20).

Deal and Peterson (1994) came very close to Rodin's ideas when they sketched out a picture of "artist-principals." These leaders were seeking to

> define reality, capture and articulate symbols that communicate deeply held values and beliefs, and engage people in ritual, ceremony, theatre and play. Their primary motivation is to instill a deep sense of meaning that makes the school a place of the heart as well as the head and hands. (p. 8)

Evidence of "artist principals" is supplied from school leaders who not only turned around troubled schools but established national models with low socioeconomic status students in such personages as Deborah Meier (1995), principal at Central Park East in Harlem, and Sandra Dean (2000), principal of South Simcoe in inner city Toronto, Canada. Both of these innovative and courageous women were role models for what Debra Meyerson, a professor at Stanford University's Graduate School of Business, would call "tempered radicals" (Church, 2002). Tempered radicals are leaders who become change agents, but "they want to rock the boat, and they want to stay in it" (Church, p. C-1). These leaders are patient; they pursue their change agendas through accumulated little actions that add up over time. John Gardner (1968) observed the same phenomena when he said, "We have all seen men with lots of bright ideas but no patience with the machinery by which ideas are translated into action. As a rule, the machinery defeats them . . . [because they] will not take the time to understand the social institutions and processes by which change is accomplished" (p. 130).

The Necessary Alliance: Leadership and Management

It was this same John Gardner (1968) who observed the following over 30 years ago: "The sad truth is that a great many of our organizations are badly managed or badly led " (p. 133). Carnes Lord (2003) also observed the following:

> The day-to-day management of the machinery of administration is the single most important thing that governments do most of the time, and whether it is done well or badly directly affects the fortunes of regimes and those who rule them. (p. 116)

Schools remain in desperate need of both leadership and management. In 1996, Thomas Sergiovanni observed that an emphasis on "org. theory" taught in graduate programs resulted in the goals of schools being pursued as if principals and superintendents were engineers and "we know that it is not engineering but leadership that schools need to improve" (p. 45). Nearly three decades of observation indicate that schools are not working for a large segment of the population (Hunter & Bartee, 2003; Jencks & Phillips, 1998; Popkewitz, Tabachnick, & Wehlage, 1982; Sedlak, Wheeler, Pullin, & Cusick, 1986). To manage them more efficiently and effectively makes little sense until they are fundamentally changed.

Managers are conservative about changes. While they may embrace change within schools, they may be reluctant to engage in alterations where the fundamental borders of schooling are concerned. And they may be cautious or even negative about making changes in their own roles within school organizations since that would be tampering with their own job security. When it comes to internal change, managers are faced with a dilemma. One of their major responsibilities is to secure and maintain organizational stability. They can't overturn the organization without endangering its capacity to exist. No matter how poorly the organization is performing, managers can't close it down, especially an organization fulfilling a social function such as education.

It is perhaps for this reason that Deming (1986), the father of TQM (total quality management), indicated that significant change in an organization could never be brought about without outside intervention because, "as a good rule, profound knowledge comes from the outside, and by invitation. A system cannot understand itself. The transformation will require leaders" (p. 94). Internal managers just have too many vested interests in the status quo. They may tinker inside the boundaries, but they cannot be the ones to engage in fundamental changes. Deming's commentary indicates that leaders are the ones who can understand boundaries and fundamental questions and they are theoretically prepared, not simply experienced operationally.

Figure 1.4 shows "the manager's dilemma" in this regard. There is an intricate interrelationship between managerial roles, organizational stability, and school boundaries, which defines organizational functions within the existing political system, socioeconomic structure, legal system, and state certification requirements. The relationship between social stratification and schooling has been established by research (Cookson & Persell, 1985; Labaree, 1988; Lucas, 1999; Sapon-Shevin, 1994). Creativity is also constrained within this nexus. Any proposed organizational change cannot seriously entertain radical role changes or social functions without calling into question the stability of the organization itself.

From this perspective, it can easily be seen that most so-called "reforms" of education today can be placed squarely within existing school boundaries and alterations of internal school operations. For example, such changes as block scheduling alter the way time is allocated within schools, but they do not alter any other changes outside of schools. Block scheduling does not change the socioeconomic structure or the legal system that defines the dimensions of schooling. As such, block scheduling is a "refinement" of the status quo. Table 1.1 shows a partial list of educational "reforms" that are popular today and the extent to which they do or do not alter the fundamental assumptions of schooling. If a proposed "reform" functions exclusively within the system of schools as they exist, and does not change any of the relationships of schools to larger socioeconomic, legal, or political systems, then the change is purely "within the box." If the proposed change has the potential of challenging assumptions beyond the traditional role of schools, then it has the potential of being an "out of the box" change and may legitimately

❖ **Figure 1.4** The "Manager's Dilemma," the Foci of Organizational Stability

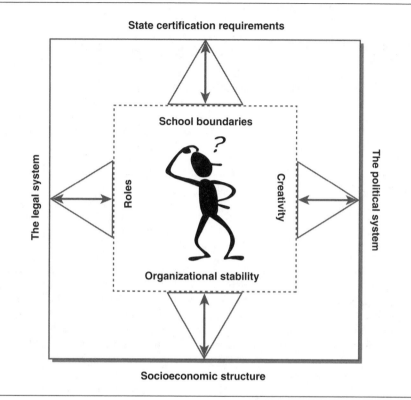

be called a "reform." For this reason, many educators confuse "reforms" with "refinements." From the perspective of leadership versus management, and paraphrasing Warren Bennis (1989), leaders challenge the boundaries of the organization while managers are captured by them (p. 44). Managers are less likely to think "outside of the box."

For this reason, this book first examines the nature of leadership outside of organizations. This stance is based on the premise that future school leaders must understand something about leadership in the human experience before examining the specific requirements of leading or managing schools as organizations. It is important that future school leaders come to see the many limitations imposed on schools so that decisions they may make that reinforce how schools are now working are made with an informed perspective (see Spady, 2007). The status quo is not acceptable. Nearly all the critics agree that change is necessary. The nature and type of changes are what are at stake.

Fullan (2002) indicates that the idea of the principal as an instructional leader is "too narrow a concept to carry the weight of the reforms that we need for the future" (p. 1). Fullan argues that future school leaders are those that "can create a fundamental transformation in the learning cultures ... and the teaching profession itself" (p. 1). Transforming school cultures is a very broad sweep of the educational environment. It includes the idea that current notions and boundaries of the social educational function

❖ **Table 1.1**   Leadership Versus Management: A Partial List of Possible Changes in Schools: Refinements or Reform?

Proposed Change	Description	Refinement? [management]	Reform? [leadership]
Block scheduling	Enlarges modules of time for scheduling subjects within schools.	Yes–impacts the scope of curriculum within schools as well as mode of instructional delivery.	No–does not change any of the boundaries of schools or alter fundamental socioeconomic conditions.
Cooperative learning	Places students in groups to help one another in learning.	Yes–functions within the existing curriculum and existing constraints.	No–does not change any conditions in the socioeconomic, political system in which schools function.
Pay for performance or certain "value added" schemes for rewarding superior student performance on designed criteria or tests	Various schemes in which teachers or principals are rewarded for superior test scores of students–usually with increased pay in the form of bonuses.	Yes–pay for performance schemes assume that organizational roles are okay; the problem is motivation, which is solved with compensation schemes that recognize effort or "results" in the form of improved test scores.	No–pay for performance schemes propose no boundary changes and assume that current forms of schools are either efficient or not, leaving a discussion of such changes to the vagaries of the marketplace, that is, for schools to become "better" forms of schooling they will get "better results" but will not challenge the efficacy of the system in which they function.
Closing the achievement gap-curriculum alignment	The idea that the "gap" between students based on race is unacceptable and must be closed by whatever means that would enable this to occur, usually by a tighter "fit" between the test and the curriculum.	Yes–educators are urged to adopt whatever tactics have been shown to improve test scores; developing a tighter relationship between the tested, taught, and written curriculums reinforces the efficacy of the tests, which have been shown to reinforce the socioeconomic plight of poor children.	No–the tactics educators are urged to adopt do not challenge the conservative nature of schooling in reproducing the society itself with its built-in socioeconomic differentials. All of the solutions are "in the box."

Proposed Change	Description	Refinement? [management]	Reform? [leadership]
Looping	Students stay with the same teacher at the next grade level.	Yes–this is a variation of assigning teachers to students within schools.	No–there are no fundamental changes involved with schooling and social reform or political change.
Vouchers and charter schools	These changes represent the move toward privatization of the public schools.	Yes–such schemes must function within existing law and serve to reinforce the existing socioeconomic class distinctions, although in theory there could be changes. Both ideas do not embrace radical internal changes in schools.	No–in theory, vouchers could be used to foster reform; in practice they have not done so. Charters have not brought about fundamental changes in school boundaries.
Parental involvement	More involvement of parents in school operations is argued to truly reform them.	Yes–parent involvement can improve certain aspects of school functions. There is no evidence any fundamental reform has been fostered by increased parental involvement.	No–parent involvement has ushered in no fundamental changes in school boundaries or larger socioeconomic conditions or relationships.
Strategic planning	The use of strategic planning can serve to improve school risk taking.	Yes–strategic planning can incorporate many useful tactical changes within schools.	No–strategic planning usually takes as "givens" school boundaries and legal covenants.
Writing across the curriculum	An approach in which all teachers in all subjects teach writing.	Yes–this change is simply one in which curriculum is assigned to teachers differently within schools.	No–this approach to curriculum fits well into current models of schooling and instruction.
Phonics	A highly politicized approach to teaching reading that does not challenge any fundamental questions of schooling.	Yes–a curriculum issue confined to reading.	No–important questions of school in the larger society remain unchallenged and unchanged.

(Continued)

❖ Table 1.1 (Continued)

Proposed Change	Description	Refinement? [management]	Reform? [leadership]
The middle school	The introduction of a different grade configuration than 7-8-9 for a school in-between elementary and high school.	Yes–changing grade configurations is part of redefining what schools will house what age-graded students.	No–middle schools make no fundamental changes to the nature of schooling and the existing division of labor between schools and society.
Constructivist approaches in teaching	The idea that curriculum should be put together with the idea that learners construct meaning and bring much to the classroom in the way of prior experience.	Yes–constructivist approaches are ways to teach different ways to think about creating curriculum and altering assessment practices within schools as they exist.	No–constructivism proffers no fundamental ways that schools should function in society.
Accountability/testing plans	Any approach to improving student test scores that links such results to persons in schools or their functions.	Yes–accountability plans may increase the use of testing and force personnel to pay more attention to tests than before.	No–accountability plans accept the way schools function now. Such plans foster any behavior within schools that leads to test score improvements.
Zero-based budgeting (ZBB)	An approach to constructing a budget in which no budget category begins with any amount except "zero."	Yes–if nothing else ZBB changes budgeting practices.	No–ZBB functions well within existing schools, boundaries, and socioeconomic and political relationships.
Group counseling	An approach to clustering students with similar needs together to promote the exchange of ideas on a common topic.	Yes–changes the way counselors work within schools.	No–works well within schools as they now exist.
Clinical supervision	An approach to supervision of teachers that includes a planning conference, observation, and feedback conference.	Yes–changes the way principals and other supervisors may work with teachers in doing required evaluations of them.	No–purely an in-school change in the way principals observe and evaluate teachers. No changes in schools are required.

Proposed Change	Description	Refinement? [management]	Reform? [leadership]
Gifted education	An approach to thinking about student differences on mental abilities using some tests as the discriminating instrument.	Yes–special classes for the gifted, or pullouts, are usually implemented within schools.	No–gifted education requires no changes in the functions of schooling and may reinforce socioeconomic inequities.
Team teaching	The use of more than one teacher in performing instruction with students in a common instructional situation.	Yes–sometimes a change in scheduling is required or may involve curricular departmentalization.	No–team teaching is a "within-school" alteration of clustering teachers and students in pedagogical situations.
Differentiated instruction	The creation of a wide variety of instructional practices that include learning styles, cultural backgrounds, and prior knowledge.	Yes–fosters a wider diversity of instructional techniques and classroom approaches that are located within the existing school structure.	No–there are no changes in the functions of schools or schooling, although some attention may be paid to specific instructional goals. These are assumed to be within the current capacity of schools.
De-tracking	The abolition of the means to "track" or "stream" students on the basis of some common criterion, usually a test score.	Yes–portends a change in scheduling practices and perhaps pedagogical practices.	Borderline–while de-tracking occurs within schools, the refusal of the school to track by IQ usually confronts a bias in the clustering or grouping of students by socioeconomic status.

may have to be reconsidered and perhaps even redefined. This is a radical idea of the scope of changes that may be required of educational leaders in the future. In closing for the moment the discussion regarding leadership and management, Lord (2003) comments that there is a tendency today that "managers" are simply bureaucrats compared to leaders, who are the more active participants on the stage. However, it is more complicated than that. Lord notes that "in reality, however, few important administrative decisions are without consequences for policy" (p. 117). And, concomitantly, "bureaucratic managers cannot be, and should not consider themselves, simply neutral technicians. At least at senior levels, administrators are inextricably involved with policy and in a position to exercise genuine leadership" (p. 117). Drawing this discussion to a close, perhaps the best way to describe the difference between leadership and management is to say that while they are different, they come together. If organizations are not managed, they cannot be led well either. While leadership can exist outside organizations, once it enters organizational life, it must initiate procedures that enable management to become a reality or the organization and the social functions it performs are likely to perish over time.

Pursuing Learning Extensions of the Chapter

The learning extensions of the chapter involve a film experience about a complete leader: Mahatma Gandhi.

Gandhi (1982), Color, DVD, Columbia Pictures, 3 Hours (Contains Some Original Newsreel Footage, Including Verbal Footage of the Real Gandhi)

Based on the Louis Fischer (1950) biography, the Academy Award–winning Richard Attenborough (1982a) film begins with the event that served as the catalyst for Gandhi to begin his evolution from a partial leader to a complete leader. That event was being thrown off a South African train because he was sitting in the first-class section and refused to take a seat in the "colored" car designated for nonwhites.

While Gandhi considered himself to be a physical coward, he could not accept the government-imposed color line. Although he was but 24 years of age, Gandhi began organizing Indians in protest. Twenty years later he left South Africa as a hero to undertake a return to India and the role of leader to gain Indian independence. It is perhaps from his South African experience that Gandhi remarked the following: "Strength does not come from physical capacity, but from indomitable will" (Attenborough, 1982b, p. 13).

This film can be watched on many different levels and with many different objectives in mind. Here are some of them:

Gandhi's South African awakening or his "transformation." The early part of this film is perhaps the most crucial for Gandhi's development as a leader. The viewer is able to see an unsure Gandhi become a resolute leader. He had a fierce temper that he had to learn to control and he began to put together the idea of communal living in the ashram or farm. It was also in South Africa that Gandhi took up *Brahmachary*, or celibacy. It was part of his vow to focus his life and be lifted above material concerns (Fischer, 1950, p. 73). Above all else, Gandhi learned in South Africa that "one man with truth on his side could wield immense moral power" (Woodcock, 1971, p. 55). Gandhi's South African experience has been called "his transformation" (Fischer, pp. 58–73; Kytle,1982, pp. 64–88). The depth of this personal transformation has been explored by Eric Erickson (1969, pp. 176–226) in his provocative book *Gandhi's Truth: On the Origins of Militant Nonviolence*. Gandhi came step by step to a position of nonviolence in his political protests, whereas later his nonviolence was copied by Martin Luther King, Jr., in the American Civil Rights Movement. Gandhi worked out this posture as he reacted to his role in the Boer War, in which his medical treatment given to the Zulus when no one else would treat them. Gandhi chose the name *satyagraha* to describe his outlook, which meant "truth" and "force" and not "passive resistance" as it is sometimes known. But there was nothing "passive" about this method, as Gandhi was to demonstrate time after time in South Africa and later India. The film speeds up Gandhi's transformation, which took 20 years.

Questions to Consider

1. Describe Gandhi's motives for engaging in social protest. How did he see his actions?

2. How did Gandhi's own code of action, that is, actionable beliefs, become translated into actions in deed?

3. From the film's portrayal of Gandhi's 20 years in South Africa, describe Gandhi's development from a protester or partial leader to the complete leader of a movement.

Attenborough's film is also an illustrative vehicle for understanding how Gandhi's moral principles guided his actions in India, how he sought out confrontation with British authorities to demonstrate to them and to his followers the folly of their continued presence in his country. Gandhi used all the tactics described by Saul Alinsky (1971, pp. 126–164) when a less powerful social force confronts a powerful one. Here is what Alinsky (1971) observed:

> Power is not static; it cannot be frozen and preserved like food; it must grow or die. Therefore, in order to keep power the status quo must get more. But from whom? There is just so much more than can be squeezed out of the Have-Nots—so the Haves must take it from each other . . . Here is the vulnerable belly of the status quo. (p. 149)

More than any other film, *Gandhi* is about moral leadership and it demonstrates many of Greenleaf's (1977) tenets about what is now called servant leadership. In addition to the film, there are abundant books about Gandhi that are worth reading to more fully understand this remarkable human being.

Writing in Your Personal Reflective Journal

To begin creating your own personal reflective journal about the book, you may start your entry with reflections on when it first came to your own awareness that others thought what you said or did was important. Could you be called a partial leader? Perhaps it occurred in athletics or coaching, or perhaps in other endeavors related to hobbies or other activities. Try to recall how you felt about this experience. How important is it that others looked to you for guidance or wanted your opinion? How do you feel about it now?

A second part of leadership growth uses Gandhi as an example (his transformation in South Africa). Human growth, especially in leadership, is about the discovery of self, of answers concerning the most intimate aspects of living, material things, confronting human mortality in death, and relating such matters to larger purposes and meanings. Gandhi was aided by his religious teachings in Hinduism and its attendant practices, notably *Bramacharya* or celibacy, which in Indian thought meant "in search of Brahma or God" (Fischer, 1950, p. 73). *Bramacharya* meant restraint not only sexually, but in diet, emotions, and speech. And it meant abstinence from "hate, anger, violence and untruth" (Fischer, p. 73). Identify your own life beliefs and indicate the extent to which your religious teachings have influenced them. These beliefs constitute your own inner core.

A Review of Key Chapter Concepts

Use a review of these key chapter concepts as a way to test your own understanding of the premises, ideas, and concepts that are part of this chapter.

artist-principals—This refers to a group of administrators who approach their duties from the perspective of creating mutually satisfying symbolic rituals, ceremonies, and interrelationships based on the creation of shared values (see Deal & Peterson, 1994; Willower & Licata, 1997).

bureaucracy—This is a type of organization with distinctive characteristics that include a job hierarchy, separate roles with differentiated salaries, and administration based on meritocratic appointments. Often attributed to Max Weber (1864–1920), a German sociologist (see Collins, 1986, p. 34).

coercive power—This is the capability of certain officers in an organizational hierarchy to compel obedience through fear, intimidation, rejection, punishment, ostracism, or physical or mental abuse.

craft knowledge—This is information that is considered useful in the practice of educational administration but that is not the result of formal, empirical study. May also refer to the "wisdom of the field" as to what practitioners believe and do but which is not the result of "scientific study" (see Blumberg, 1989).

leadership as a science and an art—The key idea here is that there are two aspects to studying leadership, one that is organization centered and focused and involves management, and a second that is nonorganization centered and involves influencing and interacting with people in common causes apart from formal organizational life. The science of leadership involves behavioral and social psychology as well as branches of sociology. While certain aspects of leadership can be approached within the realms of science, its essence remains elusive to a traditional approach and methods of so-called "scientific" disciplines. For an example of a work that sits on the border of science and art in examining leadership, see Erik Erikson's (1969) *Gandhi's Truth*.

mask of command—This is the idea that the public face and persona of a leader is carefully constructed to be what the followers require and need to engage in the enterprise at hand. A "mask" is not a phony shield of falsity, but rather a construction of self that is displayed externally. The "mask" may involve other aspects of persona such as distinctive clothing or other personal accoutrements, as for example, Franklin Roosevelt's extended cigarette holder (see Wills, 1994, pp. 23–38).

native or indigenous leaders—This refers to leaders that are part of a specific culture or subculture that arise within the customs, traditions, and practices of that culture or subculture and are usually "informal" as opposed to the result of formal, bureaucratic rituals in an organization-centered culture.

organizational theory ("org. theory")—This is a body of information, some of which is based on formal inquiry, that centers organizations as the prime source for understanding leaders, leadership, and the challenges facing leaders. "Org. theory" is primarily descriptive in nature, but has moved toward prescriptive perspectives based on what is "good" for the organization (changing cultures or introducing "reforms"; see Argyris, 1972; Hills, 1968; Senge, 1990).

paradigm—This is a norm of behavior that applies to scientific investigation in which investigators/researchers share certain assumptions about what is or is not worth researching and how best to go about the process of inquiry (see Kuhn, 1996).

partial/complete leader—This is terminology created by Saul Alinsky (1969) to describe the difference between leadership in "the rank and file" as opposed to leaders selected by outsiders or by some formal process endorsed by organizations/bureaucracies. Partial leaders do not have to acquire formal academic training to become leaders. They are leaders by virtue of having some capacity, ability, insight, or cause that appeals to and is applauded by others like them.

point of scientificity (POS)—This is a historically constructed and specific point in time when it is assumed or alleged that a discipline or a field became a science (see English, 2002).

social capital—This term refers to a relational and interactive codependency and mutually constructed social network that can be called on for support when a leader must build a coalition of support or sustain a position in times of conflict.

spiritual leadership—This aspect of leadership in the book is concerned with how educational leaders internalize values that motivate them and retain their steadfastness and vision, which leads to leadership resiliency over time. It does not refer to religious perspectives, although it may contain elements of religious values.

tempered radical—This refers to a person who does not simply uphold organizational rules and norms but is actively engaged in challenging and changing many, only in a progressive fashion that is evolutionary instead of revolutionary.

the knowledge base—This concept refers to the assumed presence of a coherent and consistent theoretical platform or body of information (facts, theories, practices) that has its roots in empirical research. Information that exists outside a knowledge base is not given the same weight in leadership preparation or practice.

TQM (total quality management)—This is an approach to management created by W. Edwards Deming (1986) in his work in Japan after World War II. TQM involves strict analyses of production by statistical methods and a rigid adherence to shaving costs to the bare bones without compromising a manufactured entity by whatever means are used to determine quality. The language of TQM has infiltrated educational administration through the development and imposition of the ISLLC (Interstate Leaders Licensure Consortium; see English, 2000).

transactional leadership—This is an interaction between a leader and a follower based on some exchange of goods, services, or psychic or emotional needs that both parties seek from the other (see Burns, 1978).

transformational leadership—This is an interaction between a leader and followers that is premised on the active participation of both in which a cause or problem uplifts both and in which leader and followers are mutually influential (see Burns, 1978).

2

Archetypes of Leadership in the Human Experience

This chapter focuses on the issue of the source of human leadership at the nexus in which educational leaders must function within every society. Understanding the origins of leadership begins with every human being's personal journey in life. Each society's set of values has been selected among many present and past in human history. Remnants of past choices surface in mythology, archaeology, and psychology. Particular cultural stories continue to influence social behavior in organized religion, a traditional fount of morality and values. Understanding these sources enables educational leaders to see leadership as a phenomenon of the universal and the contextual, and as a living and vibrant manifestation of the cultures that shape our lives. Such an understanding becomes the foundation on which academic preparation and the internship build to enable educational leaders to construct schools that are humane, caring, and nurturing places for all children.

❖

While the origins of educational leadership in the schooling context most of us know are perhaps directly traceable to the creation of the graded school in Quincy, Massachusetts, in 1848 (Tyack, 1975, pp. 44–45), pursuing the origins of human leadership within the larger landscape of humanity proves more difficult. The first hurdle to examining the role of leaders in human societies is that only about 0.4% of the total span of humanity's journey on earth is really knowable from written records (Mann, 2003, p. 34). The remaining 99.6% disappears into the primordial mists. However, from very ancient cave drawings, some artifacts, and the collected folk tales recalled in human memory viewed through the prisms of mythology, archaeology, and psychology, we can make some intelligent guesses about the origins of human leadership. The full panoply of this fundamental quest is deeply etched into the human mind and manifests itself in a revealing archaeology that is locked inside each human being's life journey. Educators are not apart from this longer path from remote beginnings. Their understanding of their part in the journey is central to enabling schools to be humane, caring, and compassionate places for children and young adults.

Emerging through culture and context, the leadership life journey is cast and recast and takes on the specific manners, dress, and cultural contours unique to each tribe, people, and culture. From this perspective, we can trace the visages of leadership in the gigantic Olmec stone heads recovered in southern Mexico; the Mayan bas-reliefs on cylindrical monuments hacked from the encroaching jungles of Tikal and Chichen Itza; the eight square miles of walls, street, and brick pyramids of the Chimu in Peru; the luxury and splendor of Teotihuacan, the Aztec capital that stood for 10 centuries and at its height boasted a population of 125,000 amid great apartment dwellings, temples, wide boulevards, and a complex system of waterways; the paintings and obelisks of the Pharaohs at Luxor and Karnak; and the temples and monasteries of Cambodia and Tibet. We can touch the ancient wood carvings from the Sudan and Nigeria and find the leadership journey in cave paintings deep in the French Pyrenees.

The person who is credited with unlocking the universal journey of leadership is Joseph Campbell (1904–1987). Campbell found, in the work of Carl Jung (1960) and Adolf Bastian (1826–1905), the keys to unlocking humankind's universal search, which is every person's leadership journey (Larsen & Larsen, 1991, p. 257). The basic idea is that the human mind in its evolution over thousands of years contains forms that Bastian called *elementargedanke* ("elementary ideas"). Jung called them *archetypes* and he differed between these *primary images* or *urtumliches Bild,* which were the "collective unconscious," and the often suppressed images, which were the "personal unconscious" (Campbell, 1987, pp. 31–32).

In her best-selling book, *Women Who Run With the Wolves* (1992), Clarissa Estes, a Jungian analyst and a cantadora storyteller, further expands the idea of archetypes by explaining that it is centered on "a knowing of the soul" (p. 9) and that "wild" does not mean out of control, but "natural," and represents a woman who has reconnected with herself to discover a healthy balance based on her "innate integrity" (p. 8). She then proceeds to describe its benefits:

> With Wild Woman as ally, as leader, model, teacher, we see, not through two eyes, but through the eyes of intuition which is many-eyed. When we assert intuition, we are therefore like the starry night; we gaze at the world through a thousand eyes. (p. 12)

Anticipating the skepticism of some regarding the idea of the *Wild Woman,* Estes remarks as follows: "People may ask for evidence . . . They are essentially asking for proof of the psyche. Since we are the psyche, we are also the evidence . . . We are the proof of this ineffable female numen" (p. 14).

An archetype is a combination of an elementary image that has its roots in human unconsciousness, and an independent form that is then fixed in a certain culture and time. To unlock and to recover these deeper images means to turn inward and to listen. It means in Estes's (1992) words, *llamar o tocar a la puerta,* to open the door to the psyche (p. 6).

To the untutored eye, in the stories and myths all that might be seen is a pantheon of distorted torsos and visages. Campbell (1973) found, however, a "standard metamorphoses as men and women have undergone in every quarter of the world, in all recorded centuries, and under every odd disguise of civilization" (p. 13).

Campbell's (1973) basic outline of the Jungian archetype is called the *nuclear unit of the monomyth* (p. 30). This "nuclear unit" was the fundamental kernel of the human quest, which became manifested in a myriad of ways and led to Campbell's titling his work *The Hero With a Thousand Faces.* By this he meant that there was only one hero, but that the face of the hero was cast in an endless repetition of guises, disguises, and forms within a universal building block (the *mono*myth) comprising a common quest over all time and virtually everywhere humans have lived or traveled. This is a powerful theory and helps explain that leadership first and foremost involves a search for personal understanding and meaning deeply rooted in all of us, something that has been validated by other authors describing leadership (Barber, 1985, pp. 1–8; Gardner, 1995, pp. 22–65).

Campbell's (1973) nuclear unit of the monomyth is shown in Figure 2.1. It involves four distinct phases separated by a threshold dividing most humans' awareness that the opposite of life is death. The "other side" of conscious life awareness is the impenetrable mystery, the great void. The basic fear and anxiety of all living persons is the confrontation with the thought that their existence will inevitably be forever expunged. The moment of sensate recognition that as a person one is unique but mortal is a constant source of tension, an awareness that one day the eyes, mind, and touch will cease to function.

❖ **Figure 2.1**   The Leadership Life Journey in Universal Myth

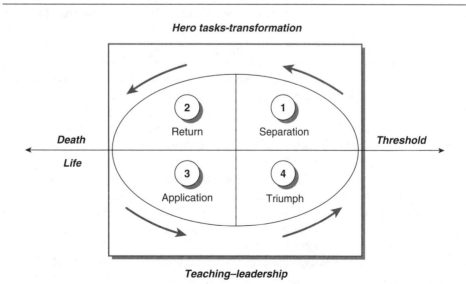

The source of the nuclear unit of the monomyth is the eternal mystery of death, and the great task of living humans is to come to terms with it. The leadership life journey begins with a separation from life with some jarring or unusual experience. Such a separation crosses the threshold of life into a mysterious unknown. Here the one separated encounters tasks and trials as well as strange beasts and persons. Along the route the individual is transformed by the experience. He or she finds a way to return and crosses back over the threshold into the world of the living to apply some new form of knowledge. The application of this new knowledge is acclaimed and the individual triumphs over the obstacles and becomes revered and honored. This story forms the basis for nearly every great religion of the world: Christianity, Judaism, Islam, and Buddhism.

Figure 2.1 represents the nuclear unit of the monomyth without some of the variations that appear in the mythology of cultures over time. It should be indicated that by using the term *myth* we do not infer that there is something false about them. Joseph Campbell (1973) said that " . . . myth is the secret opening through which the inexhaustible energies of the cosmos pour into human cultural manifestation" (p. 3) Campbell asserted that symbols embedded in mythology were not "manufactured." (p. 4). In fact, he denied that they could be ordered or invented. From a Jungian perspective, they were the permanent wellsprings of the mind coming to terms with its unconscious roots. The unconscious served as a bridge into the unknown that promised connection and unity, and an understanding of the meaning of totality. In some cultures that totality is called *God*.

Figure 2.2 is an enlargement of cells 1 and 2 from Figure 2.1. Let us review some specific examples from Campbell (1973) to serve as illustrations. As a human being exists in the lifeworld, he or she receives a "call" (No. 1 in Figure 2.2). This initial awakening or occurrence contains a "herald" of some sort (No. 2 in Figure 2.2). In fairy tales, the "herald" may be an ordinary creature such as a frog or a fox that displays extraordinary capacities by speaking to the person and issuing a challenge or a puzzle. In some stories, the herald may be a supernatural creature such as a dragon or a snake. In the popular Harry Potter books and films, the original awakening is signaled by the presence of a white owl. In religious meditation, the herald or call can be a startling insight of some kind. In Jungian terms, the "herald" is merely the awakening of the self.

Crossing the threshold involves images of swirling water, dark forests, dense mists, or in the Greek story of the minotaur and the labyrinth, an impenetrable maze that contained a fierce beast that devoured young men and maidens. The minotaur is the multifaceted tyrant-monster that is part of so many cultural myths across time that the variations fill volumes. The tyrant-monster can be a minotaur, the shaggy Jinns, which were eerie beasts of the desert, or simply the wolf that ate Red Riding Hood in the familiar children's fairy tale (see Walker, 1983, p. 520). In psychic terms, these ogres and monsters are failings of self, the obstinate extensions of ego, greed, ignorance, and arrogance, and stand as obstacles to overcome in the leadership life journey.

Once the journey has crossed the threshold into the darkness and the unknown, the first figure encountered is a protective one (No. 3 in Figure 2.2). The modern myth told in the *Star Wars* films featured Yoda, a wise and protective figure. In *Lord of the Rings,* a variety of friends some with supernatural powers, help the young Frodo.

❖ **Figure 2.2** Finding Critical Demarcations in Campbell's Universal Leadership Journey

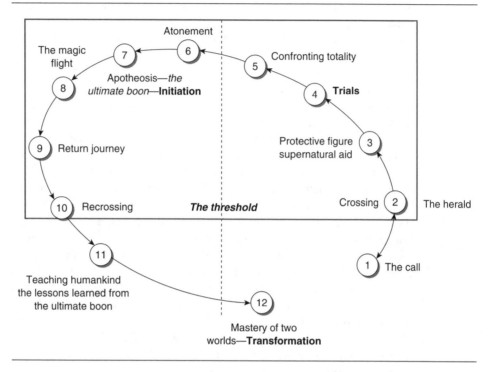

After the arrival of the supernatural aid, the leader is tested by a series of trials (No. 4 in Figure 2.2). The trials may be fierce monsters or seductive sirens as in the tale of Ulysses. In the story of the Buddha, his trials involved leaping a river and assuming the garments of a beggar so that he could transcend the eight stages of meditation.

The trials of the world's great religious figures are well known. For Moses it was the journey to Mt. Sinai to receive the Commandments. For Jesus it was a long journey in the desert, and for Mohammed the Haj. For Buddha, the long passage of time under the Bo Tree involved the mysteries of the mind and learning how to invert thought.

After the trials and tests, the leader confronts Totality (No. 5 in Figure 2.2). The figure of Totality is God. For medieval saints, the figure of Totality was the Virgin Mary (Campbell, 1973, p. 71). But the idea that the original universe was a virgin female plays an important pivotal role in many cultures, from the Aztec to the folk tales from the Tonga. The reason she is a virgin is because " . . . her spouse is the Invisible Unknown" (Campbell, 1973, p. 297).

The creation of new life is mystical and the union of child and mother is "the basic image of mythology" (Campbell, 1990, p. 1; Walker, 1983, pp. 183–185) and represents "the participation mystique" in which there is a complete union with the universe. For some contemporary religions today, God is male and referenced in the masculine gender. However, male–female gods are not uncommon and mean that the Totality contains both sexes because earthly dualisms are resolved. For example, Shiva, Lord of the Cosmic Dance in India, assumes the form of a masculine person on the right side and a feminine person on the left and is known as Ardhanarisha, "The Half-Woman Lord" (Campbell, 1973, p. 154).

The Judaeo-Christian God is masculine and the state in which man and God are united is atonement (No. 6 in Figure 2.2). For Christians, the words from John 6:55 in the New Testament are a vivid image of transformation and unification: "He that eateth my flesh, and drinketh my blood, dwelleth in me, and I in him." The practice of transubstantiation by the Catholic Church in which the bread and wine literally become Jesus's flesh and blood was the focal point for conflict and the Protestant rebellion. Two early Protestant rebels, John Huss and Jerome of Prague, were burned at the stake for denying the doctrine of transubstantiation. Protestants referred to Catholics as "God-eaters" and declared them worse than cannibals (Walker, 1983, p. 1013).

Once the leader has connected with the Great Totality he is transformed (No. 7 in Figure 2.2). When Gautama became the Buddha and was Enlightened, he sat spellbound for 7 days in complete bliss. Buddhists believe that the highest form of Enlightenment is not communicable because it is beyond identities and dissolves all the binaries that confuse humans in their day-to-day struggles. In Judaism it is said that when Moses returned from Mt. Sinai with the Divine Laws, the land was wracked with earthquakes and severe storms and peace was not restored until the first words of the Decalogue were spoken and the earth was calmed by them (Campbell, 1973, p. 34). Apotheosis represents the stage where the leader "to be" receives the "ultimate boon." This "ultimate" knowledge is portrayed as powerful and encompassing, sometimes with a weapon of war that is completely devastating to earthly enemies or in others the introduction into a heavenly paradise.

The next chunk of Campbell's (1973) universal leadership journey is represented in No. 8 (in Figure 2.2), "the magic flight." In this segment, the future leader is confronted with the task of bringing back to the real world the prize of the leadership journey. This can become a struggle if the gods have been offended in some way, or the guardians of the prize decide to take revenge for their lost secret being stolen. In Greek mythology, Perseus, the son of Jupiter and Danae, was sent to kill Medusa, one of three Gorgon sisters that sported huge teeth, claws, and snakelike hair. After Perseus killed Medusa, he fled for his life from the remaining two Gorgon sisters who pursued him. Perseus flees to the kingdom of Atlas where, after being denied rest, he turns the king into stone by flashing Medusa's severed head in his face. Toward the end of the tale, Perseus kills a sea monster and is pursued to a banquet where a great battle ensues and more combatants are turned to stone by Perseus's use of the severed Medusa's head (Martin, 1991, pp. 104–108). This sequence of events is No. 9 (in Figure 2.2), "the return journey."

No. 10 (in Figure 2.2) in Campbell's universal leadership journey is the recrossing of the threshold. Perhaps no story is so bold of crossing and recrossing this threshold as the Egyptian story of Osiris and Isis. Osiris and Isis are brother and sister, the children of Hem and Nut, the earth and the heavens (Campbell, 1990, pp. 82–92; Seyffert, 1995, pp. 438–439). As they were gods, the Pharaohs married brother and sister. Also brother and sister and of Hem and Nut were Set and Neftis. According to Egyptian myth, Osiris slept with Neftis and conceived Anubis, the jackal-headed god.

However, Set was so angry with Osiris that he devised a fiendish plan. First he had a huge sarcophagus made to fit Osiris. Then he inveigled Osiris to try it and when Osiris was inside, had it strapped tight and taken off to be dumped in the river.

Isis sets forth to find her husband. Osiris has come ashore in Syria, where the sarcophagus has been enveloped in a tree that is cut down and made into a pillar in a Syrian palace. Isis finds Osiris and brings him back encased in the pillar. Opening the pillar, she lies on the dead Osiris and conceives Horus, the god represented by a hawk. Osiris has crossed back into the living. However, Set discovers Isis and Osiris and once again destroys him, cutting him into 15 pieces and scattering his remains over Egypt. Isis patiently gathers the pieces and puts Osiris together again. In this stage, Osiris is conceptualized as the Nile, which overflows its banks and each year fertilizes Egyptian fields. Osiris becomes the judge of the dead, wherein each passing Egyptian's life is weighed in the balance, the heart against a feather. A heart with sin will be heavier than a feather. Every dead person is called Osiris and is united with the god. So in this tale, Osiris was twice killed and twice crossed over the threshold. From this story, the Egyptian practice of embalming is supposed to have originated.

An Example of a Personal Leadership Journey: The Story of Miyamoto Musashi

The mythology of every culture and time revolves around the energies that emanate from you. In the words of Joseph Campbell (1990), "Deities are symbolic personifications of the very energies that are of yourself. These energies that are of yourself are the energies of the universe" (p. 106). The first act of leadership is coming to grips with yourself, who you are, where you are, and what is of value to you, and shaping yourself by acts of conscious will into what you want to become.

Clarissa Estes (1992) reminds us that there never is a "right time" for this to occur. It takes an act of courage to initiate the process. "If this were not so, " she says, "we would not have needed to create the words *heroine, hero,* or *courage*" (p. 145). Of what kind of courage is the cantadora speaking? "Courage means to follow the heart" (Estes, p. 242). Gandhi (Iyer, 1973) also explained this point by noting, "Truth is what we believe in our hearts, not what we profess" (p. 169).

Gandhi was also a great believer not in heroes but in the necessity to engage in heroic action, that is, a perspective that is heroic involved "the pursuit of honor through action" (Iyer, 1973, p. 135) and that nothing had ever been achieved without "direct action" (Iyer, 1973, p. 325).

Stories of actual people who undertook this adventure abound. Some have assumed legendary proportions. Here is one. Miyamoto Musashi is one of Japan's greatest heroes. He participated in the Battle of Sekigahara in 1600, one of the seminal clashes in all of Japanese history (Turnbull, 1996, p. 120). According to Eiji Yoshikawa (1995), after Musashi is awakened on the battlefield in the aftermath of the siege, he finds himself wounded and bewildered (Campbell's "the call"). Struggling home ("the threshold") he encounters a Zen monk who captures him ("the herald"). He is freed by a lovely woman ("protective figure"), but is recaptured and cast into solitary confinement ("the trials"), where he passes his time reading the classical literature of Japan and China ("confronting reality"). When he is set free he rejects becoming a traditional samurai and instead works on his mind ("the atonement").

What Miyamoto Musashi learned was that a great warrior had to create an internal and stable "inner platform" (Ratti & Westbrook, 1999, p. 376). Developing such an "inner platform" meant developing character and remaining cool and very observant to react correctly and quickly to any situation. This mental attitude, called *bujutsu,* drew heavily on resolving some of humankind's most compelling problems in facing death. Control over an opponent involved first learning to control one's self.

The principle task involved the idea of "intrinsic energy" (Ratti & Westbrook, 1999, p. 381). Inner energy could come about only if a person engaged in disciplined introspection in which the inner human was consolidated and became transcendent by recognizing that true strength was centered on becoming, development, and ultimately transformation. This "life center" is known in Japan as "ki," in India as "prajna," and in China as "ch'i" (Ratti & Westbrook, p. 381).

Once he gained the insights into his inner center and learned to blend the self with cosmic force, Musashi evolved into Japan's greatest swordsman using two swords in each hand, a style of fighting that few could master ("the recrossing"). Paraphrased, here are Musashi's guidelines for attaining the proper mental attitude ("teaching humankind"):

1. Determine what is correct and true.

2. Place science into daily practice.

3. Know the arts. Honor the crafts.

4. Realize that everything has positives and negatives. Search them out.

5. Acquire the capacity to observe things accurately.

6. Know that important things are not always obvious.

7. Attend to the smallest detail.

8. Avoid extraneous activities. (after Cleary, 1992, p. 38)

Kenjutsu in Japan is the art of the sword (Ratti & Westbrook, 1999, p. 389). We can say it also represents the art of leadership in the culture of the time. Kenjutsu involves understanding and mastering the technical knowledge and the moves and sleights of hand required in master swordplay. But technical knowledge is not enough. The other half of kenjutsu is the "art" of performance centered in the inner human being. The mind has to be freed from external attachments during an encounter, including the sword itself.

Chief among the development of the art was the mental set involving preventive awareness that is grounded in keen perception. Such acute mental awareness involved the ability to sense an attack coming without any obvious signs of one. A modern example of "preventive awareness" and the display of a calm internal platform occurred in the 2001 Paramount film *Lara Croft Tomb Raider.* In the opening scene, Lara tests herself against a monster robot as she stays one step ahead of it and anticipates its moves in a ferocious duel. Throughout this spectacular combat scene, she demonstrates *bujutsu.*

The Origins of Leadership

The origins of leadership are buried in every one of us. As each human being comes to terms with the meaning of life, the hidden meanings and issues in confronting death are the first challenges. Sometimes the challenges are avoided with devastating psychological effects, leaving a kind of collective rage. Clarissa Estes (1992) describes the trials for a woman in searching for a way back from having been buried by social conventions, by being forced to take on the mantle of feigned female helplessness imposed by a male-dominated culture. As a woman begins taking control of her life, "she is learning to wake up, pay attention, stop being naïve, uninformed" (Estes, p. 252). Estes adds, "If you want to re-summon Wild Woman, refuse to be captured" (p. 255). Some humans spend their lives running from the dilemma, burying themselves in work or in mental boxes that prop them up and reassure them of purpose. Mental rigidity stems from fear and the basic fear is a refusal to take up the self. Before a leader leads others, he or she must come to terms with his or her own mortality and with the central moral issues of their times.

James Barber (1985), a professor of political science at Duke University, has long held that he can predict the performance of U.S. presidents. His leadership model is shown in Figure 2.3.

To understand presidential leadership, one must first describe the person's character, world view, and style. By character is meant "the person's stance as he confronts experience" (Barber, 1985, p. 5). The major aspect of character is how a person faces himself or herself. World view is how a leader perceives his or her environment and "particularly [his] conceptions of social causality, human nature, and the central moral conflicts of the time" (Barber, p. 5). Style is the way a leader acts upon his world view. Corresponding to human maturity, Barber comments that, as a human matures, "character has its main development in childhood, world view in adolescence, style in early adulthood" (p. 7). The interaction of these internal variables with the mediating variables such as the power situation and the climate of expectations produces one of four different types of leadership

❖ **Figure 2.3** James Barber's Presidential Leadership Model

performances. By *power situation,* Barber is referring to the political forces already in play when a president takes office. These forces may be the balance of parties in the Congress, the strength of the U.S. Supreme Court, and the activity and strength of various powerful lobbying interests and their influence on Congress and other government agencies. By *climate of expectations,* Barber (1985) refers to "the predominant needs thrust up to him by the people" (p. 6). In this area Barber points out that there are three aspects to the climate of expectations.

The first aspect of the climate of expectations is that of reassurance. Here the need of the people is to be told that everything is going to be all right, even in times of great tragedy. The second is the requirement for the people to sense that the president is going to engage in progress and action. Here the president must display himself as a person who is a "take-charge man, a doer, a turner of wheels, a producer of progress" (Barber, 1985, p. 6). Finally, the president must convey a sense of legitimacy, that is, that he is the "defender of the faith," or the "American way of life." This is the place where the president must take the moral high ground. It is the opposite of "politics as usual." In this situation, the president must stand for all of the people and the nation. Examples of where presidents have responded to all of these challenges are Franklin Roosevelt's address to Congress following the attack on Pearl Harbor or George W. Bush's speech to Congress following the attack on the Twin Towers in New York City on September 11, 2001.

In human history, similar leaders have essentially modeled the same response to a climate of expectations. Take the following, for example: Pericles' (495–429 B.C.) funeral oration given to salute fallen Athenian soldiers in the first Peloponnesian War (Kagan, 2003, p. 73); the confession of Queen Elizabeth I, "I know I have but the body of a weak and feeble woman; but I have the heart of a king," in arming her country against the Spanish Armada in 1588 (Safire, 1996, p. 85); Sojourner Truth's poignant 1851 address to the Ohio Woman's Rights Convention in which she asked rhetorically four times, "And ain't I a woman?" (Safire, p. 627); Winston Churchill's famous 1940 speech to parliament in which he proffered, "I have nothing to offer but blood, toil, tears and sweat" (Copeland, 1942, p. 460); Martin Luther King, Jr.'s, famous "I have a dream" speech of 1963 (Safire, p. 535); and British Prime Minister Margaret Thatcher's 1982 address to a conservative women's conference in which she defined British action in the Falkland Islands and said, "Let us, then, draw together in the name, not of jingoism, but of justice" (Safire, p. 151).

Evidence of Barber's concept of leadership development is drawn from a recent and compelling ethical biography of Abraham Lincoln by William Lee Miller (2002). In his revealing analysis of Lincoln's early life, and especially his development as a moral thinker, Miller traces the young Lincoln's humane treatment of animals, including his refusal to hunt or fish; his declination to formally embrace the dogma of any established religion; his abstention in the use of tobacco, alcohol, swearing, or gambling without being pretentious about it; his demurral to engage in nativist rhetoric; and his living within a social world that was racially prejudiced and soft on slavery, which he always opposed, as documentation of an independence of thought and of his own success in educating (shaping) himself (pp. 43–44). Lincoln did not read widely; such texts were not available on the frontier. But what he did read he knew well. That included the King James Version of the Bible and the plays of William Shakespeare, as well as a few additional texts on elocution, history, and biography, the latter most notably a famous but inaccurate version of the life of George Washington (Miller, 2002, pp. 50–52). As a one-term congressman from Illinois, the young Lincoln spent his "spare time" not in drinking, gambling, smoking, or going to church, but burying himself in the book stacks of the Congressional Library. For this activity, he earned the contempt of some of his fellow legislators as a "book worm." But as Miller explains, by young adulthood Lincoln had developed "moral self-confidence" (p. 52).

It was the kind of moral confidence that was displayed from his very first days in the U.S. House of Representatives in the form of a blistering personal attack on President James Polk (1795–1849) for starting and continuing the Mexican War, a conflict that Lincoln perceived as an unadulterated program of conquest (Miller, 2002, pp. 182–183).

However, when it came to moral principles, Lincoln was not a pacifist. When, after his election as president he had an opportunity to choose between war or the extension of slavery into the rest of the nation, he refused to budge on the issue of human bondage and the most terrible war in American history was the result. And Miller (2002) reminds his readers that as a generally merciful man, Lincoln refused to consider any leniency for Nathaniel Gordon, the only person ever put to death for engaging in slave trading by the United States government (p. 266; see also Donald, 1996, p. 342).

The Barber model is a dynamic view of how the internal and mediating variables, some part of the inner human and others embedded in context, culture, and the times, mix together a unique potion called leadership. As Samier (2005a) has observed, " . . . there is no universal charismatic character—it is contextual bound to the conditions, values, and institutional structure of society" (p. 73). This is one type of outcome orientation Barber (1985) calls "active-positive." Such a leader with this orientation possesses high self-esteem, and confidence in relating to his or her environment. The "active-positive" leader is not rigid. He or she selects the dance that is right for the music of the times. He or she places an emphasis on rational mastery of his or her job. "Active-positive" leaders are motivated by results. They are supremely goal oriented.

The "active-negative" leader puts forth a huge amount of energy but is unable to find much emotional recompense for his or her efforts. The "active-negative" leader knows that life is hard. He or she is strongly upwardly mobile. He or she seeks power as a reward. He or she often holds a perfectionistic perspective about work. The primary motivator for "active-negatives" is to obtain and retain power.

Barber (1985) then examines "passive-positive" leaders and finds that their lives represent a search for compassion and affection. They want to be known as being humane and cooperative. They seem to have low-self esteem, sometimes showing a false or paper-thin optimism. They want to be admired and loved. They are often disappointed with a life in politics.

Finally, "passive-negative" presidents believe they should be leading because they think they should be. It is a way a person finds meaning in an otherwise useless life. "Passive-positives" don't like conflict. They appear withdrawn and resort to procedures and protocols to make decisions. They sometimes picture themselves as guardians of the right and moral way because it serves to assuage their consciences and helps them rationalize the sleazy nature of politics in which they are embedded (see Barber, 1985, p. 10).

Leadership Is Universal—But Leaders Are Contextual and Culturally Specific Actors

While the leadership life journey is duplicated through the ages, the faces of leadership are buried within each culture, its languages, mores, and customs. Leadership is about culture and is stirred along the lines of cultural traditions. Leadership is reflective of the dominant sexual and personal mores of those cultures. It reflects each culture's gender roles as well as the customary ideas of attire, etiquette, and definitions of courage. From this perspective, a "good" leader is always "good" within the boundaries of his or her culture and tradition. A. R. Radcliffe-Brown (1933) indicated the following:

> A society depends for its existence on the presence in the mind of its members of a certain system of sentiments by which the conduct of the individual is regulated in conformity with the needs of society . . . The ceremonial (i.e., collective) expression of any sentiment serves both to maintain it . . . in the mind of the individual and to transmit it from one generation to another. (pp. 233–234)

Howard Gardner (1995) echoes these sentiments about leaders when he observed that leadership occurs "within the minds of individuals who live in a culture" (p. 22). Gardner concentrated on the exchange of stories within a common culture. Leaders and followers swim within a social structure that is culturally specific, relying on stories that all understand. The great common pieces of literature, the fairy tales, myths, folklore, and wisdom that every culture possesses, become the common symbolic bonds between leaders and followers.

Yet as the tales and myths of each culture permeate its art and its artifacts with universal longings and fears, leadership can be understood only in context. This point was dramatically underscored by the eminent military historian John Keegan (1987) when he was discussing the desire of the founding of Western military academies to abstract the lessons of generalship so that they could be taught to each new generation, an approach not unlike the current strategy with the ISLLC Standards (Interstate Leaders Licensure Consortium), which are used to evaluate and ultimately accredit university programs that prepare educational leaders (see Hessel & Holloway, 2002).

As Keegan (1987) points out in his criticism of behavioral studies from the social scientists, they labor to extract into general principles and laws "what is stubbornly local and particular" (p. 1): "Generalship is . . . much more than command of armies . . . For an army is . . . an expression of the society from which it issues . . . A general . . . will in the last resort act as a man of his time and place . . . context . . . is all" (pp. 2–3).

Keegan (1987) concedes that military leaders usually possess certain physical traits of endurance and raw physical courage, but this alone does not and will not explain their successes or failures. What is more important is "to ask how the societies to which they belonged expected such qualities to be presented" (p. 11). For answers, we return to the murals of the early Tiahuanaco in Peru; stone carvings in the Indus Valley, India; the delicate white ware of the Shang, China, exhibiting two-wheeled chariots; and even stretching to contemporary America. The same powerful psychic forces that propelled humans through time to engage in describing their personal leadership journey are at work today. A stunning combination of religion, image, and symbols in describing leadership is the successful struggle of the Mexican American labor leader Dolores Huerta. Her story is of a schoolteacher and mother of 11 children who quit teaching to become a passionate social justice leader who pushed aside traditional strictures of gender roles to engage in tireless work to improve the lives of Mexican American farm workers. It is inspiring and testimony to the power of individual human agency to bring about profound changes in the human landscape.

Biography Box 2.1

Dolores Huerta (1930–)

She Quit Teaching to Lead a Labor Movement

Dolores Huerta (1930–) is a former schoolteacher who finally quit the classroom because she could no longer tolerate the conditions in which her children came to school, hungry and without shoes. Huerta was born in Dawson, New Mexico. Her father was a Mexican American miner who was later blacklisted because he engaged in union activities (Schiff, 2005, p. 299). When her parents later divorced, Dolores moved to Stockton, California, with her mother and her siblings. She witnessed her mother's participation in the 1938 cannery worker's strike. Dolores was pushed by her mother to be independent and she did not follow the traditional gender roles in which the girls had to cook and wash clothes for their brothers. She participated in Girl Scouts and it was there she learned about leadership.

Dolores's schooling experience was not always positive. Some of her teachers questioned whether she had actually written the papers she was turning in because they were "too good" for Mexicans. Her mother took her to Mexico City and she learned about her heritage. Dolores's father kept in contact. Her served in the navy in the Korean War and at age 51 he graduated from college.

Dolores married her high school sweetheart, had two children, and divorced. Later she married Ventura Huerta and had five more children. She became active in community organizing, going to public meetings and nursing her children in the public restrooms in between. Dolores organized the Agricultural Workers Association as the only way to upgrade farm workers' lives and their economic gains. She found people resistant to the idea of a woman running an organization and tried to take a back seat while urging trusted men and family to take the leadership role. And the continuing demands for leadership, child bearing, and her passion for the cause led to her second divorce. This time there ensued a custody battle in which her husband accused her of being a negligent mother. She threw herself more fervently into her work and battled to keep her children. During this time she renewed her religious faith and went to church. She believed that while she labored for farm workers, God would take care of the rest.

In 1962, Dolores Huerta and Cesar Chavez started the United Farm Workers Union (UFWU). When she went recruiting for the UFWU, she took her children, slept in her car or on the ground, ate from hand to mouth, and also sacrificed time

(Continued)

(Continued)

with her children. But her passion was her cause. And she had great grassroots organizing skills, which the union sorely needed. Huerta took advantage of the fact that, from her perspective, women's egos were not as involved as men's and women were more open to compromise. Compromise is the key to successful unionism, in keeping the rank and file together and in making progress toward sought-after objectives in contract negotiations.

Dolores Huerta has never tired of being an activist, although it has often placed her in personal danger. She has been jailed over 20 times. In 1988, during a peaceful protest against the policies of President George H. W. Bush, she was hit by police batons that broke two ribs and ruptured her spleen. She continues to be an indefatigable labor leader and was inducted into the National Women's Hall of Fame in 1993.

The American Monomyth in Action

Jewett and Lawrence (1988) assert that there is an American monomyth, that is, the presence of "an archetypal plot pattern emerging in which a community threatened by evil is redeemed through superheroism" (p. 308). The outline of the American monomyth begins with a peaceful representation of Eden, usually a small town in the Midwest calmly going about its business until it is attacked by evil. Such a disruption must be resolved by the creation of a superhero. The superhero exists in the form of the town marshal or sheriff, or a single stranger. In a modern context set in a large city, we have the motifs of plots of the films *Batman* and *Spiderman*.

The American monomyth also involves the concept of *redemptive resolution* in which a siege is relieved or a group of innocents is saved by vigilantes or cowboys. The redeemer figure of the town sheriff standing up to outlaws and other desperados pillaging and plundering Eden echoes through such westerns as *High Noon* and many of Clint Eastwood's spaghetti westerns such as *For a Few Dollars More* and *The Good, the Bad and the Ugly*, directed by Sergi Leone. The idea of the lone cowboy riding into town and cleaning it up is behind many westerns, including the popular TV series in the late 1960s anchored by Richard Boone, *Have Gun Will Travel*. The "face off" in the street between the "good guy" and the "bad guy" is legendary in American films. The figure of the redemptive lawman who has repressed or renounced his own sexuality is an implicit theme. The American hero verges on sainthood. While Europeans ridicule the image of the "cowboy" in describing the behavior of George Bush or Ronald Reagan (Cava, 2003, p. 2A) as aberrant, American images of the cowboy rarely have such resonances. If anything, the cowboy is a romantic metaphor and not one signifying that someone is "crazy."

Jewett and Lawrence (1988) summarize the American monomyth as the following: ". . . vigilantism without lawlessness, sexual repression without resultant perversion, and moral infallibility without the use of intellect. It features a restoration of Eden for others, but refuses to allow the dutiful hero to participate in its pleasures" (p. 196).

The idea of a paradise restored "by heroes larger than life has appeals far deeper than reason, particularly to a culture believing itself besieged by ruthless foes" (Jewett

& Lawrence, 1988, p. 196). Americans have long held their form of government and their way of life to be under attack by vicious despots and dictators. This theme is embedded in the nation's Declaration of Independence, which cites the king's "abuses and usurpations" of the American Colonists (Jewett & Lawrence, p. 175).

The Declaration of Independence was formal recognition of what the American Colonists had come to see as a grand plan of enslavement of their way of life. Historian Bernard Bailyn (1992) indicates that after 1763, Americans came to believe that there was a strategy to eradicate their society. He cites a Boston Town meeting in 1770 as an example: "A series of occurrences, many recent events . . . afford great reason to believe that a deep-laid and desperate plan of imperial despotism has been laid . . . for the extinction of all civil liberty . . . The dreadful catastrophe threatens universal havoc . . ." (p. 94).

The interposition of divine help for Americans was noted by the Boston Committee of Correspondence when it wrote that God had "wonderfully interposed to bring to light the plot that has been laid for us by our malicious and invidious enemies" (Bailyn, 1992, p. 122). This concept of rapacious evildoers bent on destruction of America was what "in the end propelled them [the Colonists] into Revolution" (Bailyn, p. 95). In this sense they were propelled by such incendiary and influential writings such as Tom Paine's *Common Sense,* which labeled the English monarch "the Pharaoh of England" (Maier, 1997, pp. 31–33).

On September 11, 2001, an event once again offered convincing evidence of a plan to erase the American way of life. Foreigners do not appreciate the vitality of the American monomyth in explaining the destruction of New York's Twin Towers. Innocent victims were saved by the police and firefighters (the heroes) who came to the rescue and were themselves cut down. American heroes were also in the skies as they resisted the takeover by terrorists on one of the airline flights headed to Washington, DC, which subsequently crashed in Pennsylvania. The wives of those heroes were saluted by President Bush in Congress before a national and international audience where he warned that an "axis of evil" was at work to destroy America. As Americans responded with an invasion of Afghanistan and Iraq, some European allies were mystified and then alienated. Their cultures were not animated by the American monomyth.

In a prescient analysis, Francois Heisbourg ("Dissent Over Iraq," 2003), a French director of a think tank in Paris for strategic research, said

> The biblical references in politics, the division of the world between good and evil, these are things that we simply don't get . . . They [Europeans] don't understand what 9/11 meant for the U.S.—a terrible shock that affects the whole world outlook of Americans. (p. A-8)

The roots of the American monomyth in the American Revolution were inexorably stirred by September 11, 2001, and Europeans were decidedly anxious by "the crusader-like tone of the Bush administration" ("Dissent Over Iraq," 2003). Mythologies are not fake or amusing stories. They are the real glue that holds peoples and nations together. For many they [myths] are integral in sustaining personal and social psychic health. In the Western world, the myth supports the "system" or the "establishment," and the establishment in turn sanctions the myth (Larue, 1975, p. 200).

Like all world cultures, America has need of contemporary myths. Popular myths live on in film and music. One need only take a look at the Great Seal of the United States, which is on the back of the American dollar. Above the pyramid on the left side of the dollar is the "all-seeing eye" of ancient Egypt. This symbol once belonged to *Maat,* the goddess of truth and justice from which the syllable *Maa* was translated to mean "to see" (Walker, 1983, p. 294). The all-seeing eye became the infamous "evil eye" when the female spirit was demonized in the Christian and Islamic religions. The word *ayin* means "eye" and became the "evil eye" in Arabic writing. Syrians use the words *aina bisha,* meaning "the eye witch." In Christian lore, during the Inquisition, condemned witches had to walk before their male judges backward so that their "evil eye" could not lay a curse on them (Walker, p. 294).

Myths contained in religion remain a strong force in America, mostly Christianity in the forms of Protestantism and Catholicism, but also with Judaism and Islam, the latter being a dynamic and growing force in the United States. All these religions contain cultural images of the lands and peoples from which they emanated. As such they are cast from cultural mirrors as double images, particularly in gender roles. In nearly all the dominant U.S. religions, the gender of God is male. Since religious mythologies give rise to cultural, economic, and political manifestations, it is important to recognize contemporary mythologies as defining forces because myths shape our attitudes toward facts and what we claim is "reality" (Highwater, 1990, p. 14). If we are to understand the special problems culture and mythology hold for women, we have to examine gender roles at work in the myths in which we currently believe. And modern American society does believe in its special narratives or mythos. A 1998 Harris Poll revealed that 66% of non-Christian Americans believed in miracles and 47% similarly believed in the Virgin Birth. The figures for Christians were much higher. At least 45% of all Americans believe in the Devil. Seventy-one percent of fundamentalist Protestants, according to a 1999 *Newsweek* magazine poll, believe that the world will end in a titanic battle (Armageddon) between Jesus and the Anti-Christ (Judt, 2003, p. 27). Most cultures believe that their special myths are good, are true, and represent "reality." America is no different than others in this respect.

A more modern and educational example of a hero in the American monomythic tradition is the life and career of Harold Howe II, former U.S. Commissioner of Education shown in Biography Box 2.1.

Gender Barriers in Mythos and Religion

Patricia Reilly (1995) wrote a best-selling book titled *A God Who Looks Like Me.* It is a painful remembrance of a young girl growing up in a Judaic-Christian tradition in which God was "the Father" and the image of woman was lodged in an immoral Eve in the Garden of Eden. These early images, combined with the figure of a male savior in the form of Moses, Jesus, or Mohammed, help lay the early groundwork for female guilt, submission, and acceptance of men as the "natural" leaders of women. They become enormous psychic barriers for women and give men a false sense of their own "natural" leadership abilities. Reilly notes that "religious language is very powerful and exerts a lasting influence on our lives. The language of traditional religion permeates our society" (p. 51). Reilly's reflections about gender are poignant when she

BIOGRAPHY BOX 2.2

Harold Howe II (1918–2002)

The Southern Segregationist Senators
Called Him "The U.S. Commissioner of Integration"

Harold "Doc" Howe II (1918–2002) served as U.S. Commissioner of Education from 1966 to 1968 in the Lyndon Johnson administration. He was sponsored by the Secretary of Health, Education, and Welfare, John W. Gardner, himself a famous educator who authored several notable books on education, social issues, and leadership (Gardner, 1961, 1963, 1968, 1991). Harold Howe was born in Hartford, Connecticut, the son of Reverend Arthur Howe, then a professor at Dartmouth and formerly president of the Hampton Institute in Virginia. Howe's grandfather, Samuel Chapman Armstrong, was a Union general in the Civil War and founded Hampton as a trade school for freed slaves.

Harold Howe II grew up on the campus of Hampton and developed a good rapport with African Americans and a passionate zeal for equal opportunities. He graduated in 1940 from Yale, where he excelled in athletics, and began teaching at a private school. He later was captain of a Navy minesweeper during World War II. He received his master's degree in history from Columbia University and did postgraduate work at Harvard and the University of Cincinnati. He became a high school principal before moving to Scarsdale, New York, as the city's superintendent of schools, a position he held from 1960 to 1964.

In the early 1960s, he directed the Learning Institute of North Carolina while he was an adjunct professor at Duke University. He worked hard on the social problems of poverty and racial segregation. As U.S. Commissioner of Education, he became a strong advocate in the Great Society program to rid the nation of racial segregation under the auspices of the 1964 Civil Rights Act. In these labors, he was derided by several segregationist southern senators as the "U.S. Commissioner of Integration."

That sobriquet was earned because Howe set minimum integration goals that school systems had to meet to receive federal funds, and he pushed through the establishment of tough deadlines and procedures that school districts had to meet. He was particularly interested in the status of teachers and school administrators. After his Washington stint, he affiliated with the Ford Foundation as an advisor to India and lectured at the Harvard Graduate School of Education (*The New York Times*, 2002).

remembers that "the maleness of God and the inferiority of women were woven into the religious literature, instruction, and ritual that surrounded us in childhood" (p. 166). The domination of men over women in the Judeo-Christian mythos continues into present times. For example, Israel's Supreme Court recently ruled that Jewish women could not worship at the Western Wall and read from the Torah. Ultra-Orthodox Jewish tradition bars women from reading the Torah ("Women Barred," 2003, p. 7A). Southern Baptist missionaries were also recently informed that they had to swear "that they believe in wives' submission to husbands and oppose female pastors" ("What's News," 2003, p. A1).

But God was not always male. Jamake Highwater (1990) indicates that there were certain pre-Hellenic mythologies dominated by female earth spirits and that the notion of a supreme male deity occurred about 2500 B.C. in the form of the Greek god Zeus, and later the figure of Abraham emerged from the Old Testament (p. 32). Barbara Walker (1983) indicates that "all the most ancient mythologies speak of a Creatress rather than a Creator because living things could be made only by a female . . ." (p. 680).

Even in early Christian literature, in the Gnostic creation myths, God was portrayed as female (Walker, 1983, p. 184). All religions have developed narratives regarding creation. In the Christian tradition, Jehovah is the male God who engaged in creation. However, Jean Austric, an 18th-century French Catholic physician and scholar, claimed that the Book of Genesis contained two versions of creation. One version, called by scholars the "E" strand, spoke of "plural creators, *elohim,* male and female deities" (Walker, pp. 184–185). The second or "J" version has come to be the accepted interpretation today. The multiple interpretations of the Bible occur for many reasons, not only because of the many amendments to the document that happened over many centuries, but because the fount of stories contained have been derived from many sources over the same time period. In fact, the Archbishop of Canterbury acknowledged that the Christian Bible is full of myths and legends (White, 1955, p. 359).

The erasure of female divinities was not confined to Christianity. Prior to the rise of Islam in the Mideast, the tribes of Arabia were governed by a matriarchal culture. The name of God in Islam, *Allah,* was derived from *Ah-Lat,* part of a female trinity in Arabia. Mecca, now the holiest site in Islam, was the place where the Goddess Shaybah or Sheba was worshipped in the form of a black stone, now a shrine called the *Kaaba.* The stone was "a feminine symbol . . . and covered like the ancient Mother by a veil" (Walker, 1983, p. 51).

Deborah Rhode (2003), the director of the Keck Center on Legal Ethics at the Stanford Law School, summarizes the legacy for women through time when she says, "For most of recorded history, women were largely excluded from formal leadership positions" (p. 3). Despite being excluded, women have exerted enormous influence, but not by being selected for such formal leadership positions. They worked through men within networks dominated by men. Such dominance has very deep and wide roots in gender stereotypes that are codes of behavior within the dominant mythos of our times. Such codes prescribe what is appropriate for men and women in social contexts. Despite our understanding of gender stereotypes, " . . . the characteristics traditionally associated with women are at odds with the characteristics traditionally associated with leadership" (Rhode, pp. 8–9). They are even steeper for women of color.

The dearth of women in the top educational leadership positions has been noted in the previous chapter (see Blount, 1998, 1999, 2003). The same is true in other spheres. For example, Ruth Mandel (2003) cites the startling statistic that in 2002 there were 7,424 people in the top educational leadership positions, of which 22% were women. Among legislators age 35 or younger, there were 320 in the top educational leadership positions, of which 36 were women. Mandel ruminates that "...women who set out on a road to top leadership will still travel in domains designed by and for men, replete with the residues of men's leadership for centuries" (p. 73). The contribution of the dominant mythos and its pervasive influence on governing the social relations between men and women and the apportionment of power by gender in that mythos exerts a deep and wide impact on both sexes. The dominance of gender role stereotypes has served to reproduce the idea of *heteronormativity* in schools and in schools of education (Fraynd & Capper, 2003).

Mary Cranston (2003), a nationally known and accomplished attorney named to the National Law Journal's list of the most influential lawyers in America, confronted her own anger about the issue by coming to terms with the fact that she was "...unconsciously conceding men that power...when instead I could have been looking within...Ironically, the cultural bias was in my own head as well as in the culture" (p. 177). Similar stories have occurred in education where women have been barred from executive positions based on their gender (see Tyack, 1974, p. 266) or called "hysterical" when they objected to male decision content or decision making (see Spring, 1986, pp. 265–269). Such biases are also consciously or unconsciously dealt with by educational administrators who may be gay, lesbian, bisexual, or transgendered (Koschoreck, 2003; Lugg, 2003).

The idea of dealing with the problems in one's own head as the first barrier to confront in facing the challenges of leadership is contained in *bujutsu*, the concept of attaining a stable internal platform to combat one's external foes successfully. While the code of the warrior has undeniable male trappings in feudal Japan, it is applicable today to signify becoming aware of the obstacles in one's own culture that have not yet come to conscious awareness, as Mary Cranston's testimony shows, and the necessity for "identity management" for sexually minority administrators (Fraynd & Capper, 2003, pp. 103–106).

The crucible of leadership lies in the living dreams and memories of all humans in all times and places. The creation myths of many cultures contain references to darkness in which light suddenly occurs representing universal "memories of birth trauma" in which the lumination of the world shines into the eyes of every newborn for the first time (Walker, 1983, p. 184). At the core of all myths lies the child/mother relationship. The living memories of the human experience have been cast and recast through the ages in symbolic form. Joseph Campbell (1973) reminds us of the following: "For the symbols of mythology are not manufactured; they cannot be ordered, invented, or permanently suppressed. They are spontaneous productions of the psyche, and each bears within it, undamaged, the germ power of its source" (p. 4).

The myths of our age contain references to the universal human experience, but they have been shaped by specific historical and cultural forces. They assume forms within the culture and context of the times. While myths are neither right nor wrong, they contain references and relationships that influence contemporary behavior in the home; the workplace; the church, synagogue, and temple; or in intimate, interpersonal human situations. Leadership, as a phenomenon of the universal and the contextual, is likewise a living and vibrant manifestation of the same relationships and forces in our lives. It can never be extinguished as long as humans are who they are.

Educational leaders are part and parcel of the general cultural and contextual fabric of the times in which they work. Schools represent specific and sanctified forms within each culture as it defines, protects, and seeks to extend itself into the future. Educational leaders are cultural leaders and it is important that the culture that binds them be made more inclusive than it has been in the past. The roots of leadership lie in each leader's personal journey toward self-knowledge. Academic preparation and a practicing internship simply build on this foundation.

Pursuing Learning Extensions of the Chapter

The nuclear unit of the monomyth is amply demonstrated in many popular films. Part of the learning extensions of this chapter involve reviewing these films and learning to "see" them differently. Here are some of the films that are recommended as learning extensions of this chapter:

The Lord of the Rings: The Fellowship of the Ring (2002), Color, DVD, New Line Cinema, 2 Hours 40 Minutes

Based on J. R. R. Tolkien's best-selling triology, the *Lord of the Rings* involves the classic Joseph Campbell's nuclear unit of the monomyth (see Figure 2.2). Tolkien was an Oxford Don who, as a medievalist, also wrote scholarly works concerning Chaucer and Beowulf. Tolkien was very familiar with the narratives of myths and folk tales. This film can be analyzed using Campbell's nuclear unit of the monomyth.

Lara Croft Tomb Raider (2001), Color, DVD, Paramount Pictures, 1 Hour 40 Minutes

Based on a popular video game, the heroine of this film also follows Joseph Campbell's nuclear unit of the monomyth as she sets forth to search for the "triangle of light," a historic invention that is able to alter time and space. Lara, played by Angelina Jolie, crosses gender lines in her exploits. She is strong, skilled in the martial arts, tough, resilient, shrewd, and although portrayed as feminine and sexy by conventional standards, takes on the attributes of the American monomyth by being uninterested in romantic interludes. Lara is all business and easily outfoxes if not outfights all of her male opponents and enemies. Lara Croft is the female equivalent of Campbell's male hero in the customary heroic adventures of men being tested in the monomyth.

Crouching Tiger Hidden Dragon (2000), Color, DVD, Sony Pictures, 2 Hours

Set in 19th-century China, Ang Lee's film is based on a 1930 Chinese *wuxia* novel that represents classic portrayals of Joseph Campbell's archetypal characters. The hero is Li Mu Bai, a legendary swordsman who uses his great weapon, called *Green Destiny*. He is aided by a female warrior, Shu Lien, as they confront their ruthless and deceptive enemy, Jade Fox, also a female.

As opposed to American films in which the heroes and heroines are sexless saints, both Mu Bai and Shu Lien are attracted to each other, but because of the warrior's code they follow, must remain uncommitted and passionless. As Simpson (2001) notes, "*Crouching Tiger* taps so deeply into the roots of ancient myths that it runs the risk of seeming quaint" (p. B19). The energy and power of myth are so dramatically pictured in this film that viewers have found it compelling and engaging.

Seven Samurai (1954), Black and White With English Subtitles, VHS, 3 Hours 28 Minutes

This film has been called one of the 10 best films of all time. Directed by Akira Kurosawa, it is set in 16th-century Japan and involves a journey of seven hired samurai who set out to defend a village against the transgressions of a band of bandits who have been terrorizing them. The trials of the samurai amply display a remarkable steadfastness, technical mastery of various weapons, outstanding perception, and mental stability and serenity in facing a more numerous adversary. While each of the samurai are individual warriors of skill and courage, they face the inevitability of death in a stoic and reserved manner that reveals superb discipline and training. This is leadership as defined by culture, context, and a dash of mythic narrative.

The Seventh Seal (1957), Black and White, VHS, Janus Films, 1 Hour 36 Minutes

Called Ingmar Bergman's greatest film by many, *The Seventh Seal* was shot in a studio in 35 days. The film involves a struggle with death and evil and is set in medieval Europe. A knight has returned from the Crusades with great doubts about his faith and his belief in God. As he enters his homeland, he discovers that his country is being ravaged by the Black Plague. The knight confronts Death in a chess game and is granted a brief reprieve to continue his journey home. The country is thoroughly in the throes of the clutches of religious fanatics who have blamed the pestilence on the wrath of God.

Bergman (1944/1990) calls the central theme in *The Seventh Seal* of confronting two perspectives, one of his childhood religious faith "alongside a harsh and rational perception of reality" (p. 238). These two perspectives are pitted one against the other as the knight continues to play chess against Death. In Bergman's own introspective journey, he recounts his own fears about death that were behind *The Seventh Seal:*

> The fact that I, through dying, would no longer exist, that I would walk through the dark portal, that there was something that I could not control, arrange, or foresee, was for me a source of constant horror. That I plucked up my courage and depicted Death as a white clown, a figure who conversed, played chess, and had no secrets, was the first step in my struggle against my monumental fear of death. (p. 240)

This is a film that lies behind all personal leadership journeys, the awareness by humans that death is everyone's ultimate and permanent fate.

A Film Epitomizing the American Monomyth: The Classic Western

Unforgiven (1992), Color, DVD, Warner Brothers, 2 Hours 11 Minutes

Clint Eastwood starred in and directed this classic Western with a distinctive "antiviolence," profemale theme. Although Big Whiskey, Wyoming, is not the equivalent of Eden, it is run by a sheriff totally devoted to law and order who maintains his control over the town until Eastwood, playing a former gunman turned brief bounty hunter, turns up to avenge the loss of his sidekick. The image of William Munney, the former killer trailing two rampaging cowboys who cut up a saloon prostitute, is far from the romantic cowboy, but his sexless character is filled with the kind of grit and determination that is the trademark of the American monomyth. How this film shapes Americans' image of their country on the world stage today as the sole remaining superpower should give everyone pause to think.

Writing in Your Personal Reflective Journal

Write in your personal reflective journal the story of your own leadership journey. What are the events that were most important to you in desiring to become a leader? If you have had recurring themes in your imagination or in your dreams, can you relate these images or thoughts to that journey?

If you are a woman, have you ever found the dominant themes in our culture's mythology a hindrance to your own aspirations? Did you ever question them or wonder about their origins? If so, how were your queries answered? Do you find them troubling now?

It should also be clear that leadership can be directed toward good or evil causes.

A Review of Key Chapter Concepts

Use a review of these key chapter concepts as a way to test your own understanding of the premises, ideas, and concepts that are part of this chapter.

archetypes—This was created by Carl Jung to explain the concept that humans carry in their minds fundamental ideas or primary images of experiences that may be lodged in the unconscious.

atonement—This is a phase in the leadership life journey in which the human and the Divine are united.

crossing the threshold—This is within Joseph Campbell's concept of the nuclear unit of the monomyth: When the hero/heroine goes from the world of the living to the supernatural world (often of death or representations of death), the transition is referred to as "crossing the threshold."

heteronormativity—This is the idea that "normal" sexual relations between humans is heterosexual (male/female) and rarely or never homosexual (same sex).

identity management—This is the notion that gay/lesbian educators must conceal their sexual identity to others for fear of reproach or retribution in their jobs or lives.

inner platform—This is the concept that a great warrior had to attain a form of internal peace to be able to concentrate on engaging an opponent successfully. Control over an opponent begins with learning to control one's self. This mental attitude is called *bujutsu* in Japanese.

myth—This is a story, tale, or narrative to which to the persons located in the indigenous culture from which it emanated may be considered to be authentic and true. Fundamental myths are often the stuff of religions and of religious observances.

the American monomyth—This is the idea that there is a kernel unique to and nearly always present in the stories, films, and narratives that are understood by most Americans. The American monomyth has roots in the American revolution.

the creatress—This is the idea that God was feminine instead of masculine, near universally held in all ancient cultures because only women could usher forth new life.

the leadership life journey—This is the idea that leadership begins with a confrontation with death and a reconciliation of how life and death are to be understood and resolved by every human being. The roots of leadership and followership are connected in this universal journey set within the context of culture and time, which provides the bridges of communication, symbols, and imagery necessary for the dynamic connection between leaders and followers to exist.

the nuclear unit of the monomyth—This is the basic kernel of all myths over time, although they may vary in many other aspects, such as gender of the hero or heroine or to specific cultural trappings, garments, instruments, weapons, or food.

the Wild Woman—This is a reference to a woman representing a "natural state" in which she is connected to her "innate integrity" as a woman.

Mental Prisms of Leadership

Performance as an educational leader is dependent on how the leader "sees" events, situations, and challenges. The core values of a leader help him or her know how to respond, which challenges to accept or to ignore, and how to shape the practice of leadership in schools. In many cases a leader only "sees" what his or her values permit to be seen at all. This chapter explores the pivotal points of how leaders discern what is good and true, and how to move toward revealing their personal "blind spots," which all humans possess. It is about peering inside the mind to discern how "reality" is defined prior to perception. Such inquiry is difficult but it is the key to the idea of "critical, reflective practice." The chapter provides the conceptual tools to engage in that quest for enhanced self-knowledge and it shows what assumptions have been used in the past to anchor leadership thought in education.

❖

The art of leadership is performance. Performance, however, is anchored in the essential core of every leader's deeply held beliefs that not only guide him or her in a role of leadership, but actively shape the world and define the issues in it. These beliefs are the "mental prisms" in which leadership is defined, situated, and socially contextualized by language and culture. All the beliefs are fixed in what a human being believes to be good and true. So what counts as good and true are the touchstones of educational leadership practice.

The world is not a static entity perceived the same way by everyone. Rather, the world is a dynamic place in which different cultures, languages, and contexts shape perception to become congruent. In other words, "reality" is not "out there." Rather, reality is "in there," meaning in the leader's mind. And the leader's mind is set firmly within his or her linguistic frame and all its attendant conventions, idiosyncrasies, and cultural blind spots. Between the internal world of the leader and the external world's demands is the space where any leader decides what to do and how to respond to circumstances. If, for example, an educational leader values the kind of curriculum that includes the arts, poetry, and literature but sees the accountability laws driving them from the curriculum, what course should the principal or superintendent pursue? The discrepancy between the core values of a leader and his or her role demands make up the agenda for action. It is the lynchpin to define practice (Kelleher & Van Der Bogert, 2006).

We saw in the last chapter the work of political scientist James Barber (1985), who put it this way about the leadership of the U.S. president:

> A President's world view consists of his primary, politically relevant beliefs, particularly his conceptions of social causality, human nature, and the central moral conflicts of the time. (p. 5)

Barber (1985) differentiated between a "leadership style," which he defined as a president's way of acting, and a "world view," which is how a president's perception is shaped. "World view" is a president's anchor. It's any leader's anchor. And it's an anchor because it moors a leader in all kinds of weather. The world can be a turbulent place. To keep from being buffeted about, a leader has to be able to ride out the inevitable chaos. Those who follow leaders expect them to offer reassurances, defend their beliefs, and point out a course of action (Barber, p. 6). Leaders cannot perform these functions if they have no idea of who they are, where they are, and what they should be doing.

Ralph Keyes (1995) compiled a book of the wit and wisdom of U.S. president Harry S. Truman (1884–1972), whose stature has consistently risen since he left office. Keyes wrote the following of the 33rd U.S. president:

> Harry Truman stands in stark contrast to modern politicians who don't seem sure of what they stand for until they've taken a poll. Harry Truman knew who he was. "I've never met anyone," wrote journalist Charles Robbins, "whose idea of his own identity was clearer than Truman's." (p. 3)

Biographer David McCullough (1992) said of Truman that he held the values of the common American and that "he held to the old guidelines: work hard, do your best, speak the truth, assume no airs, trust in God, have no fear" (p. 991).

The nature of a leader's "world view" is shown in Figure 3.1. This schematic shows that within the world there are different cultures. These cultures possess linguistic/cultural differences that have shaped human perception in them.

Human perception is not a matter of peering through the eyes of a totally open lens. Humans do not "see" what is there. Rather, humans "see" what their language, culture, and context permit them to see. What we see has been actively shaped, just as an artist would "see" a landscape and then paint or draw it. Consider the differences in landscapes between Monet, Gaugin, or Van Gogh. The artist brings to the painting a complex set of understandings as well as mental images that have been preshaped, including political perspectives and gender biases (see Callen, 1995).

The external world is "trimmed" to "fit" the "world view" of the perceiver. As we have seen in the last chapter, "world views" are fed by the psychic forces of every culture's mythos, those primary beliefs expressed in the dominant narratives guiding all cultures.

In the West, the act of observation has become the dominant mode of determining "the truth." The concept of truth, the stuff of facts that were "out there," was well

❖ **Figure 3.1**   The Dynamic Nature of Leadership Within Varying "World Views"

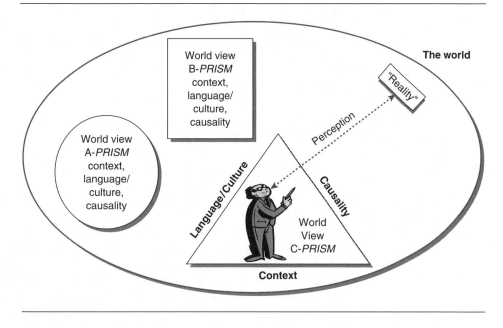

implanted in the mind of educational leaders quite early, and is partly accountable for the quest of trying to fashion educational administration into a science early in the 20th century (Culbertson, 1988; Donmoyer, 1999). An example that remains popular today was espoused by George Howland, superintendent of schools of Chicago in 1896, writing under the title of how school should develop human character:

> The pupil must know what is true and beautiful ere the conception of truth can dawn upon his mental vision, must learn of the good and the right if ever goodness and righteousness shall be to him more than empty words. (p. 114)

This former Chicago superintendent believed that what is "true and beautiful" are values that exist separately from humans and both must be "taught" to students. These values are clearly outside the student's immediate experience and must become the "stuff" of school curricula. The other revealing thing about this quotation is that it places "truth-beauty-good-righteousness" as moral equivalents on the same plane. What is one is the other. It never occurs to Superintendent Howland that the truth might be ugly, destructive, or evil. Likewise he apparently never heard of the antithesis, that "beauty is in the eye of the beholder."

Figure 3.1 demonstrates that perception and notions of truth based on perception are bound, defined, and limited by a person's language/culture and context. Notions of causality (cause and effect or what leads to what and why certain things happen) are powerful shaping forces to constrain observation. Science, as one form of human knowing, is similarly bound. Paul Feyerabend (1991) said it best: " . . . you have to approach science . . . by tracing . . . life stories . . . analogies there are—but no permanent structures" (p. 156). All cultures are situated not on an immutable intergalactic platform, but contextually positioned in a specific time and context. To return to former President Truman, for example, David McCullough (1986) reminds us that

> . . . at heart he [Truman] remained a nineteenth century man . . . He was never really happy with our twentieth century. He didn't like daylight saving time. He didn't like air conditioning. He didn't like the telephone at all; he would use his pen, or pencil. He would far sooner write a letter than use the telephone. (p. 33)

This was Truman's anchor because there are no permanent structures. Everything is fluid. Concepts of permanency are illusory.

Discerning Contemporary Notions of Perception and Truth

Figure 3.1 illustrates that there exist in the world competing perceptions and values regarding causality (shown as world views A, B, and C in the schematic). Causality is linked to historical context, which can be positioned in time and fully cloaked in linguistic/cultural traditions. The human perceiver may not recognize that his or her perception is embedded in and defined by these forces. Edward Hall (1981) describes this immersion as follows: ". . . his culture, the total communication framework: words, actions, postures, gestures, tones of voice, facial expressions, the way he handles time, space, materials, and the way he works, plays, makes love, and defends himself" (p. 42).

Culture shapes perception from the moment of birth. One has to know what one is seeing to know what it is and to learn the language needed to identify it (see F. Saussure in Gadet, 1986). "Reality" is arbitrarily and inwardly defined. The outward boundaries of "reality" are embedded in the context of time.

Within this very fluid interaction, language shifts are occurring. And the language used by the speaker is a kind of temporal space by which experience itself is separated from the act of observation. A perceiver can be observing a sunset and experience it at the same time. However, when the perceiver realizes that he or she is in the act of viewing a sunset, then he or she is not only experiencing it, but recognizing it as well. In this moment, the human perceiver differentiates the act of sunset viewing from other kinds of acts, and in the process, identifies it using language. This kind of two-pronged act creates the human concept of *time* (see Rapaport, 1989, p. 71).

Within this framework or discourse, language is both a product of, and a determiner of, temporal relationships. Language is both descriptive and prescriptive in this sense—it indicates "what is" as well as "what should or might be." Language cements the hierarchical nature of perceived relationships and other "givens." Embedded in language are concealed hierarchies and power relationships. Humans learn early on their "station" in the social structure. Perception is geared to staying within this structure and coming to see it as "natural," a point underscored by Hall (1981) when he said, "Culture hides much more than it reveals and, strangely enough, what it hides, it hides most effectively from its own participants" (p. 39). Edward De Bono (1972) calls language "our strongest patterning system" (p. 134). People using a language are often unaware of such patterns. Human thinking is shaped not by an independent reality that words represent, but by cultural metaphors without any inherent properties or fixed relations between them (Lakoff & Johnson, 1980, p. 210).

Here are some propositions about the nature of perception and the related idea that humans can perceive something called "the truth." It is an essential foundation on which an educational leader constructs his or her practice, as Jentz (2006) notes:

> . . . we do not know what we do not know, and a great deal of what we do not know is essential to our success. We can only discover what we do not know by being willing to look inside, making our minds the object of our inquiry. (p. 237)

This chapter is about looking inside our minds at the mental prisms we have erected there and subjecting them to scrutiny "because leadership for change requires pioneering steps into unknown territory in the external world" (Jentz, 2006, p. 237).

Perception and Truth Are Linguistically and Culturally Defined

Perception is neither absolute nor universal. It is encapsulated and relative to linguistic conceptual systems, part and parcel of everyday discourse and specific cultures (Lakoff & Johnson, 1980, p. 159). Because of these temporal and specific cultural conditions, "all observers are not led by the same physical evidence to the same picture of the universe" (called the *Sapir-Whorf hypothesis;* see Whorf, 1956, p. 214).

For example, the Eskimo language has four words for *snow,* the Hopi language uses the same word for *insect, pilot,* and *plane,* and some Arabic languages have nearly 100 words for *camel.* Some Native American languages have no noun/verb distinctions, and others have no word for *time.* English makes the words *flame, storm, lightning* and *spark* nouns, while Hopi represents them with verbs (see Palmer, 1986, p. 45). The ancient Egyptians used a 24-letter alphabet, but all the letters were consonant signs only (see Jensen, 1969, p. 62). What is true is culturally constructed. Truth is invented and hence not "discovered" (Eco, 1990, p. 67).

The invention of truth was forcibly illustrated in 1992 when the Yokohama Rubber Company in Tokyo, Japan, apologized to its Arabic customers for making tires with treads that resembled the word for Allah, the Islamic name for God. The Yokohama Rubber Company indicated that the tread design (called Y-814) was generated by a computer that was searching for maximization of driver safety and was not intended as a blasphemy against the Islamic Deity. The company also apologized for its ignorance of Islam (Associated Press, 1992, p. A3).

In some languages, it is impossible to separate the meaning between a written sentence and an utterance. English is one of these languages (Palmer, 1986, p. 154). A model is provided by Matthews (1965) in which the North American Hidatsa Indian language contains six examples of the meaning of a sentence determined by the mood imparted by the speaker in uttering it. In Hidatsa, if the speaker knows the sentence he relates is true, it is spoken with great emphasis. If this emphatic mood is questionable, the speaker is considered a liar. If the same sentence is delivered in the indefinite mood, it means that he or she does not really know whether it is true. If the sentence ends with a period mood, it means that the speaker believes it to be true. However, if it does not, then he or she did not lie, but was simply mistaken (Palmer, p. 152).

Political relationships are part of all texts since they are "products or inscriptions of the discursive formations of institutions or ideologies" (Felperin, 1988, p. 32). Such ideologies are usually submerged in the requirements for linearity and sequencing in speech and script. They are therefore "hidden" to those using them, and to those who may believe that they are "open" and nonprejudiced in their perceptions. This "blindness" leads to ethnocentrism, a world view that holds that people who are not like you are inherently inferior. Paul Feyerabend (1991) said the following: "Many people make the mistake of assuming that the world that arose as a response to their actions, or their history, underlies all other cultures, only the others are too stupid to notice" (p. 43).

Lakoff and Johnson (1980) indicate that "absolute objective truth is not only mistaken, but socially and politically dangerous" (p. 159).

Each human culture shown in Figure 3.1 acts on its own perceptions of reality. More than one response works. To survive, human cultures must find sustenance (response) from that reality or "Being." This is the essential function of mythos that was discussed in the last chapter. Cultures are successful in this endeavor or they perish. This concept underscores the idea that "there is no way of connecting the reactions with universal substance or universal laws" (Feyerabend, 1991, p. 43). The full implication of this linkage is that perception and hence truth are contextually dependent rather than contextually independent of any observation of "reality."

The necessity of knowing the context to understand if a sentence is true is established by trying to ascertain a sentence's meaning, independent of context. Usually, a second sentence is required—normally, a paraphrase. But how is one to know which sentence is true, or even if the two are similar without knowing the context in which both would be used (Palmer, 1986, p. 48)?

Eco (1990) affirms Charles Sanders Peirce's "principle of contextuality," that "something can be truly asserted within a given universe of discourse and under a given description, but his assertion does not exhaust all the other, and potentially infinite, determination of that object" (in Figure 3.1. as world views A, B, and C; p. 37). This means that perceivers in all three separate world views could make claims about their "realities," but none of them would exhaust the potentially infinite meanings such claims could generate.

Perception and Truth Are Relational and Circular

"To learn a language is to learn the meaning of its sentences, and hence to learn what observations to count as evidence for and against them," says philosopher W. V. Quine (1974, p. 38). The meaning of perception/truth depends on a statement's relations with other statements. The meaning of "red" is established in a network of relationships. A red cloud has no particular meaning in weather systems. However, a red traffic signal does have a specific meaning within a communication system (from Palmer, 1986, p. 3). The fact that "red" means "stop" is purely contained within that notational/communication system. It is relational and circular—that is, other signs and colors are dependent on them for the same reason.

A perception that is considered "true" is positioned within a "web" of other statements and assertions. True statements are linked to others and within larger frameworks or paradigms. These are circular in nature—that is, all definitions lead back to assumptions on which the paradigm rests and also to undefined words, like spokes in a wheel. For this reason, Popper (1979) has indicated that most theories contain their own "truth" and are therefore unable to predict any situation that involves their own rejection (p. 67).

However, when undefined words are used to indicate meaning in the act of definition (and there is no end to this process called *infinite regress*), boundaries are created for what is considered true to be indexed, like a dictionary within a language. But, since there is no end to the shifting from one word to another undefined one, there can be no final or authoritative, transcendental meaning possible, because such a meaning is infinitely postponed (see Eco, 1990, p. 27).

Perception/truth is confined to language syntax and its content-meaning will vary from language to language. This circularity to "boxed" meanings within languages (not always translatable to others) is reinforced by the fact that languages are indeterminate in categorizing "reality" to the point where "there is no absolute line . . . between what is in the world and what is in language" (Palmer, 1986, p. 32). This concept was reinforced by Dick Littlebear, a North American Cheyenne:

> We need our land and we need our language. The two are inseparable . . . There are references to the land that can be articulated only in the Cheyenne language. I believe that once these sacred references can no longer be expressed . . . These vital links will no longer exist in the tribal consequences. (Crawford, 1992, p. B5)

Language indeterminacy shrouds perception and truth in tentativeness, and denies anything resembling a stable "objectivity" within one language or across other languages. It negates the search for causation because decisions are independent of one another and are not connected (although they may be connected in each culture's mythos). The idea of a "free will" and the arbitrariness of all linguistic conventions is underscored and affirmed by linguistic scholarship.

The discovery of the Rosetta stone is one of the most famous examples of language indeterminacy. The Rosetta stone was a chunk of black basalt found in 1799 at the mouth of the Nile River in Egypt by a French engineer with Napoleon's army. The broken tablet contained three separate scripts: Egyptian hieroglyphs, demotic (a kind of secular and condensed form of hieroglyphs), and Greek. Inasmuch as the Greek script was describing a royal event (the reign of King Ptolemy Epiphanes, 204–181 B.C.), it was assumed that all three texts were similar (Jensen, 1969, p. 74).

The Rosetta stone promised a way to break the hieroglyphic code of the ancient Egyptians, which up to that point appeared impenetrable to analysts. The translation was a lot more difficult and took longer than anyone imagined. The definitive dictionary of hieroglyphics was not published until 1926—120 years after the Rosetta stone discovery in the land of the sphinx (Jensen, 1969, p. 78).

The first attempt to translate the Rosetta stone obviously moved from the Greek to the second script, the demotic. This involved changing proper names in Greek to proper names in demotic. But this translator incorrectly assumed that demotic was an alphabetical text when it was not. The next move by a subsequent translator occurred in 1815 when a demotic alphabet was created. After this, the move to hieroglyphics was attempted. Again the proper names were deciphered in ancient Egyptian, which yielded only six hieroglyphic letters with phonetic equivalents. All work then came to a halt. No one could go any further.

The person credited with the breakthrough was a young Frenchman named J. F. Champollion (1790–1832). His diligence and hard work eventually paid off. Champollion's strategy was based on an intensive study of Coptic, one form of linguistic evolution from ancient Egyptian. By comparing forms of Coptic to demotic, and an even earlier type of hieroglyphic called *hieratic,* he could trace the development of the language.

In the deciphering process, Champollion noticed something that contradicted a previous assumption he had made about the Egyptian hieroglyphs. Initially, Champollion thought the hieroglyphs were pure picture script. Then, he discovered that this portion of the Rosetta stone contained three times as many signs as the Greek words contained. It was apparent to him that each hieroglyphic sign could not be a whole word. He worked from Greek to demotic to hieratic and into the hieroglyphs, and then found the name of the king: P,T,O,L,M,I,S. This insight eventually unlocked the secret of ancient Egyptian writing, but even the details eluded Champollion's exacting mind (Jensen, 1969, pp. 76–77).

It was not until 1867 that further scholarly work unveiled the place of determinatives in ancient Egyptian texts. These were certain picture-sign extensions with written phonetic additives that indicated a generic sphere of concepts to which a word belonged. This graphic-phonetic combination limited the meaning to only one of many possibilities. Ancient Egyptian texts therefore contained around 700 different kinds of signs. These consisted of word-picture signs and from some of these determinatives, double-consonant signs for phonetic groups labeled syllable-signs. Others were single-consonant signs or letters.

The dramatic story of the unlocking of ancient Egyptian texts from the Rosetta stone underscores the arbitrariness of language development. It also illustrates the patent difficulties in attempting a language-to-language translation based on the many assumptions of parallelism in human experience, perception of reality, or oral and written expressions and conventions.

Another bit of history regarding the Rosetta stone is supplied by Asante (1990). Because of the prejudice and ignorance of the European historians and archaeologists regarding Africa, the Rosetta stone was believed to unlock the key to ancient Egyptian writing, which was classified in England as an "Oriental" language rather than an African one. Africans were not believed to have developed a written language. Because the Arabs had conquered Egypt by the time the Europeans had arrived on their military expeditions, they saw hieroglyphics as Eastern rather than African, although this ancient language predated Arab conquest (pp. 59–68). The belief that African civilizations were not as advanced as European civilizations in the development of writing is still a prevalent myth, even among educated people.

As a final commentary, when languages are translated, some small points on which arguments may hinge can be lost. In 1925, in the famous Scopes trial in Dayton, Tennessee, when Charles Darwin's evolutionary theory tangled with the Biblical version of Genesis and classroom science teaching (two competing narratives for social mythos), the defense team tried to raise the issue of linguistic distortion (English & Zirkel, 1989).

The original Hebrew translation of Genesis did not read, "In the beginning God created the heaven and earth" (remember the J for *Jehovah* version of Genesis cited in chapter 2?). Instead, the literal words read, "When the gods began to set in motion the heavens and earth" (the so-called E or *elohim* version; DeCamp, 1968, p. 178). The difference is significant. In the first translation, it is God who is fusing the materials to fashion a heaven and an earth. In the second, the heavens and earth already exist and the gods (female as well as male) are merely putting them into place. Darwin's theory of evolution clashes with the J version but not with the E version. Presumably, the E version translated as "set into motion" the heavens and earth—the exact translation of Genesis in Hebrew is not at odds with evolutionary theory.

The difference between the two texts was the result of a power shift in ancient Hebrew society. The Hebrew priests of the storm god Yahveh (Jehovah) became the dominant group around the sixth century B.C. and suppressed the worship of all other gods, including those that were female. Hebrew society at this point was polytheistic. With this translation, it became monotheistic and male-centered. God possessed only one gender. The texts of the time were rewritten into the *Book of Law* in the reign of Josiah in 621 B.C. (Eiselen, Lewis, & Downey, 1957, p. 92). The texts were changed to shift "gods" to "God" to show that the Hebrews were monotheists all along. In southern Israel, God was named *Jehovah*. In northern Israel, texts show God to be called *Elohim* (Eiselen et al., p. 218).

The Hebrew language is a difficult one to translate. It has 22 letters, all consonants, and "some of these can scarcely be represented by our English letters, or spoken by our vocal organs" (Eiselen et al., 1957, p. 100). Furthermore, Hebrew uses few particles and compounds and eschews independent pronouns and tenses. Acts are either completed or not completed, without any reference to time: "It is not easy for the modern interpreter to put himself in the place of the ancient writer" (Eiselen et al., p. 99).

Perception and Truth Are Theory Embedded

What any perceiver believes is true is usually linked to larger stories or narratives, either explicitly or implicitly. In some cases, these can be called "theories," where they are offered as statements open to refutation (see Popper, 1965). Where such statements are offered as tenets (matters of true belief), the only avenue open is to accept or not accept their authenticity. These "stories" are not open to refutation. Most stories embedded in mythos (religion) are not open to refutation. In fact, disbelievers are called heretics or infidels. Stories not open to question may be called dogma. Figure 3.2 shows this difference. Human perception, even in science, occurs within sociocultural rules that remain linguistically dependent. Science is not value-free. Statements judged within the rules of science may be false because as Feyerabend (1991) indicates, "theories very often contain hidden assumptions one is not even aware of" (p. 20).

The practice of medicine is full of stories about wrong theories or stories within larger theories. These are "stories within stories" (Cherryholmes, 1988, p. 156). In some cases, the larger theory may be wrong and discourage a correct practice from being applied. For example, during the American Civil War, doctors understood that infection could eventually kill a soldier. They believed that infection was caused by foul air

❖ **Figure 3.2** The Rules of Refutation in Science

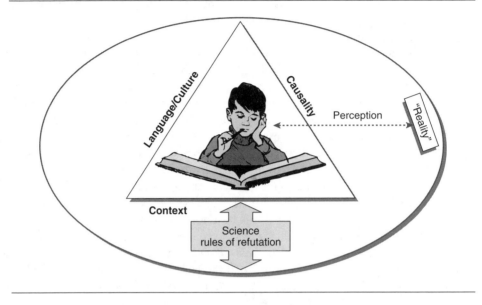

or to some unseen contagion. The concept of asepsis or sterilization to prevent bacterial infection was unknown (because bacteria were unknown). Some observed medical conditions were simply misread. A preliminary infection in which pus was produced near a wound was labeled "laudable pus" and was believed to be a sign that the patient was recovering (Duffy, 1979, p. 222).

When gangrene was discovered among 50 soldiers after the battle of Antietam in 1862 (the bloodiest battle in American military history—Sears, 1983), doctors were ordered to wash their hands after treating such cases. Many were outraged at this command. Although no new cases of gangrene were reported after extensive hand washing, no orders were given extending the procedure to other types of wounds or patients (Tschanz, 1992, p. 37). Thus, in this historical story of medical practice, a true statement (hand washing) was not understood because it was embedded in a larger narrative that was false (infection being caused by foul air). Medical doctors of the day were incapable of comprehending the nature of infection because they believed it to be the product of the sum of symptoms and did not understand the cause (Peirce, 1955, p. 51). The continued misreading of infection caused the death of one U.S. president. In 1881, when President James A. Garfield was shot in the third rib by an assassin, his doctors probed the bullet wound with their fingers (insuring infection), and noted "laudable pus" developing 3 days after the incident. As the infection developed into abdominal peritonitis, they were still not worried. President Garfield died 11 weeks later from infection (Duffy, 1979, p. 249).

Human perception is not only filtered by existing narratives (stories), but defined but them. We do not "see" things we do not believe are there although they may be there all the time. For example, it was once widely believed that peptic ulcers were caused by excess nervousness, personality disorders, or chronic anxiety (LeFanu, 1999,

p. 151). These disorders caused excess stomach acid to be secreted, which in turn led to peptic ulcers. The Freudians even got involved by theorizing that persons with peptic ulcers possessed a secret desire to remain dependent on their parents. Domineering mothers and meek fathers were hypothesized to be the causative agents. Experiments with monkeys that were placed in decision-making contexts for other monkeys and given electric shocks showed that the animals developed peptic ulcers. In addition, after the turn of the century, the rate of individuals developing peptic ulcers was 1 in 10 adult men. Explanations were offered that the rise in the complexity and intensity of modern life led to this condition of excessive stress and the result was increasing cases of peptic ulcers.

Then in 1983 in Australia a young medical intern, without training in research, found a small "crescent-configured" bacterium in the lining of the human stomach. This discovery was thought impossible because it was believed that no bacteria could live in the acidic environment of the stomach. That was the reason that the presence of peptic ulcers "had" to be accounted for by something else. But Dr. Barry Marshall, the young intern, discovered that when he gave a patient with a chest infection the antibiotic tetracycline, the patient reported that his stomach symptoms were much improved. Dr. Marshall worked to isolate the stomach germ called helicobacter and when successful devised a treatment plan that completely cured 50 patients of peptic ulcers. Dr. Marshall even infected and cured himself with this treatment. James LeFanu (1999) comments as follows:

> There was now no escaping the scale of their [medical practitioners] earlier collective self-deception, for not only had they failed to see these bacteria even though they were present in virtually all their patients, but they had systematically misinterpreted the many clues pointing to the fact that peptic ulcers must be caused by an infectious organism. (p. 155)

Scientists are human and humans do not directly see what is in any particular conceptual "field." Perception is determined by belief. One "sees" what one expects to see and does not see what is not expected to be "there." There can be no true "objective" view of reality.

Perception and Truth May Be False

Even if perception is anchored to something that is true (at least for the moment), the extension of the perception may be false. We pause here a moment to consider Darwin's notion of natural selection-adaptation being used to support and promote a variety of social doctrines, including shady business practices in the name of competition, and even religious ones: "God picks out a select few" (see Ruse, 1979, p. 264). In Feyerabend's (1991) words, "But ideas (such as true statements), like butterflies, do not merely exist: they develop, they enter into relations with other ideas and they have effects" (p. 163). Nowhere was this more amply illustrated than in the effects of Darwin's ideas on all aspects of British life, from its political system to its economic base (see Ruse, 1979).

Darwin's ideas generated a host of fallacious theories in other fields, notably the false "truth" of recapitulation (Gould, 1981, p. 114). The idea embodied in recapitulation was that "ontogeny recapitulates phylogeny," or that growth of a human retraces the growth of the species itself (Gould, 1977). Thus, the true observation that, at a certain point in time, a human embryo possessed slits in the head like fish gills provided "evidence" that humans were passing through the "fish stage" in their evolution to the current level of development.

With recapitulation, all animals could be ranked on the same scale. Humans could be ordered into groups that were "higher" or "lower." The American paleontologist E. D. Cope was a recapitulationist. He theorized that humans could be sorted into four lower classes beneath Nordic white men: nonwhite races, all women, southern European men, and lower classes within superior races such as the Irish (Gould, 1981, p. 115). The classification of the human family by race on a scale of development was endorsed by the founder of anthropology, J. F. Blumenbach, who devised a scheme of sorting the races into groups on the basis of intelligence and perceived degree of "civilization" (Gould, 1981, p. 32). Cornell West (1999) was therefore correct when he declared that the origins of contemporary racism lie within science (pp. 55–86).

Blumenbach's racism entered American schoolbooks, among them an 1881 geography text, *Appleton's Standard Higher Geography,* which displayed the five racial categories, noting that the white was "the most intellectual and civilized race, and embraces the leading nations of the earth" (p. 14).[As "proof" of the premise, three human skulls are shown with the most "developed" being the white, followed by the Mongolian and then the Ethiopian. The use of skulls to demonstrate intellectual capacity emanates from a now defunct school of thought called *craniometry,* based on Darwin's theory of evolution, and within it, the related concept of recapitulation, which was supposed to be one of the undergirding "truths" supporting it.

Paul Broca (1824–1880) was professor of clinical surgery on the faculty of medicine in Paris. Through meticulous calculation of the size of human skulls, Broca would stake out a claim to the "superiority" of white men and the white race. Jay Gould (1981) carefully researched Broca's experiments in measuring human skulls. He found no statistical difference in one of Broca's key samples (p. 95), while Broca claimed this same sample "proved" his observations of white race "superiority." Broca worked from predetermined perspectives (tenets) and filtered his data to support his preordained conclusions, all the while denying he was doing so. His collection of statistical data was voluminous. All of it appeared to confirm his conclusions, yet all of it was bogus in supporting a patently false theory.

In summing up Broca's mistaken concept, Gould (1981) warns of the following: "Broca was an exemplary scientist; no one has ever surpassed him in meticulous care and accuracy of measurement. By what right . . . can we identify his prejudice and hold that science now operates independently of culture and class?" (p. 74).

Because of Broca's "research," American history books such as Ridpath's (1874) *History of the United States* could open their texts with the following statement: "The western continent was first seen by white men in A.D. 986" (p. 13). This statement ignores the fact that Native Americans were already on the continent and had "seen" it thousands of years earlier. The "ladder" of ranking the races linearly following advances by Darwin remains in the popular American mental mainstream to present times. It is advanced blatantly by white race supremist organizations and remains firmly lodged in education with concepts of IQ and the "bell curve" (Hernstein &

Murray, 1994; see a rebuttal in Kincheloe & Steinberg, 1997, pp. 3–50). Reformers in the first half of the 20th century couched their educational aims for centralized control to "elevate the inferior race" (Apple, 1991, p. 18). Once established by supposed facts, false narratives (theories) and statements often die hard, and leave vestiges of intellectual debris scattered across many generations that may not perish until the civilization itself dies.

Perception and Truth Produce a Situated "Reality"

Human perception or "world view" is inevitably grounded in a specific time, linguistic/cultural and contextual frame. Humans cannot perceive outside of their own humanity and its linguistic/cultural traditions, although humans may become conscious of their presence. Notions of causality are especially grounded in larger metanarratives, either scientific or cultural mythos (religions). Scientific narratives are constantly changing, and a look at historical narratives reveals the changing nature of religious perspectives as well. For example, Biblical scholars studying the Gospels have indicated that 82% of the words allegedly spoken by Jesus were not actually his.

> Not even the fundamentalists on the far right can produce a credible Jesus out of the allegedly inerrant canonical gospels. Their reading of who Jesus was rests on the shifting sands of their own theological constructions. (Funk, Hoover, & the Jesus Seminar, 1993, p. 5)

Human perception always produces a world view of potential "realities" that are situated. This means that human world views are locatable and can be "fixed" within spans of history that are bound by culture and language. In the sense of a "world view," the most important histories are conceptual/metaphorical. This is critically the case with human moral development.

What is true must be regarded as a statement or proposition, often to refutation, that no one has yet been able to show is false. No statement can be forever "true" in this sense. It is merely accepted as a temporary truce in the never-ending struggle to find a test that will eventually show that the statement is false.

The idea of subjecting statements to continual attempts at refutation has been called by Karl Popper (1979) "the critical method" (p. 16) or the doctrine of falsification (Popper, 1965, p. 229). Popper concedes that in a case in which an infinite number of theories are possible, no method can deduce which theory is true. The perceiver is then faced with a situation in which any number of narratives or theories may be true or false. In this situation, there can be no permanent mystical entity called "objective reality" that will finally be "discovered" by a scientist or anyone else. It should be clear that human perception is invented. Reality is a *syncheism,* that is, a situation in which no person or group can ever exhaust the possibilities of determination, or as Peirce (1934) concludes, " Reality is a continuum which swims in indeterminacy" (p. 171).

It is due to this indeterminacy that Newton's theories still work. They still predict the tides. They don't explain some of the phenomena that Einstein's theories do, yet Newton's theories are not false. They are simply not as "true" as Einstein's. In time, Einstein's theories may be similarly pushed aside.

It is often difficult for scientists to differentiate between theories and to assess their overall truth content. In fact, theories or paradigms are never in themselves testable. They simply contain too many possibilities to test, and for some statements, there is no way to test them directly. It was because of this dilemma that Karl Popper (1968) commented, "I do not demand that every scientific statement must have in fact been tested before it is accepted. I only demand that every such statement must be capable of being tested" (p. 48). Devising appropriately rigorous tests of statements derived from a theory may be exceptionally difficult.

A recent example of a well-accepted theory that is not able to account for all the phenomena under its aegis is the case of the pink lady's slipper orchid that grows wild in Virginia's great Shenandoah Valley. Zoology professor Douglas Gill, an evolutionary biologist at the University of Maryland, has been systematically gathering data about this plant that has baffled traditional Darwinists (McDonald, 1991, p. A6).

Darwin's premise—that organisms survive and reproduce in proportion to their adaptability to their environments—does not explain how the pink lady's slipper orchid manages to survive in the Shenandoah Valley. Professor Gill found that none of the 1,200 orchids he studied in a 1-acre plot had been pollinated. Over 14 years of observation, Dr. Gill found that of 3,300 plants, only 1,000 flowered and only 23 had been pollinated. The mystery was how this plant reproduces itself to survive in its environment. Its incapacity to do so would reject Darwin's natural selection thesis.

At first, Professor Gill thought that the flowers were in some way not attracting bees for pollination purposes. This proved correct. How then does the orchid attain pollination? Many orchids self-pollinate. The type of pink lady's slipper orchid studied by Gill is not one of them. He says, "There is no way I can show in this orchid a significant pattern of natural selection for certain flower morphologies" (McDonald, 1991, p. A8).

Gill and most of his biology colleagues still accept the main premise in Darwin's seminal 1859 work, *On the Origin of Species by Natural Selection.* Even Darwin himself, who wrote a book about orchids in 1862, was stumped by some orchids that defied his own theory The inability of a theory to account for every possible variable does not necessarily invalidate it or lead to its abandonment. "Every scientific theory, interpreted in a literal way, is in conflict with numerous facts." says Paul Feyerabend (1991). The following occurs as a result:

> You will no longer think of a theory as a well defined entity that says exactly what difficulties will make it disappear; you will think of it as a vague promise whose meaning is constantly being changed and refined by the difficulties one decides to accept. (Feyerabend, 1991, p. 72)

It seems clear that theories as a special kind of metanarrative involved in the work of science must be dissembled into propositions to be tested. The dissembling takes the form of "deducing from them statements of a lesser level of universality. These statements in their turn, since they are to be intersubjectively testable, must be testable in like manner—and so ad infinitum" (Popper, 1968, p. 47).

At the same time, the manner in which various tests are devised to assess whether statements or propositions are true is at least partly determined by theories about truth and its nature. It is to this matter that we now turn.

How Do We Know What We Perceive Is True? Theories of Truth

As opposed to verification of tenets by affirmation or disbelief similarly, science proceeds by raising questions concerning the nature of human perception itself. How would humans know if their perceptions about something were "true"? An affirmation with roots in faith is its own confirmation. One simply has to believe intensely enough and doubt can be overcome.

Science, on the other hand, inquires about its own ability to know. One of the first quandaries regarding theories of truth lies in determining by what means one knows if one's representation of truth or "reality" is in fact the truth and the reality. The situation of the perceiver is shown in Figure 3.3.

In the instance shown in Figure 3.3, a person engages in the act of perception. A relationship or a proposition is formulated. The perceiver formulates a hypothesis about what is true. The first way a perceiver might know if his or her perception or observation was true was to compare it to already known "facts" that were similar and generally accepted as true. If the observation "corresponds" to that which is already known, then the observer could conclude that his or her proposition was also true. This "theory of truth" has a long history in science. It is called the *correspondence theory* of truth.

Correspondence theory consists of designing procedures for verification. Such data are normally sensory or experiential information. The idea behind science utilizing the correspondence theory is that of empiricism. Empiricism holds that there is no knowledge possible (or worthwhile) outside of the human senses. Empiricism denies that there is any such thing as inborn, innate, or a priori knowledge that is unable to

❖ **Figure 3.3** The Correspondence Theory of Truth

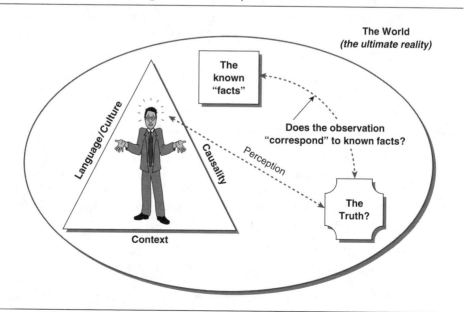

be ultimately demonstrated (usually seen/observed). It rejects the notion "that there are universal or necessary truths" (Runes, 1984, p. 105).

House (1991) has delineated the traditional and largely positivistic tenets involved in defining educational research linked to the correspondence theory of truth as the following (paraphrase):

1. All scientific propositions are founded on data and facts in which hypotheses are verified against the facts.

2. Scientific theories are those using hypothetical-deductive methods which assume their meaning via linkages to observations and definitions stated in performance terms.

3. The activity of research is itself atheoretical; the most important aspect of a theory is its ability to predict events, occurrences, or results.

4. Causality is that which links events with contingencies.

5. Explanation and prediction are considered parallel forms. (pp. 2–3)

The correspondence theory has a number of problems, chiefly the ambiguous nature of the "facts." Securing agreement about the "facts" is often a matter of perspective and is not theory-free but encapsulated in a theory itself, or in the words of Evers and Lakomski (1991), "our knowledge of how we know the class of epistemically privileged items is not itself epistemically privileged" (p. 228).

Any theory of truth that is language dependent has a number of built-in problems at the outset. We shall comment on this problem shortly. Finally, the unreliability and subjectivity of human experience in "verifying" truth is also a problem.

Karl Popper (1968) comments on the instability of the scientific enterprise in words that ought to create skepticism that what is "scientific" is permanent and lasting:

> Science does not rest upon solid bedrock. The bold structure of its theories rises, as it were, above a swamp. It is like a building erected on piles . . . and if we stop driving the piles deeper, it is not because we have reached firm ground . . . we are satisfied that the piles are firm enough to carry the structure. (p. 111)

There are no granite substructures on which to build science, and experience is a mercurial substructure at best.

Linguistic Difficulties With Theories of Truth

The simple discernment of truth is not as "simple" as it seems. Those who insist that it is simple usually have an agenda that cannot stand sustained scrutiny. Simple approaches require only simple solutions. The question of what is truth has been taken up by scores of philosophers over the ages. The answer is—it all depends. Aristotle defined truth in the following way:

> To say of what is that it is not, or of what is not that it is, is false, while to say of what is that it is, or of what is not that it is not, is true. (from Haack, 1988, p. 88)

In attempting this definition, Aristotle was caught in a definite language quandary: "To say of what is [to speak about something] that it is not [that is not true] or of what is not [to say something that is not true] that it is [but which is true] is false [is not true], while to say of what is that it is [to speak about something which is true, and it is true, and therefore true] or what is not that is not [or is false and therefore false] is true [is really false and therefore true]." This explanation is reminiscent of the very famous language problem called *the liar's paradox,* a version of which is also called Epimenides paradox (Haack, 1988, p. 136).

The liar's paradox occurs if one person should say to another, "Everything I tell you is a lie." If, however, this is true, then the person has not lied to you. On the other hand, if the person tells the truth, he has lied to you, but he has told you the truth. Aristotle's definition contradicts the liar's paradox, yet by saying, "truth is what is true and therefore not false," he has not explained very much.

The transparency of language, and the inability to explore reality through it, was discussed by Ludwig Wittgenstein (1989–1951) in *Tractatus Logico-Philosophicus* (1961). In this work, Wittgenstein declared, "What finds its reflection in language, language cannot represent. What expresses itself in language, we cannot express by means of language" (p. 26).

"Semantic theories" of truth are the descendents of Aristotle's version of the nature of truth. Semantic theories have to take into account two major problems in discerning what is true from what is not. The first problem is that natural languages (English, French, German, Spanish, Italian, Chinese, Arabic, etc.) are semantically closed, that is, even with correct use one can fall into the trap of antinomy.

Antinomy is the condition in which two correct inferences can be equally and validly drawn from the same passage, resulting in contradictions such as the liar's paradox. Alfred Tarski (1956) indicates that "natural languages contain their own meta-languages, so that truth cannot be defined without running into paradox" (from Haack, 1988, p. 120).

The second problem facing those using natural languages in their search for truth or "reality" is that words must follow formal patterns of logic. This requirement is a formidable one for most natural languages, which are idiomatic and not logical. Logical truth must be independent of the world and not be bound by experience. It is the gap between logic and experience that creates the grounds for paradox (meaning one statement can stand for two contradictory interpretations). Logicians are interested in the world as it should be and not the way the world is. The result is modal logic (see Palmer, 1986, p. 192).

The difference between modal logic and experience produces two kinds of truth. The first kind is analytical. The second is synthetic. Analytical truth is dependent on logic and not on experience. The example provided by Palmer (1986) of an analytical truth is "All bachelors are unmarried" (p. 204). This statement would be true on Mars, the moon, or Earth. It is not dependent on experience.

Synthetic truth is world dependent. It would be represented by the statement "All bachelors are happy" (Palmer, p. 204). To support this statement one would have to gather a lot of world-related data (empirical) to ensure its accuracy. Theories of semantic truth end up using disambiguated language, which is logical but often difficult to follow because the meaning is not experience dependent.

Willard Van Orman Quine (1980) has disputed the whole idea that there is any such thing as analytical or synthetic truth. Quine posits that the phrase "No bachelor is married" is nothing like a truth statement grounded in some ulterior factual or logical world. To use language as Tarski (1956) employs it simply is the result of "language synonmy," that is, replacing synonyms for synonyms (pp. 20–23). This kind of language game is rooted in common observations within the same language. Finally, "the old champions of a verification theory of meaning went wrong in speaking too blithely of the meaning of individual sentences. Most sentences do not admit separately of observational evidence. "Sentences interlock" (Quine, 1974, p. 38). The interlocking of sentences means that when considering what is true based on some sort of observation, the researcher has to decide which sentences are false and which ones should be considered to remain as true. Quine (1980) insists that "the unit of empirical significance is the whole of science," and not individual sentences, one by one. To this matter he adds, "it is nonsense . . . to speak of a linguistic component and a factual component in the truth of any individual statement": (Quine, 1980, p. 42).

Critics of the semantic theory of truth also attack it as another form of correspondence theory. If one insists that what is true is simply what is perceived as true, then the truth is actually what corresponds to what is perceived as true. Other critics aver that the use of semantic theory as presented by Tarski (1956) is an example of "physicalism," that is, a movement to reduce all phenomena to that of concrete, physical objects and their relations. Such a scheme is utterly useless in describing a non-physical object like "leadership."

The semantic theory of truth is as contextually bound as the correspondence theory that it attempted to supplant. Languages are contextually sensitive and even Tarski (1956) noted that what was true in one language may be false or inconsequential in another. The only "truth" that exists may be in the metalanguage. Truth is therefore relative (Haack, 1988, p. 114).

Pragmatist Theories of Truth

The pragmatist theory of truth was enunciated by Charles Sanders Peirce (1955) as "a method of ascertaining the meanings of hard words and of abstract concepts" (p. 271). The term *pragmatism* comes from the Greek word meaning *action*, from which the English words *practice* and *practical* are derived. The "pragmatic method" is an approach to truth that determines it by defining "what conduct it is fitted to produce: that conduct is for us its sole significance" (James, 1991, p. 23). Having defined pragmatism, James then indicates that "theories thus become instruments, not answers to enigmas" (p. 26).

The great American pragmatists of science were John Dewey, Charles Sanders Peirce, and William James. Pragmatism is a form of correspondence theory, but it is a form of the idea that insists the meaning of a concept is that it ultimately makes a difference in the real world. If there is no difference, then there is no meaning. This idea was Peirce's concept of the "theory of inquiry," which formulated a scientific method that was superior over others such as authority or a priori beliefs. Such a method ultimately led to "stable beliefs, beliefs which will not be thrown into doubt" (Haack, 1988, p. 97).

The notion of correspondence in the pragmatic theory of truth is that the scientific method will be constrained by reality, and therefore what it produces will correspond to that reality. The definition of truth is very much part of the method of discerning it. It was regarding this problem that Karl Popper (1965) commented that the search for theories that were simply powerful instruments (methodologies) may be quite well supported by false theories as well as true ones (p. 226). None of the pragmatists believed in absolute truth. Dewey described truth as "warranted assertibility," (1938, p. 345) and, like Peirce, believed it to be stable, that is, safe from doubt. Peirce (1955) proffered that knowledge was never absolute and existed in a state of uncertainty and indeterminacy, in fact, "all things so swim in continua" (p. 356).

Coherence Theories of Truth

A coherentist perspective on truth takes a position on two views: (a) the truthfulness of a statement or theory can be judged only in a context of other statements (a kind of contextual set), and (b) trying to return to an experiential base of verification to discern the matter of truthfulness will be neither productive nor definitive. The criteria for determining a superior theory are those that Evers and Lakomski (1991) indicate are "extra-empirical" (p. 37). A superior theory is one that is more consistent, comprehensive, simple, conservative, and fecund, and possesses greater explanatory unity than others. This is an adaptation of correspondence. A superior theory is one that adheres or "corresponds" to these requirements better than others. It is assumed in turn that superior theories are world descriptive as well, and can be verified empirically (adhere to the facts).

The problem with coherency theories is, according to Karl Popper (1979), that they confuse consistency with truth, that is, a statement is considered true if it corresponds to other statements we have accepted as true. This procedure is a very conservative one; "entrenched knowledge can hardly be overthrown" (Popper, p. 309).

Lakatos (1999) called "coherency" a form of "simplicism" because at its base the position assumed that when confronted with two theories or explanations, one had to assume that they were roughly equivalent. If equivalent, then one could determine which one was "simpler." Lakatos then commented, "Simplicity seems to be relative to one's subjective taste" (p. 174). Despite Lakatos's admonitions, coherence retains a powerful appeal to some leading thinkers in educational leadership such as Lakomski (2005).

Redundancy Theories of Truth

Frank Ramsey (1931) took the position that the distinctions between object language and metalanguage were unnecessary, that is, they were redundant. Alfred Tarski (1956) made such distinctions to avoid the problem of paradox.

Ramsey discerned that he could eliminate the words "true," or "false," from nearly all expressions. For example, the expression "It is true that p" can be written as "means the same as p" or "For all p, then p" (Haack, 1988, pp. 127–128). Ramsey therefore proposes a more simplified approach to language expression regarding truth or falsity. In his process, he is able to bypass the problem of "objects of relief." For example, the statement "It is true that p . . . is true" includes the idea that it is a predicate (the part of a sentence or clause that expresses what is said of the subject). It is an object of belief that truth is a property of something. However, by eliminating the word *truth*, it is no longer necessary to know what it is a proper of, so the belief is redundant (Haack, p. 128). The solution to such semantic riddles and problems—even applying the logic of the redundancy theory to language—has not eliminated the problem of paradox so far, which Tarski's (1956) theory was developed to do.

The Uses of Truth in Science

There are few absolutes in science. Karl Popper (1965) has indicated that there are two points of view about the use of truth in scientific activities. The first use of truth is to prove things, that is, that facts or propositions can be believed if they can be verified. In the process of verification they become worthy to be believed. Belief (Dewey's warranted assertibility) is the absence of doubt. To arrive at this state, one must produce positive evidence. Logical positivism or scientific empiricism lies behind this view of how truth is established. Popper's (1965) view is that such concepts have been discredited because positive reasons can never support the belief in a theory, whether buttressed by observation or probabilities in statistical manipulations (p. 228).

A second view is proffered by the falsificationists. This perspective is that theories are never held to be true from empirical evidence. Rather, they are held in a state called *verisimilitude,* after rigorous testing has failed to dislodge them for the moment. Falsificationists, to which Popper belonged, are concerned only with testing theories in proposition form, and in continuing to test them ad infinitum. All theories are most likely to be shown false in time. So truth is that which has not been shown to be false (so far); "We are not interested in establishing scientific theories as secure, or certain or probable," says Popper (1965, p. 229).

BIOGRAPHY BOX 3.1

Barbara McClintock (1902–1992)

Iconoclastic Thinker, Nobel Prize Winner, Passionate Pursuer of Truths

The famous "corn lady" of science, Barbara McClintock, not only epitomized a passion for pursuing mysteries that intrigued her, but learned how to endure in a world that demeaned her work and erected barriers to her career and her personhood because she was a woman.

The youngest of three daughters, Barbara recalled that her mother expressed disappointment because she was not a boy. Barbara recalled that she felt she didn't really belong in the family because she was the odd member (McGrayne, 1993, p. 147). Throughout her life, Barbara's mother worked to persuade her daughter to give up the academic life and her work in science. Her father raised her as a boy, however, so she was free to pursue whatever activities she found compelling. "I didn't play with girls because they didn't play the way I did," Barbara recalled (McGrayne, p. 148). When she graduated from high school, Barbara wanted to go to Cornell, but her mother blocked the idea, fearing a higher education for her daughter would make her unattractive for marriage. Securing the approval of her MD father, Barbara went to Cornell and enrolled in the College of Agriculture there because tuition was free.

Slim at 90 pounds and 5 feet tall, Barbara wore her hair bobbed, sported knick-ers, and smoked. Already a free spirit, she rejected sorority bids because some of her Jewish friends were not invited to join them. Cornell researchers specialized in a study of corn not only because of its importance as a crop, but because the way it grew permitted controlled studies of genetic changes rather quickly. Barbara McClintock forged to the front in corn research, working with corn chromosomes. Only one male colleague recognized the significance of her work. "Hell, it was so damn obvious. She was something special," he remarked. At 25, Barbara earned her PhD at Cornell and set forth to work in the academic world. At this point she rejected the idea of becoming a wife to her beau of the time, commenting, "Men weren't strong enough. I knew they would want to lean against you . . . They're not decisive" (McGrayne, 1993, p. 154).

But the new "Dr." McClintock found the going tough. While she earned a "post doc" at Cal Tech in 1931, the first woman to do so at the famous institution of science, she was allowed only once into the university's faculty club.

Later, as an assistant professor at the University of Missouri, McClintock had a crusty reputation with students. She expected them to work as hard as she did. She regularly had students in the lab past university curfew hours, and she wore pants all the time. She was excluded from faculty meetings and was told that once her chair quit she would most likely be fired. She left Missouri and never went back to a university again.

Finally, in search of a place to continue her research, she found a location at Cold Spring Harbor on Long Island, New York, where geneticists around the world studied in the summer. Securing a very modest stipend, Barbara moved in. It was here that she was relieved of her teaching responsibilities and had complete intel-lectual freedom to pursue any line of inquiry that made sense to her. Living in a nonheated room over a garage, Barbara McClintock began her corn gene research program that eventually led to the Nobel Prize in genetics. For her work at Cold Spring Harbor, she was elected the first woman president of the Genetics Society of America in 1944.

But her research was so complicated and filled with data and empirical evi-dence that it was often difficult for her male colleagues to follow. Once in 1951 after she gave a symposium in which her conceptual frame of genetics revolved around the fact that genetic systems were moving and exceptionally complex rather than stable and simple, a biologist remarked, "I don't want to hear a thing about what you're doing. It may be interesting, but I understand it's kind of mad." Another leading scientist ridiculed her as "just an old bag who'd been hanging around Cold Spring Harbor for years" (McGrayne, 1993, p. 168). Later, when she summarized her research in a very lengthy scholarly piece published in 1953, only three individuals requested copies of her work. She concluded that publishing was a waste of time and she ceased giving seminars.

Barbara McClintock is a near perfect example of a thinker who challenged prevailing thought orthodoxies. Accustomed to being ostracized because of her sex, she forged on with her research and the pursuit of anything that interested her,

(Continued)

(Continued)

from studying certain kinds of toads to studying extrasensory perception (McGrayne, 1993, p. 169). Her environment on Long Island provided her with the intellectual/conceptual freedom to let her thoughts go in any direction. In her 80s she was still putting in 12-hour days and traveling to South America for her corn research. Her discovery of genetic transposition in corn turned the idea of genetic chromosomes existing as immovable elements to current images of genes as dynamic and exceptionally fluid systems that could be re-ignited even if they were believed to have expired in some environments.

Barbara McClintock was the seventh woman in history to win a Nobel Prize. Her research was considered one of the two greatest discoveries in genetics for her times; the other was the exploration of the structure of DNA (see Watson, 1996). A female colleague recalled that Barbara McClintock was a tiger to survive in the scientific world dominated by men because women had to have those characteristics "to abide in a world where they weren't wanted . . . You're not going to find any weeping willow making it" (McGrayne, 1993, p. 162).

One might think that Barbara McClintock's story was atypical for science, which professes to be neutral on so many counts. Female scientists working at universities today still encounter significant obstacles based on their gender and social stereotypes of "women's work." Laurie McNeil, a physicist at the University of North Carolina, says that continued discriminatory barriers mean "You're neglecting half your talent pool, and science is not going to be the better for it" (Heady, 2003, p. 9).

Popper's perspective puts a different emphasis on theories of truth. If one is interested in "proving" something to be true, the various theories of truth are disconcerting. They show that there are few ways to conclusively do so. All of them are flawed to some extent, either logically, or in leading one into a morass of semantic traps and paradoxes that are difficult to resolve; some of the resolutions produce such minutia as to appear trivial in the real world.

On the other hand, if one is not trying to "prove" something, but is interested in testing it, the various theories of truth are illuminating. They suggest various ways to probe for weaknesses in arguments, lines of logical development, and inadequacies in presenting evidence or "correspondence." If one is not searching for certainty or even stability, but is in pursuit of a temporary state (verisimilitude), then the various theories of truth are quite useful in demonstrating what problems remain in that pursuit, what fallacies to avoid, and what remaining avenues are still open.

As researchers work with theories, they may produce evidence that does not "correspond" to predictions made by the theory. Contrary evidence never outright invalidates a theory. Rather, as Quine (1986) has shown, there is not a one-to-one relationship between data and propositions. Theories are comprised of bundles of hypotheses. Rarely are data able to identify which one may be false. Theories are usually underdetermined by data, "and not only by the observations we actually have made and will make, but even by all the unobserved events that are of an observable kind . . . our theory . . . is underdetermined by all 'possible' observations" (Quine, 1986, p. 6). So, even if some data do not correspond exactly to a theory, researchers will continue to use the theory until more and more of it is invalidated. This prospect is called the *Duhem-Quine thesis* (Phillips, 1987, p. 13).

Sometimes discarded theories come back to life. The process may taken centuries. For example, Paul Feyerabend (1991) indicates that the theory of the motion of the earth existed in antiquity. It was criticized by Aristotle (384–322 B.C.) and was in disrepute until Copernicus revived it. A similar story can be told about atomic theory. Originally the creation of Leucippus in the 5th century B.C., it was refuted by Aristotle (342–322 B.C.) and was rejected in the 19th century. "It is good not to be guided by experience and experiment alone," comments Feyerabend (p. 8). Despite its obvious shortcomings, correspondence, in its variety of forms, continues to be one of the major ways of deciding whether a theory is worth pursuing.

Pursuing "Truth" in Educational Leadership

Early workers in the field of educational leadership were influenced by classical Greek philosophy, notably Plato's concept of the *ideal world,* which was fixed and impermanent. Culbertson (1988) notes that two of the discipline's earliest thinkers—William Torrey Harris and William Harold Payne—were devoted to making education a "new science . . . for a new management" (p. 4). They were trying to engage in a quest for science that would envision schools as organizations that reflected a multidisciplinary perspective such as history, political science, sociology, and law. While Payne and Harris searched for a compatible "new science," they soon found that one was emerging and were swept aside in the move toward logical positivism, as expressed in the ideas of August Comte and Herbert Spencer. The ideas of Comte and Spencer were cresting in the late 19th century. Spencer wrote the following in 1860:

> Science is organized knowledge; and before knowledge can be organized, some of it must first be possessed. Every study, therefore, should have a purely experimental introduction; and only after an ample fund of observations has been accumulated, should reasoning begin. (p. 119)

The idea that science and the scientific method were quite superior to anything to be included in a school was captured by Spencer in this paragraph:

> By science, constant appeal is made to individual reason. Its truths are not accepted upon authority alone, but all are at liberty to test them—nay in many cases, the pupil is required to think out his own conclusions. Every step in a scientific investigation is submitted to his judgment. He is not asked to admit it without seeing it to be true. (p. 79)

Spencer's admonition about science bespeaks his view of it. Truth is established objectively by "seeing" it. This is verification by observation—the experimentalist position. Truth is established inductively, not by accepting a teacher's view or some deductive principle, but rather by "testing" for it. Here, we have the correspondence theory in abundance.

As schools of education began growing (see Clifford & Guthrie,1988, pp. 47–84), they added departments of educational administration that initiated the practice of surveying school systems to establish "the facts" (see Tyack, 1974, pp. 182–198).

Data gathered from these procedures were supposed to be "representative" of the "real world." It was from such information that scholars could create scientific laws and could establish a true management science for schools (see Tatsuoka & Silver, 1988, pp. 677–701).

Culbertson (1988) notes that between 1901 and 1925, educational administration was dominated by the desire of academics to find legitimacy in their new places in American higher education. The tool to accomplish this purpose was seen as gathering the data empirically. In the mid-1930s, a second generation of educational administration professors began looking to the social sciences as models of inquiry. The role of the school survey was soon envisioned as too narrow, so experimental techniques were proposed as the appropriate tools to determine the truth.

Among the national leaders were Paul Mort, Arthur Moehlman, and Jesse Sears (Culbertson, 1988, pp. 12–13). It was Sears (1950) who advanced the thesis that schools should be seen as organizations that are parallel to government and business. Sears's ideas led the way to the present dominance of organizational theory as the contemporary theoretical umbrella for the study of educational leadership. We see this continuing dominance of theoretical thought in the works of Peter Senge (1990) and Bolman and Deal's (1991) *Reframing Organizations,* which are simply the latest of the continuing ripples of the 1957 "theory movement" in educational administration (Culbertson, 1995, p. 41).

Figure 3.4 shows the impact of the "theory movement" in the ideas concerning educational leadership that remain regnant. Methods of inquiry and truth seeking are intimately related to this historical moment (Heck & Hallinger, 1999, pp. 141–162).

The "theory movement" in educational leadership was an offshoot of the "unity of science movement" powerfully advanced by a group of philosophers and thinkers associated with the Vienna Circle (Mises, 1956; Runes, 1984, p. 302). This group blends the theories of many philosophers, among them Hume, Mill, Helmholtz, Duhem, Frege, Whitehead, Russell, and Einstein (Runes, p. 302). The notion of the "unity of science" was indebted to linguistics and to the world of Ferdinand de Saussure (Gadet, 1986).

The Vienna Circle was a bastion of scientific empiricism and empirical structuralism, a perspective that only by viewing a while could any part make sense or "mean" anything. One of the leading members was Herbert Feigl, whose ideas were incorporated into the birth of the "theory movement" in educational administration in the time period 1960 to 1980 (Evers & Lakomski, 1991, p. 3). As many of the Vienna Circle thinkers sought asylum in the United States from the rising Nazi movement in Germany, the impact on leading U.S. academics was accelerated and profound. The areas of psychology and sociology were deeply influenced by scientific empiricism. Because these are root disciplines to educational administration, it was not long before professors of educational administration such as Jacob Getzels, Dan Griffiths, Andrew Halpin, and Egon Guba were propelling the field toward a new direction (see Lipham, 1988, pp. 171–184).

This new direction for educational administration was centered in the following key ideas:

- Observation must take precedence in scientific inquiry over intuition or imagination.
- Methods of inquiry in the natural sciences should become the model to use in investigations in the world of human affairs.

❖ **Figure 3.4** The Continuing Influence of the 1957 Theory Movement on the Methods of Inquiry Regarding Educational Leadership

		Science	Leadership	Results	
Nonscience	**November 10, 1957**	→ Logical positivism	→ Leader behaviors	→ Low to no prediction in leadership studies	**Visible**
		→ Natural science methods			
		→ Theory based	→ Structures	→ Loss of leadership-substitution of management	
		→ Hypothetico-deductive systems	→ Roles		
		→ "What is"	→ Processes	→ Theory-practice gap because theories don't predict	
		→ Unified science	→ Tasks		
Root disciplines or assumed centers	Tenets of scientific management	–Behavioral psychology –Organizational sociology –All administration contexts	–Major and modernistic research traditions –Emphasis on "what is" *the real world* –Renames and reifies the status quo		**Invisible**
Foucault's three fields	*Field of memory*	*Field of concomitance* transferability based on assumptions of similarity	*Field of presence*		

SOURCE: From "The Fateful Turn: Understanding the Discursive Practice of Educational Administration," in *The Changing World of School Administration: 2002 NCPEA Yearbook* by English, F., 2003, p. 48. Reprinted with permission from Rowman and Littlefield Education.

- Mathematics was considered the most neutral and most robust of disciplines to pursue observation and truth (hence the preference for forms of quantitative inquiry).
- "Theory" meant "hypothetico-deductive" systems which would guide research.
- The goal of the extension of science to educational administration was a "unified field" in which the most important outcome was the application of laws and principles across all fields of administration: public, business, and education (see Culbertson, 1995, pp. 36–41; English, 1994, pp. 204–208; Greenfield & Ribbons, 1993, pp. 137–138; Thompson, 1958, p. 31).

Figure 3.4 shows these continuing influences. The impact of one idea of "right science" for leadership has been to focus organized inquiry on "behaviors" within "organizational structures" and the result has been that the subject of leadership has been subsumed to the tasks of management and the sociology of structures (see Argyris, 1972; Rost, 1991, pp. 14–36). The lasting dominance of behavioral psychology and organizational sociology are also testimony to the continuing virulence of the Vienna Circle and its adherents in educational leadership thinking. Figure 3.4 also shows Foucault's (1972) ideas that in a "field," there are three moments in time to be considered. The first is a field of presence. In this "field," statements are determined to be truth and involve exact description. They are examples of "well-founded reasoning" (Foucault, 1972, p. 57). A field of memory, on the other hand, are those ideas, thoughts, and concepts that are believed to be false or unworthy of any further consideration. These represent the "theoretical discard pile" of a discipline. A field of concomitance represents a place where statements are made in similar areas or other fields that are also assumed to be correct and proper. The idea of "transferability" in a field of concomitance made it possible for the works of Herbert Simon (1945) to cross over from public administration to educational administration (English, 1994, pp. 204–208).

Tracing the Influence of Herbert Simon and the Doctrine of Efficiency

Herbert Simon's (1945) seminal work *Administrative Behavior* was a watershed in the consideration of educational leadership. In retrospect it has been largely negative in fostering a greater understanding of leadership, and it has fueled an immense wake in the later half of the last century with the accountability movement and all if its many facets and ramifications (English, 2003b).

Simon blended together the perspectives on human relations and decision making of Mary Parker Follett (1924; see Biography Box 3.2), Roethlisberger and Dickson (1939), and Elton Mayo (1945), and coupled these perspectives with the new emphasis on logical positivistic behavioral theory contained in the social psychology of Talcott Parsons (1951), to attack the old "principles" as "unscientific," and to offer the new as, again, truly scientific instead of simply as paradoxical proverbs. Yet even Simon's new theoretical science contained as much doctrine as the old one that he was attacking and debunking.

BIOGRAPHY BOX 3.2

Mary Parker Follett (1868–1933)

Prescient Management Thinker;
Precursor of "Distributed Leadership"
and the "Learning Organization"

Mary Parker Follett was an idealist who rejected conceptions of the state and of management that subordinated the individual to those of society or to "experts." Her ideas about administration and organization were far ahead of their times.

Born to a family of modest means, Mary early on exhibited great intellectual strength. Graduating from high school at 15, she received her higher education from the Society for the Collegiate Instruction of Women taught by professors of Harvard. Later she studied in England at Newnham College, Cambridge University (Crawford, 1971, p. 640).

Mary Parker Follett was a tireless social worker and pioneered the idea of using schools as community centers as well as the notion of providing vocational guidance for Boston school students. Her work in this area emanated from her belief that the neighborhood provided the best source for social organization. Miss Follett was not a believer that social justice would be the result of management/labor conflict, and she did not support labor strikes because such activities were oppositional to creative ways the individual and his/her employer could resolve problems.

Described as a large woman, well over 5 feet tall, with brown hair and blue eyes, Mary Parker Follett was highly religious, although she belonged to no church. In 1925 she began lecturing on issues in industrial management, which made her famous. Miss Follett began her thought on management by disagreeing with her contemporaries about authority. Authority was not hierarchical, she thought, but rather it was pluralistic. Responsibility was therefore cumulative and not something parsed out in standardized tasks or delegated. Today her ideas resemble what may be called *distributed leadership* (see Smylie, Conley, & Marks, 2002, pp. 172–173; Spillane & Louis, 2002, pp. 83–104).

Mary Parker Follett viewed management as a social process centered around the notions of evoking, interacting, integrating, and emerging (Massie, 1965, p. 395). Evoking was the leader's duty to draw out the fullest potential of every individual with whom he or she worked. Follett insisted that subordinates should not be trained in followership, but in working with a leader (Massie, 1965, p. 395). Follett saw interacting as a fluid and dynamic process in which individuals and the situation were constantly changing and adjusting. Follett emphasized that individuals were interacting not only with one another (one on one), but with a whole complex of other persons. Relationships were not linear but circular. Her concept of organization sharply differed from that of classical managerial thinkers in this regard. Instead of seeing the usual line/staff and organizational boxes arrayed in hierarchical relationship, Follett saw a continually emerging set of interactions that were a continuous process. In this respect she anticipated what is called today *the learning organization* (Senge, 1990). Mary Parker Follett is an example of a pragmatic discipline "border crosser." Her thought wove together ideas from political science, psychology, public administration, and industrial management. The force of her work is obscured by the fact that she was very far ahead of her time (Massie, 1965, p. 395).

During the latter part of her life, Mary Parker Follett lived with Dame Katharine Furse, an international leader in the Red Cross and director of the Women's Royal Naval Service in World War I (Crawford, 1971, p. 641).

Simon utilized the criterion of efficiency as the most important of all principles in developing an adequate theory of administration (not leadership, which was too subjective a term for him). Despite taking pains to dissociate himself from the work of Frederick Taylor (Simon, 1945, p. 180), he defined efficiency as "the ratio between input and output" (p. 180) and one in which "to be efficient means to take the shortest path, the cheapest means, toward the attainment of the desired goals" (p. 14). Efficiency for Simon involved the metaphor of the balance sheet and conceded that "the criterion of efficiency is most easily understood in its application to commercial organizations that are largely guided by the profit objective" (pp. 172–173).

In this scenario, what is most efficient is simply the cheapest route because the attainment of goals is simply maximizing profit. In this economic model, the means and the ends match. The less money is spent up front on costs, the more money one has at the end, or as Simon (1945) put it, "In practice, of course, the maximization of income and the minimization of cost must be considered simultaneously—that is, what is really to be maximized is the difference between these two" (p. 173).

Simon's (1945) theoretical base is derived from this model of efficiency. From it, he defines *rational organizational behavior* on the part of management: "The efficiency of a behavior is the ratio of the results obtainable from that behavior to the maximum of results obtainable from the behaviors which are alternative behavior to the given behavior" (Simon, p. 179).

The implicit value that underscores this identification of efficient behavior is that of scarcity of resources. Administrative behavior is rational if it maximizes results at the lowest cost.

To do this, Simon (1945) casts out the human dimension of his proffered theory of administration. He eliminates personality as a domain outside of science, and ethics along with it. He engages in a false bit of posturing when he declares that a science of business has no ethical content. The statement "Alternative A will lead to maximum profit" is a scientific statement, he asserts. However, he insists that the statement "To maximize profit is good . . . has no place in any science" (Simon, p. 250).

By defining the maximization of profit as the "best" alternative because it maximizes results (profit) with the lowest cost, the outcome is the same, that is, what is good is the greatest profit. In this self-deceptive tautological stratagem, what is ethical (non-science) is subsumed under a rational alternative that is stipulated as factual without the so-called ethical component being present. Simon's approach has simply suppressed the ethical component instead of eliminating it. The logic becomes "what is cheap will maximize profit." The greatest profit is the highest goal of a commercial organization. It is therefore the "best" of all possible alternatives. By default, it is the greatest good to be desired by the organization and its management.

The fallout of this kind of logic is best exemplified by a perfectly rational example of administrative decision making in which profit and cost define and inform "rational and scientific decision making" in an organization. It is an example of Simon's (1945) "economic man"—"one who selects the best alternative from among all those available to him" (p. xxv).

When the Ford Motor Company discovered that its Pinto automobile exploded sometimes when rear-ended by another car, it calculated the expense of correcting the design problem. Using a chart to calculate the cost of burn deaths, it used the figure of $200,725 per person, established by the National Highway Traffic Safety Administration as the price of a human life. Figuring the likelihood of such accidents and resulting damages in pain and suffering, hospital costs, and absence from work of the victims to be roughly $49.5 million, and the cost of sheathing the gas tank with a rubber lining to prevent explosions at $137 million, Ford management refused to change the auto design (see Gabor, 1990, p. 133). According to Simon's model, this would be a rational decision by a purely economic man, based on the maximization of profit. It would be devoid of the problem of ethics and therefore totally "scientific." The idea that such situations are devoid of ethical implications is absurd. The whole concept of scientific rationality without ethical considerations is in itself a fantasy—a doctrine of belief that is irrational.

Simon's doctrine turns on the tenets of logical positivism and its insistence on objectivity as a condition in which the observer is separated from the observed. This condition is created when a human perceiver of phenomenon is not believed to be essential to the process of observation itself. The premise is unprovable and is therefore a statement of belief. A perceiver is necessary to create a condition of observation as an act. The "objective world" is therefore intimately bound to the eyes of the beholder and his or her politics, culture, language, and conceptual-affective awareness state, that is, consciousness. The presence of consciousness is a prerequisite to engage in perception. The observer cannot be separated from the observed. There is no objective "fact" that stands alone in a field of phenomena without the presence of a sentient human being to bring it into consciousness. Note the following words of cognitive scientist Donald Hoffman (1998):

> Vision is not merely a matter of passive perception, it is an intelligent process of active construction. What you see is, invariably, what your visual intelligence constructs (p. xii) . . . without exception, everything you see you construct: color, shading, texture, motion, shape, visual objects, and entire visual scenes. (p. 5)

So the logical positivists were wrong. There is no independent factual reality "out there" independent of our construction of it. Therefore there can be no "independent objectivity," and there cannot be separate decisions from the values that are embedded in it or the outcomes produced from it. There can be no factual grounds that exist apart from either the aims or the means, or the decision to adopt those that attain the ends, if by factual we mean able to stand alone untainted by ethical or value judgments. Where then is a science of administrative theory that pretends it is possible?

What is at work here is logical positivism's classic inability to question its own essential premises. While it insists that all things must be observable and factual to be considered scientific, the assertion itself cannot be verified by anything that is observable or factual. It is therefore a statement of belief—a powerful, nonobservable metaphysical assertion and not science at all. Devitt and Sterelny (1987) explain the following:

> One cannot theorize about anything, least of all language, without implicit commitment to a view of the world. As a result, attempts to eliminate metaphysics lead not to its elimination but to its mystification; The philosopher has to hide or deny his own metaphysical assumptions. (p. 208)

The turning on words to separate fact from nonfact results in elaborate explanations that result in logical tautologies touted as science. A tautology is a statement that is true by definition. Logical positivism's approach to discovery results in the enshrinement of tautologies. Hypothetico-deductive systems often lead back to themselves. Rost's (1991) admonition should be heeded:

> Leadership studies as an academic discipline needs to come out of the woodwork of management science in all of its guises . . . and out of such disciplines as social psychology, political science and sociology. (p. 182)

The study of educational leadership requires the creation of a counter ontology. Such a deliberately crafted view of reality would reject objectivism and any concept of truth as finality. To criticize studies in educational leadership without creating a different ontology will be futile. To successfully engage in counter ontology will require the rejection of a concept of truth, beginning with Socrates, and brilliantly extended by Plato to the dawn of the new 21st century. Thinking outside the closed definitions of Greek logic poses a challenge to the field's most creative thinkers (see De Bono, 1992). It is unlikely that there will be any major breakthrough until it occurs.

A Final Commentary About Theories of Truth

Theories of truth ground our ideas about leadership. They are the "mental prisms" that ground our actions. The pursuit of knowledge, and in particular which knowledge may be considered true, is one of the oldest known pursuits of the human species. Since the era of the ancient Greeks, the idea of how to pursue knowledge has been embedded in a process called *logic.*

Scientific activity as we understand it today arose in the 17th century and has taken on a number of traditions and methods over time. One of the legacies of scientific activity is the way in which the people pursuing science go about their business of developed knowledge, and discerning the true from the not-so-true or the false.

Scientific activity is directed by a number of often hidden assumptions, such as the concept of *determinism,* which rules out "free will" and posits that everything is caused by or connected to something else. These chains of causal events, means, and ends are discoverable if one is persistent enough and knows enough.

Most recently, scientific activity is conceded to be *indeterministic,* governed by choice and chance as much as by anything else. Indeterminism cancels out the concept of progress as it has come to be understood in the West, because change is not always for the better, and because what is considered true today may not be considered so tomorrow.

Current concepts about truth are that it is embedded in language, culture, and temporal spatial relations that deny that it may be considered universal (Lakoff & Johnson, 1980, p. 227). Truth is contextually defined and has either no meaning or a diminished meaning outside the context in which it is located.

Verisimilitude is a concept created by Karl Popper (1965) that is substituted for the concept of truth as a stable and enduring concept, fact, or idea. Verisimilitude represents the nearness to the truth rather than truth itself.

There are five major theories of truth: correspondence, semantic, pragmatist, coherence, and redundancy. Nearly all can be called versions of the correspondence theory in one way or another. The agenda of those proffering any of the five versions is to arrive at a final truth or statement about reality. Researchers and scientists can roughly be divided into two camps: those who insist on some sort of positive evidence that something is true, and those who insist that something is false and determine ways to test statements derivative from theories to demonstrate their fallibility.

An emerging viewpoint is that there is a middle road between the binary term *objective-subjective,* which is called the *experientalist* perspective. This concept revolves around the idea that truth exists only within various contextual systems, bounded by culture and context in any given period of time (Lakoff & Johnson, 1980, p. 193). This version of an ontology is a kind of grand temporality without resorting to subjectivism—the opposite of objectivity—in Greek logic. The breaking away from boxed definitions is the first step in constructing a new ontology for educational leadership and redefining the mental prisms that surround it.

Recently the National Research Council (2002) released a highly controversial publication titled *Scientific Research in Education,* which attempted to establish "rules" for what was and was not "scientific" in establishing truth about educational practices. Their recommendations were about codifying "correct science" for researchers in education. If faithfully extended to thinking and researching educational leadership, these methods would reveal little if anything new about leadership practice in schools (see English, 2007). Churchland (1985) has warned that human reasoning contains a hierarchy of heuristics that were invented mostly at random and opined, " It would be miraculous if human reason were completely free of false strategies and fundamental cognitive limitations, and doubly miraculous if the theories we accept failed to reflect those defects" (p. 36). For this reason it is even more important to probe deeply the mental prisms educational leaders employ to improve the practice of leadership in the schools. The purpose of this chapter has been to provide the basis for a continuing, critical probe into those prisms.

Pursuing Learning Extensions of the Chapter

The learning extensions of the chapter involve the films listed later. Films have been shown to be powerful learning tools to highlight chapter learnings in class work or pursued individually (see also Clemens & Wolff, 1999; Trier, 2003). Most of the films listed can be rented at a minimal cost at a comprehensive video rental store.

Inherit the Wind (1960), Black and White, VHS, 2 Hours 8 Minutes

This is a powerful film about the 1925 Scopes trial in Dayton, Tennessee, in which William Jennings Bryan (twice a candidate for U.S. president) and Clarence Darrow, famous Chicago lawyer and avowed agnostic, squared off over Darwin's theory of evolution being taught in the public schools. The use of Darwin's theory of evolution is still a controversial topic in schools today (see Manatt, 1995). One result is the advocacy of so-called "scientific creationism" as an antidote in science curriculums (Numbers, 1992). The rise of "scientific creationism" resulted in the Kansas State Board of Education, in 2000, junking its science curriculum and eliminating teaching the theory of evolution, the Big Bang Theory, and geologic time because it contradicted Genesis in the Bible, 75 years after Scopes (see Baringer, 2000). One of the most critical scenes in the film, which closely followed actual events (see Weinberg & Weinberg, 1980, pp. 317–329), is the cross-examination of Bryan by Darrow over how Biblical text must be interpreted and cannot be taken literally. It is a powerful example of how language is subject to context and culture and "truth" is situated and therefore dependent rather than independent of such factors. Darrow's use of argumentation involves one or more theories of truth, which can also be analyzed. This film still resonates with audiences and will be the launch platform for vigorous discussion.

Medicine Man, Color, VHS, Buena Vista, I Hour 45 Minutes

While this film is primarily about the disappearance of the Amazon rain forest, it features the story of eccentric scientist Dr. Robert Campbell, who has accidentally discovered a cure for cancer from rare flowers growing atop the tall canopy of jungle trees. However, Campbell can't replicate his findings after repeated tries. Into the film comes a female coworker to assist him. The film involves a clash between modern civilization and its values and those focused on the primitive culture in which the medicine man rules. The film portrays the role of observation in scientific trials and how missed clues led to an incorrect conclusion. The story line also exposes how, even if followed, the so-called "scientific method" isn't infallible, an important factor in trying to make progress in the war against disease. The symbol of the medicine man is also one of traditional "faith" versus modern science.

The Magician (1959), Black and White, VHS, California Video Distributors, I Hour 41 Minutes

This is one of Ingmar Bergman's very successful films and was originally called " The Face" (Bergman, 1944/1990, pp. 161–172). This is a film that contrasts the ways of science and the ways of faith/magic. The plot involves a magician who is travelling with his wife and other companions who is stopped by police and must demonstrate his supernatural powers. The magician, played by Max Von Sydow, is humiliated by the police chief and a health official, Vergerus, a doctor who epitomizes early positivistic scientific attitudes toward anything that cannot be logically explained. Vergerus says to the magician's wife, " . . . you represent what I hate most of all: that which cannot be explained" (Bergman, 1944/1990, p. 167). In the final scene in the film, the magician corners Vergerus in the attic and quickly surrounds him with fear, revealing his scientific faith to be quite shallow. There is much science cannot explain. This is a wonderful film to explore the many meanings of perception and truth.

Gorillas in the Mist (1989), Color, VHS, Universal Pictures, 2 hours 9 Minutes

This is the inspiring film of the life of Dian Fossey, a former physical therapist who gave up a comfortable life in the United States to live in the African mountains to study rare gorillas. Dian learns gorilla ways and becomes familiar with their habit patterns. She constantly fights poachers who kill gorillas for their hands and heads. In the end she is mysteriously killed on her mountain. The film is descriptive of a courageous woman who braves the wilds and death to follow her dream and to protect her "family." While Fossey was not a scientist in the Barbara McClintock mold or a political scientist in the Mary Parker Follet category, she offers a glimpse of the kind of single-mindedness and courage both exhibited in their lives.

Writing in Your Personal Reflective Journal

The section in your journal around this chapter should deal with what you believe to be true and beautiful, and how you know or have verified what is true and beautiful. Try and separate what you believe from what you can verify through one of the forms of correspondence described in the chapter. With which form do you feel most comfortable? Why?

Consider Karl Popper's (1965) idea of *verisimilitude,* that is, the notion that what is believed should be "near" the truth as opposed to the truth itself because one can never directly perceive what is true due to the presence of linguistic paradoxes and cultural filters at work. How are your perceptions "shaped" by language and culture? Have you ever noticed the cultural shaping process at work in schools? Were you aware of it in your own classroom as a teacher? If so, how?

Consider the dividing line between science and faith as portrayed in Ingmar Bergman's 1959 film *The Magician* or the 1960 film *Inherit the Wind.* Where is this dividing line in your own life or are you aware of it? Are there things about which you require some form of verification? Are there other areas where you are satisfied without these forms of verification? To what extent should human life be governed by the rules of science and verification? As an educational leader, how would you inform your faculty colleagues of your belief systems regarding science, research, and skepticism? Is there a place in your view regarding leadership for faith? If so, describe it.

A Review of Key Chapter Concepts

Use a review of these key chapter concepts as a way to test your own understanding of the premises, ideas, and concepts that are part of this chapter.

absolute objective truth—This is the idea that there is a final statement or situation that is true for all places, all time, and all persons independent of human perception or will. The Greek philosopher Plato (428–347 B.C.) is usually credited with the creation of this notion, called *idealism* (Smith & Smith,1994, p. 22).

antinomy—This is a condition in a natural language in which two or more inferences can be drawn that are equally correct.

coherence theories of truth—This is the view that experience (empiricism) is not a definitive base on which to select a superior theory. Rather, superior theories contain qualities in greater abundance than inferior ones. Superior theories are more complete, consistent, simple, comprehensive, and rich in content than inferior ones. This concept was disputed by Imre Lakatos (1999), who called the idea that a "superior theory" was also "simpler" *simplicism.* One of the problems was that to judge a theory as better because it was simpler meant that the two theories were equivalent on all other counts, something that was not likely to exist (pp. 174–175).

correspondence theory—This is the idea that the truth can be discerned when it "fits" or is congruent with the facts, known evidence, or other statements believed to be true. The notion that "more" data becomes conclusive in establishing truth content is related to this idea.

counter ontology—Ontology is the study of reality, or of the question "What is real?" A counter ontology is one that would reject the idea that reality is either objective or subjective. It would posit that reality may be something other than these binary terms suggest.

criterion of efficiency—This is a principle advanced by Herbert Simon (1945) that the metacriterion for sound decision making was to take the shortest path to desired goals (pp. 172–173).

ethnocentrism—This is the notion that people who are not like you are inherently inferior. In the realm of religion, nonbelievers may be called "infidels" and their lack of belief may be attributed to stupidity or the presence of evil in them.

falsificationists—These are researchers or philosophers who believe that science is advanced not by positive assertions or evidence, but by subjecting statements or propositions to rigorous testing to demonstrate their falsity rather than their truthfulness.

indeterminism—This is the idea that a search for stable precedents that are causative of individual actions is futile, or that individual actions are free from a predetermined cause such as fate. Similarly applied on a political scale, no nation is selected by history to rule over others.

infinite regress—This is a recognition that when defining words of terms, such definitions are dependent on other terms that have not been defined. Since there is no end to this dilemma, the problem has been called "infinite regress." One implication is that since there is no end to this problem, there can be no final meaning of any term or word.

leadership style—This is a term that has enjoyed a wide variety of meanings and interpretations. In this chapter it refers to a term utilized by political scientist James Barber (1985) of Duke University to mean that a person performs three political roles: rhetoric, personal relations, and homework. Respectively, "style" refers to the manner of public speaking, personal relationships, and how a leader manages the "endless flow of details which stream onto his desk"(p. 5). In this reference by Barber, "style" is more than a superficial rendering sketch of how a leader "appears" to others.

principle of contextuality—This is the idea that something can be identified as truthful, but only within a specific context and only with the understanding that many other manifestations or assertions about truth could likewise emanate from the same situation. It is the opposite of absolute objective truth.

rational organizational behavior—This is a concept advanced by Herbert Simon (1945) that an organization's actions could be judged by the results obtained at the lowest possible cost (p. 179).

recapitulation—This is the notion that in the development of a human being, growth follows the general pattern of the development of the species from lower to higher order animal creation. At a certain point in human development, the human fetus has fishlike "gills." This was believed to be the human passing through the evolutionary "fish stage" of development.

semantic theories of truth—This is the idea that truth can be ascertained with either natural or formal "non-natural" languages using logic. Natural languages have their own rules, which may not be logical and lead to a variety of paradoxes (see Etchemendy, 1999, pp. 830–832).

syncheism—This is the idea that reality is so overwhelming that no person or group could ever encompass all of it. For this reason, scientific theories are most likely going to be underdetermined.

the critical method—This is a concept of Karl Popper's (1979, p. 16) that he indicated was superior to the "scientific method." The critical method was a procedure to severely test theories, with the belief that none are most likely true in the long run. The critical method was an approach to falsification rather than to establishing truth with "proof."

the liar's paradox—This is a very old problem in discerning truth, sometimes called "Epimenide's paradox." This is a paradox of semantics in which the truthfulness of a statement is being assessed when it is asserting its own falsity. It is attributed to Eubulides, who used it to object to Aristotle's correspondence theory of truth (see Etchemendy, 1999, pp. 830–832).

verisimilitude—This is a concept of Karl Popper's (1965, p. 229) that stands for "truth." The idea is that since one can never really know truth, the role of the researcher or scientist is to come as close to it as possible. In this pursuit one is apt to know more accurately what is not true.

world view—This is a term from James Barber's (1985) book on presidential performance. It refers to the way a leader "sees" things and how he or she confronts "reality." Barber stresses that "world view" is what a leader "pays attention to, and a great deal of politics is about paying attention" (p. 5).

4

Individual Human Agency and Principles of Action

The inescapable dilemma of every leader is the gap between deeply held personal beliefs concerning right and wrong, good and evil, and the requirements of working in environments in which these principles become muddled in a messy world. Emergent situations in schools do not always come cleanly labeled and categorized. This chapter is about how to parse out different perspectives regarding value orientations as educational leaders confront such problems. Many types of value orientations, from absolutist moral positions to very pragmatic compromising ones, can be effective in producing significant change.

Carnes Lord (2003) once remarked that ". . . it is well to remember that leaders are fragile instruments. As in classical tragedy, their very virtues often contain the seeds of failures and disasters; and self-knowledge is not generally their strongest suit" (p. 10). The contrast between virtue/vice and the drama between "fate and freedom, proportion and passion, the dynamic of the real in the name of the ideal," (Diggins, 1996, p. 131) was underscored in the work of Max Weber (1864–1920), the German sociologist who saw the fulcrum of the human drama embodied in acts fueled by moral imagination (Samier, 2002).

Weber developed a principle of action that, while acknowledging that "ultimate reality" or "truth" might not be knowable, proffered that humans could become real and knowable by examining their actions (Diggins, 1996, p. 120). Weber distinguished between four types of actions. These are useful when approaching an examination of educational leadership. The actions were as follows:

> Type 1: Zweckrationalitat–This type of action is known as "instrumental," and it refers to traditional educational leadership decision making in which an administrator anticipates the costs and benefits of reaching a desired set of ends or goals.

> Type 2: Wertrationalitat–This type of administrative decision is approached and engaged to attain an ethical, aesthetic, moral, or religious principle or ideal.

> Type 3: Affectual–This type of action is based on a purely emotional response to a situation.

> Type 4: Traditional–This type of administrative decision is simply that of following from past practices irrespective of whether the reason for them is apparent. Weber called this "ingrained habituation." (Diggins, 1996, p. 122)

In complex bureaucratic societies, we typically think of a leader as occupying a position to which he or she has been elected or appointed. Once in office, the inescapable dilemma of a leader is the requirement to provide advice and directions, or issue orders so that others may make decisions or follow those orders. Stephen Skowronek (1997), a professor of political science at Yale University, defines the moment of leadership as follows:

> The first thing a leader does is to situate himself in a public discourse, and construct a narrative relating what has been done previously to what he proposes to do in the moment at hand. The basic parameters of the politics of leadership are set here. . . . (p. 24)

However, knowing what to do and where one is placed in a flow of events is no small challenge. Abraham Lincoln commented on this leadership dilemma by observing, "If we could first know where we are, and whether we are tending, we could better judge what to do and how to do it" (Basler, 1953, p. 461).

The Apex of Decision Making: The Oracle of Delphi

One of the traits leaders must possess is an ability to peer into the future. Leaders develop a knack of taking information and putting it together to glimpse, sometimes only vaguely, into the mists that lie ahead. The ancient Greeks created sacred places where especially prepared individuals (mostly women) engaged in future prophecy. These were called *oracles*. The seers of the future were supposed to have the capability of consulting with the gods. There were many oracles in ancient Greece, but the most famous was the oracle at Delphi. Delphi means "womb" and the Mother Earth was worshipped under the name Delphyne. With the rise of patriarchal rule in Greece, Delphyne was supposed to have been slain by Apollo. Thereafter, the oracle delivered her responses to queries from the temple of the god Apollo, located on the slopes of Parnassus in Phocis (Martin, 1991, p. 260; Walker, 1983, p. 218).

When asked about a momentous decision a person was supposed to make, the Delphic priestess chewed leaves of cherry laurel, which induced a kind of poetic-prophetic trance since these leaves contained small amounts of cyanide. She then foamed at the mouth and showed manifestations of other signs that she was possessed of the gods (Walker, 1983, p. 46). Then she delivered a usually vague response, one that would fit most all occasions, to the anxious supplicant.

In reality, every leader, when confronted with difficult decisions, turns to and looks for guidance to some text or book, some place, a supernatural persona, or someone. But since there is no Oracle of Delphi in the modern world, the functional equivalent is the core of values that make up ourselves. This "core" is our personal "Oracle of Delphi," the voice, principles, beliefs, axioms, or truths we turn to or listen to when times get tough, and when nearly every response may carry a heavy negative consequence. This "core" or "constellation" of beliefs or principles can come from our formal education, our family values, our culture, and our personal religious or philosophical convictions. In short, our "core" is usually a complex and unique blend of personal and contextual factors that have left an indelible imprint on us along the way of our growth and development into adults. James Barber (1985) has called this our "character" (p. 8), and despite the fact that it is considered stable and enduring, it is not impervious to change. It is, however, not easily changed.

Throughout human history, leaders have relied on such combinations of prophecy, custom, education, stories, rituals, and signs of potential divine intervention to point out directions and to attract followers and persuade them to be accepted. One of the most dynamic models of leadership that describes how this happens has been developed by Howard Gardner (1995) of Harvard University.

The Gardner Cognitive Model of Leadership

Howard Gardner (1995) posits that leaders traffic in stories or narratives. His perspective moves beyond simple stimulus/response sets (behavioral models) in which leaders talk and followers listen. These static leadership models leave out the pivotal role that followers play in creating leaders. Indeed, leaders don't create followers. Rather, followers go in search of leaders that the times and context require. Leadership is an artful and purposive construct of a voice and a message that resonates with the people. Leaders are not the doers. The followers are the real doers. Leaders give voice, make sense of, and interpret and rationalize what followers are perceiving and feeling. This perspective is illustrated in Figure 4.1.

A common group of people or subgroup of people confront or are surrounded by conditions, hardships, or deprivations. Their continued interaction with these negative elements gives rise to a shared sense of community. Subgroups facing extended oppression and humiliation create a volatile caldron in which various leaders rise up to give voice to these emotions and privations. This situation is especially likely to produce what Max Weber (1968) called "charisma," a personal quality that acts like a magnet with other humans. Weber (1968) observed that "charisma is the greatest revolutionary force . . . [it] may involve a subjective or internal reorientation born out of suffering, conflicts, or enthusiasm" (p. 53). The result of the rise of charisma may be "a radical alteration of the central system of attitudes and directions of action with a completely new orientation of all attitudes toward the different problems and structures of the 'world'" (pp. 53–55).

❖ **Figure 4.1**   Creating the Social/Political Conditions for Leadership in Which Leaders Compete for Followers

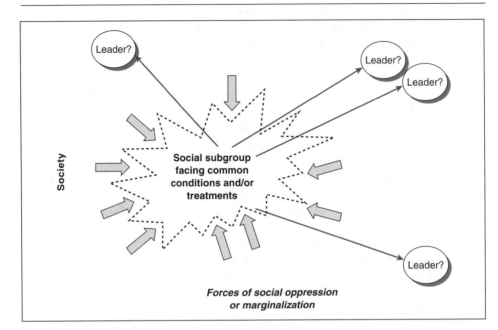

The Gardner (1995) model is radical in that it proffers that leadership (outside bureaucracies) is mostly accidental (p. 17). Leaders emerge to meet the needs of followers who are facing similar contextual circumstances. A person or persons gives voice to the emotional/psychological/cognitive fields in which the interaction and construction of leadership occurs. Its formation lies in creating a certain mass of follower opinion, which results in the fusion of a center of gravity or what might be called a movement.

Gardner (1995) believes that leaders compete for potential followers by engaging in offering narratives or stories to explain their predicament, offer a solution, point the way, and galvanize followers toward moving in a certain manner or engaging in certain acts. Thus, the leadership of the U.S. Civil Rights Movement began with the refusal of Rosa Parks to give her seat up to a white man on a public bus in Montgomery, Alabama, in 1955 (Parks, 1992). Ms. Parks did not consider her act of defiance one of "leadership." She just observed wearily, "The only tired I was, was tired of giving in" (1992). And she was not the first African American woman or women who refused to give up their seats to whites on public buses over the years. Rosa Parks commented about the political/social context in Montgomery, "I don't think any segregation law angered black people in Montgomery more than bus segregation. And that had been so since the laws about segregation on public transportation had passed" (p. 108). Ms. Parks observed that back in 1900, after a segregation law had been passed, African Americans had boycotted Montgomery streetcars until the city council changed the law. Parks also confessed that she had been put off a bus in Montgomery in 1943 for violating the practice of segregation. But the reemergence of Jim Crow laws in 1945 created legal justification for segregation. Because African Americans did not own cars, 65% of the ridership of the Montgomery bus lines were comprised of African Americans. Yet they were subjected daily to the humiliation of paying their fares in the front of the bus, and then having to walk back and get into the back bus doors. This condition was ripe for a voice that would express the feelings of potential followers. It came from a young, newly appointed minister, Dr. Martin Luther King, Jr., who said the following in a meeting to the Montgomery Improvement Association:

> There comes a time that people get tired. We are here this evening to say to those who have mistreated us so long that we are tired—tired of being segregated and humiliated; tired of being kicked about by the brutal feet of oppression. (Parks, 1992, p. 138)

Leadership by Dr. King was conferred by the boycotters and the black community. The pulpit had given him a platform from which to speak. But what he said was what potential followers were already feeling, stored away in the resentments of many years.

Howard Gardner (1995) speaks of "born leaders" and "born followers" (p. 35). Both appear to have primary needs for what he has termed social structure, a hierarchy, and a mission or purpose (Gardner, 1995, p. 35). There is a seeking on the part of followers for leaders who can provide these elements, and help them make sense of things that may often appear overwhelming. People require a sense of identity, pride, and a mission. Followers need to be reassured that their privations are not in vain. Gardner (1995) calls the narratives leaders tell "identity stories" (pp. 52–53). Identity stories are about answers to questions humans ask who are confronting uncertainty and ambiguity in nearly all situations. The more dangerous and complex they become, the more the anxiety level rises. Gardner indicates that identity stories are about "Where do I belong? And what price do I pay for where I choose to stand?" (p. 50). Gardner observes that the knack of creating a successful identity story is that it assumes the symbols, signs, and metaphors that the followers already know and understand. Gardner insists that a "story" is not simply a joke or a fairy tale, although it may use such examples in its construction. Rather, a story is "a basic human cognitive form; the artful creation and articulation of stories constitutes a fundamental part of the leader's vocation" (Gardner, 1995, p. 43). And, Gardner reveals, the simpler the story the better. They are far easier to remember.

Dr. King was not the only leader trying to create resistance to segregation in Montgomery, Alabama. There were older, more mature leaders also toiling to change things, but Dr. King was selected, according to Rosa Parks (1992), because "he was so new to Montgomery and to civil rights work that he hadn't been there long enough to make any strong friends or enemies" (p. 136). The story of the Montgomery bus boycott is marked by harassment and violence. It lasted over 350 days. Dr. King was arrested and fined. Other leaders had their homes bombed. Churches were bombed. Even after integration was achieved, buses carrying African Americans where shot at by snipers, curfews were imposed so buses couldn't be on the streets after 5 p.m., and African Americans couldn't use the buses if they had "9-to-5" jobs. Rosa Parks received so many threatening phone calls that she and her family moved to Detroit. While she remained active in the U.S. Civil Rights Movement, she was never considered a leader of that movement, despite the fact that her defiant rejection to move to the back of the bus one December day in 1955 launched it. She was only 28 years old at the time.

On the other hand, Dr. King's stories embodied Biblical narratives and metaphors. He spoke of brotherhood, dignity, and discipline. He cautioned against "drinking from the cup of bitterness and hatred" (Safire, 1996, p. 534). He spoke of "meeting physical forced with soul force" and he had a dream that "all of God's children, black men and white men, Jews and Gentiles, Protestants and Catholics" (Safire, p. 536), would be able to join hands together. Dr. King's was a powerful identity story. It reached not only into the wellspring of the African American experience, but into the deep reservoir of Christian compassion, tolerance, and forgiveness.

Rosa Parks (1992) recounted a personal anecdote about Dr. King when at one Southern Christian Leadership Conference in Birmingham, Alabama, an enraged man, later identified as a member of the American Nazi Party, leapt onto the stage and attacked Dr. King, slamming his fist into his face and twisting him around. Suddenly Dr. King dropped his hands to his sides and faced his attacker straight on. He said to his assistants, "Don't touch him. We have to pray for him" (Parks, p. 165). He spoke soothingly to his assailant and escorted him from the stage, and he refused to bring charges against him at all for his aggression.

This anecdote about Dr. King underscores a second dimension of the leader–follower dynamism. Leaders must embody the beliefs they espouse. Gardner (1995) says it best: "When leaders ask their constituents to die for a certain cause, the leaders must appear credible. Leaders must convincingly embody the stories that they tell audiences" (p. 261). In the parlance of modern times, leaders must not only "talk the talk." They must also "walk the walk." The key to credibility is congruence in action. Connecting powerfully told narratives with actions, artfully delivered in the public arena, is the essence of leadership performance. This is what Samier (2005) has called the primacy of "individual agency" in a study of leadership (p. 24). It's one of the oldest and most human of all transactions in our communicative currency. It is about the art of leadership.

There's No Getting Around Who the Leader Is and What Is Important

Despite much talk about "distributed leadership" and even doing without leadership (Lakomski, 2005), there is no getting around the need for leaders and leadership in human affairs or in educational institutions, for as Gardner (1995) asserts in his study, "I readily acknowledge my belief that individuals matter, and that a few individuals matter a great deal" (p. 295). The individual human, even in bureaucratic settings in which leadership agency is diffused throughout a hierarchy of offices, the influence of a leader who is an expert communicator, credible, persuasive, purposeful, faithful to democratic ideals, energetic, and even playful is the essential ingredient in organizational life. Faceless bureaucracies may be efficient, but they can never be inspiring or even constructed in the beginning without visionary, motivating, or charismatic human beings drawing other humans to them and who confer on those individuals the role of "leader."

Weber (1968) says that leadership legitimacy of those leaders who have attracted followers "lasts only so long as the belief in its charismatic inspiration remains" (p. 52). Such authority based on charisma runs counter to the requirements of organizational routinization, which is attained by stability and the rules of offices with predictable relationships. Indeed, Weber (1968) recognized that "in its pure form charismatic authority may be said to exist only in the process of originating" (p. 54).

With this distinction in mind, Eugenie Samier (2002) distinguished between leaders and authority, particularly leadership rooted in traditional and legal-rational forms. These latter types made it possible to say that " . . . not everyone with authority is a leader" (p. 38). Samier (2002) extends her analysis by conceding that sometimes those occupying formal positions in organizations can "exert leadership influence" (p. 38) but that "the more bureaucratized social relations in an organization become, the less room there is for charisma to play a role" (p. 38).

While there may be a reduced role for charisma within large formal organizations, to eliminate the accountability of individual agency is a mistake. Perhaps this is no more poignant than with fixing the accountability of the holocaust. The traditional structural-functional perspective eschews getting into the minds and hearts of people or even leaders in Nazi Germany. Human action is viewed from afar like watching amoeba swim about in a speck of pond scum under a microscope. In this social science view, nobody was really responsible for the holocaust. But as English historian and philosopher R. G. Collingwood reminds us, historical events are comprised of two events, not simply one. The first (the outside) is the event itself. The second is the creation of it by a human agent of action:

> To penetrate the inside of an event, the historian has to enter into the minds of the men and women whose actions make history and in effect recreate their thoughts. The minds of these agents of history are . . . as important as any battlefield or house of parliament. They are far and away the most strategic sites of history. (Dawidowicz, 1975, p. xxxii)

So leaders, within and without bureaucracies, bear special burdens and responsibilities for the decisions they make. And as has been stated, decisions are comprised of two levels. The first is the nature of the decision itself, the action involved in carrying it out. The second level represents the ideas, perceptions, assumptions, and values in which any action is embedded. Leaders not only have to decide what and when to decide. They should also have some idea of the medium in which potential actions swim in their heads, their hearts, and the language and culture that defines what they think and how they feel and perceive the outside world.

So potential decisions rest on perceptions and judgments, and ultimately they are embedded in a value system. A value system revolves around a concept of self and a base of motivation. Actions are the result of decisions regarding options, costs and benefits, and responses to pressures (Hodgkinson, 1991, p. 95). Even followers make decisions. They must decide whether to be "led" by a leader and whether or not his or her decisions are congruent (or acceptable) to them. The leader/follower, follower/leader interaction (because followers often "cue" leaders or indicate what is acceptable to them) is never static. Leaders are constantly being tested by followers, often silently because everyone can make choices, although some may be more limited than others.

The "bottom line" for a study of leaders and leadership is that there is no science that deals with morality because there is no science of values. For a leader to function as a moral one, he or she has to be guided by a constellation of values or principles. Such values cannot be established with scientific (empirical) procedures. The central problem is described by Christopher Hodgkinson (1991):

> . . . any administrator is faced with value choices. To govern is to choose. One can accept or not accept the value dictates imposed by the particular organizational culture in which one works. One can aspire to or can disdain any number of systems of "ethics" . . . one can allow, or not allow, one's leadership to be swayed by values deriving from hedonism . . . or by the prejudices and affinities one has for colleagues and peers. Each day and each hour provides the occasion for value judgments. . . . (p. 93)

Examine Biography Box 4.1 for a sketch of Arthur A. Fletcher, the father of affirmative action. Fletcher devised what he termed *the revised Philadelphia Plan* when he served as the Assistant Secretary of Labor under President Richard Nixon in 1969. A religious man, Arthur Fletcher once said, "I really hate politics and don't like politicians, and I despise the political environment. But the big man upstairs told me, 'That's what I want you to do, brother'" (Nelson, 2005, p. B9).

Fletcher was clearly guided by a belief in an enduring set of values and a supernatural power that communicated with or through him. The "common good," in this case the need for a revised "Philadelphia Plan," was enhanced by such a document.

BIOGRAPHY BOX 4.1

Arthur Fletcher (1925–2005)

"The Mind Is a Terrible Thing to Waste," The Platonic Leader at Work

Arthur A. Fletcher, the man who coined the phrase "A mind is a terrible thing to waste" when he served as executive director of the United Negro College Fund, was the son of a career military man. Born in Phoenix, he grew up all over America. He organized his first civil rights protest in Junction City, Kansas, after learning that the photographs of African American students would appear in the school yearbook only in its back sections (Nelson, 2005, p. B9).

After service in the U.S. Army where he served under George S. Patton, Jr., (see Figure 4.4), and was wounded, he went to college on the G.I. Bill. However, because he was black, he could not live in on-campus housing at Washburn University in Topeka, Kansas. He graduated in 1950 with joint degrees in political science and sociology. It was during this period he briefly played defensive end for the Los Angeles Rams and the Baltimore Colts. When an injury cut his career short, he wanted to coach, but nobody would hire an African American. He said of this realization, "That's when I knew something had to change, and if you can change the laws you can change the culture" (Nelson, 2005, p. B9).

He began a political career in the Republican party in Kansas. This was a time when the Democratic party still carried the baggage of segregation, especially in the deep South, so most African Americans in Kansas were Republicans. Fletcher served as vice-chairman of the Republican party in Kansas for 2 years, then was brought to Washington to serve as Gerald Ford's deputy assistant for urban affairs. It was under the Nixon presidency that he devised a plan that came to be known as affirmative action. It established regulations for employers doing work for the government to create timetables to increase minority persons in jobs located in their ranks. Later, women were added to these expectations. Clearly, Arthur Fletcher was about changing organizational culture by means of the law.

President George H. W. Bush (Sr.) appointed him to the U.S. Commission on Civil Rights, which he chaired for 3 years. He decided to run for president when he became angry over the attacks on affirmative action, saying that if those in support of his position would just send 5 dollars, that would help his campaign. It's slogan became "Send five and keep affirmative action alive" (Nelson, 2005, p. B9).

Fletcher's penchant for turning the appropriate phrase at the right time made him a legend, although his wife of 41 years said of him, "People find him kind of an oddball" (Nelson, 2005, p. B9). Fletcher's antidote to years of job discrimination for African Americans in the concept of affirmative action remains his most lasting contribution to social justice in the United States, and the U.S. Supreme Court also narrowly agreed that diversity remains a compelling state interest in an affirming court decision in 2001 and so "a mind is still a terrible thing to waste." Arthur Fletcher embodied the Platonic leader as a believer in enduring values, which, however, had to be embodied in human law to be made to work.

Leaders are guided by the values that have come to influence or shape them. Over the ages, there have been two camps about the values around which leadership revolves. Great and mediocre leaders, good and evil leaders, popular and reviled leaders have lived and exemplified both of these oppositional perspectives. They are an important focal point from which to discuss such issues as determining "the common good" and the shared agenda of leaders and followers.

The Antipodes of Moral Discourse

Carnes Lord (2003), a political scientist who teaches at the Strategic Research Department of the Center for Naval Warfare Studies, posits that modern notions of leadership should make use of examples from the ancient world because ". . . the character of modern leadership reveals itself fully only from a vantage point beyond itself" (p. xiv). Lord sees great continuity in issues in ancient times and our own. For this reason it is instructive to examine the dimensions of moral discourse as it has been defined in ancient times. Figure 4.2 identifies the antipodes of moral discourse. By discourse is meant written and spoken forms of communication. Fairclough (1992) has indicated that discourse theory involves a three-dimensional structure consisting of textual analysis, discursive practices, and social practices. By textual analysis, Fairclough refers to an understanding of the actual content of a written or speech act. Both are considered "texts." By a discursive practice is meant that when a human being

❖ **Figure 4.2**   The Antipodes of Moral Discourse

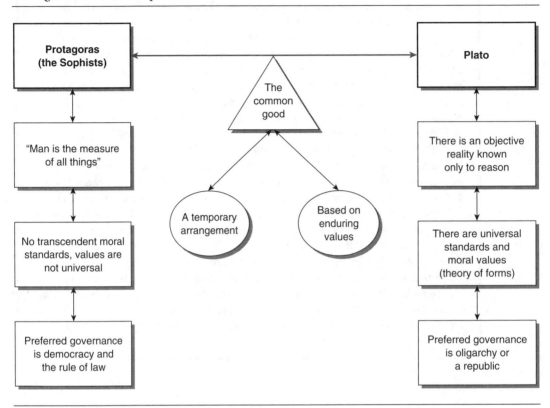

interacts with a text, there is an interpretation involved. Humans search for the meanings within any text, and such "soundings" are usually multiperspectival and occur on many levels. Finally, a social practice refers to interactions between humans and texts within organizational/institutional settings. Most of the time discourse theory involves or is situated in a network of power relations and communication works within and is designed to reinforce existing power relations.

Consider for a moment the issuance of a memorandum from an educational administrator's office, a principal or headmaster, or a school superintendent. Suppose this memo is written to teachers, reminding them of the new impact of a law, regulation, or policy that applies to them. The content of the memo constitutes the "text." No matter how clearly such a memo is written, there will be multiple interpretations of the content. Human cognition involves the whole human, not simply a narrow slice of intellect. The "whole human" is comprised of life experiences, values, motivation, perspective, and reaction to authority. So this "text" is interactive with those reading it. This is its social dimension. As a practice of communication, the memo was issued inside an educational institution, which is comprised of hierarchical offices and prescribed duties and responsibilities encapsulated in roles or jobs. The person writing the memo occupies a position within that hierarchy with defined authority. The memo silently reinforces that authority. The location of the office within the organization means that the issuance of the message is inextricably connected to the power of the office and to the overall exercise of power as the organization defines and executes it. Usually, respondents might question the content, even disagree with it. Rarely do respondents object to the role of the incumbent issuing the text, unless it involves authority that is not perceived or defined as affiliated with the office. For example, the director of transportation would not likely issue a memo defining the school's curriculum. But the director of curriculum might issue such a memorandum.

Value orientations or value poles, as shown in Figure 4.2, are the most fundamental perspectives that anchor social discourse. Power relations exist with institutional frameworks and structures around which such values define the nature of the texts issued within them, the manner of their interpretation, and often the perceived legitimacy connected to them.

Some leaders and followers see their values as fixed to standards they believe extend through time and appear to be universal to all cultures, contexts, and dilemmas. These would be adherents to the perspective of Plato. Other leaders and followers are fixed on processes that guide their actions, but are more swayed by the possibilities within immediate political or social contexts. These individuals would be persuaded by the outlook of Protagoras and the Greek Sophists.

Arguments about what schools should be doing and for what ends revolve around the antipodes of moral discourse shown in Figure 4.2. According to Bernard Gert (1999), morality involves a kind of informal public system that is comprised of moral rules, ideals, and virtues. By "informal," Gert indicates that "there is no decision procedure or authority that can settle all its controversial questions" (p. 586). The implication of this observation is that individuals in any given society may agree on how one should act in many noncontroversial issues within a framework of understood public morality, but differ on particulars. For example, in our own society, most people would adhere to the principle of not killing someone, but disagree on whether abortion constitutes murder. Gert notes that "morality does not resolve all disputes," (p. 586), and a person does not always act morally consistent with some set of beliefs or doctrine. Moral behavior is much more complex and situational than simple moral codes sometimes proffered embody. Ambiguities are nearly always present as a result.

Because schools have been formed to bring benefits to a whole society, clashes in values in schools are often quite fundamental to what the larger society professes in the way of morals and values. In a democracy, values are often placed at odds with one another from moment to moment, which is why school law often hinges on constitutional interpretations.

At the core of the discussion is the idea of "the common good." "The common good" is supposed to guide the leader in deciding among competing values. Yet there are different ideas of what composes "the common good," as Figure 4.2 illustrates. If "the common good" is the same for all time and places, then such enduring principles should guide leaders. On the other hand, what if "the common good" is more temporal and contextual? If that is the case, what should guide leaders in making decisions? Whose "common good" should prevail?

The leading proponent of a cultural and contextual approach to thinking about values and morals was Protagoras (490–420 B.C.). Perhaps Protagoras's most famous saying was that "Man is the measure of all things—of those that are, that they are, and of those that are not, that they are not" (Russell, 1955, p. 97). Protagoras's thoughts became the foundation of the Sophists, a class of professional teachers. The Sophists centered their teaching on the fact that there was no objective truth to separate virtue from nonvirtue. A belief in the absence of ultimate, objective truth laid an emphasis on democratic government and the law as the way to resolve conflicts. The Sophist perspective was that the pursuit of truth must be taken without regard to moral values because "we cannot know in advance that the truth will turn out to be what is thought edifying in a given society" (Russell, 1955, p. 98). The Sophists were of the mind to pursue truth no matter where it went. "The common good" for the Sophists consisted of many temporary arrangements worked out among conflicting elements in any society. This approach would today be called "coalition building."

The antipodal perspective of the Sophists is represented by Plato (428–347 B.C.).

Plato was born into an aristocratic, conservative family. He was educated in the traditional subjects of grammar, music, gymnastics, and poetry and excelled at writing. But his light voice and otherwise unimpressive bearing made him a poor public speaker.

Plato was much impressed with Socrates and his style of teaching, called *dialectics*, in which both sides of an issue were explored. When Socrates died Plato set forth on several journeys to Egypt and Syracuse. At Syracuse he became lovers with Dion, the son-in-law of the city's ruler, Dionysius I. Dionysius found the young aristocrat a threat to democracy and had him sold into slavery (Smith & Smith, 1994, p. 21).

But Plato's wealthy friends ransomed him and he returned to Athens and founded a school named after Academus and known today as Plato's Academy. The school has been described as a social and drinking club "with strong religious underpinnings," perhaps the forerunner of a modern day "think tank" because there were no examinations, no graduation, and no certificates issued even for attendance (Smith & Smith, 1994, p. 21). Plato's family wealth made it possible for him to avoid work. Over his life he enjoyed several male lovers and never married. He also owned slaves.

Plato's perspective on things (see Figure 4.2) was that behind the appearance of difference in the world, there was another world of ideas, which was universal and permanent. From this perspective, change was seen as an illusion. Plato's thinking was highly influenced by the Pythagoreans, a somewhat mystical sect that believed numbers possessed magic. In fact, Bertrand Russell (1955) says that " . . . what appears as Platonism is, when analysed, found to be in essence Pythagoreanism" (p. 56). Pythagoras has been described as a combination of Albert Einstein and a religious cult leader (Russell, 1955, p. 49). The idea of a theory of forms is centered in mathematics. Mathematical knowledge appeared to be "certain, exact, and applicable to the real world; more it was obtained by mere thinking, without the need of observation" (Russell, 1955, p. 53). While empirical knowledge was often inexact, mathematical knowledge represented an ideal that was simply beyond what the real world included. This is the reason that mathematical knowledge for Pythagoras as well as Plato was the key to eternal and precise truth. Any exact reasoning therefore had to involve "ideal" as opposed to "real" objects. And the pursuit of truth was independent of empirical validation.

For Plato, "the common good" had to be based on enduring and permanent values and it had to be based on disciplined thinking. Governance could not be trusted to anyone who was not so disciplined. The undisciplined would inevitably corrupt a government. When Plato tried to connect his "enduring ideals" to human social life, the result is what we call a *utopia* and it is illustrative of what his ideals would, could, or might be like if humans constructed a society around them. In this ideal, utopian society, Plato divided people into three categories: the commoners, soldiers, and the guardians. Only the guardians were allowed to have political power. Boys and girls were educated exactly alike. Marriage, however, was transformed. Brides and bridegrooms were selected by lot on eugenic characteristics. The most physically and mentally fit were to have the most children. Children were taken from their parents at birth and brought up by the state. Sexual relations outside these marriages was permissible, but abortion and infanticide were "to be compulsory" (Russell, 1955, p. 133). In a society in which no one knew their parents, a person's devotion was to be to the state and not to his or her family.

While there were courts and laws in Plato's utopia, they were not concerned with equality or fairness. The principle reason for the law and for the courts was to adjudicate the paying of debts and to deal with property rights. In Plato's world, there would be inequality but not injustice because only the guardians, the wisest, possessed political power. Bertrand Russell (1955) summarized what he thought Plato's society would achieve:

> . . . what will Plato's Republic achieve? The answer is rather humdrum. It will achieve success in wars against roughly equal populations, and it will secure a livelihood for a certain small number of people. It will certainly produce no art or science, because of its rigidity; in this respect, as in others, it will be like Sparta. (p. 136)

Perhaps one of the most important issues regarding moral discourse is whether one believes in Plato's theory of forms. Plato argued against the position of Protagoras by using a rationale that consisted of examining its social consequences (Johnson, 1996). Plato poses a question as to what kind of society there would be if anybody's opinion was as good as anyone else's. What if there were no lines between right and wrong, justice and injustice?

Bertrand Russell (1955) found this tack of Plato's reprehensible and contradictory. Russell (1955) criticized Plato because "he is hardly ever intellectually honest..." (p. 99). If a doctrine is judged against its social consequences and not by the standards Plato professes to be universal, then he has forfeited a defense of them and used whatever standards of the day in whatever context they may be found to support his case. In sum, he has used nonuniversal standards and situations to build his case for why universal standards exist.

Russell (1955) has also refuted Plato's use of arithmetic and pure mathematics as representing any kind of "objective reality" (p. 177). To be able to understand if a mathematical expression is correct one does not have to know anything about the world, Russell argued, one has to know only about the symbols in use in the mathematical expression itself. Such a "mathematical truth" may be independent of perception, "but it is truth of a very peculiar sort, and is concerned only with symbols" (p. 177).

The strongest argument for the existence of universal standards advanced by Plato was a linguistic one. Even Russell (1955) conceded it was partially based on logic (p. 143). Plato advanced the thesis that the human mind "sees" things in general terms. If you were asked to envision a four-legged creature that hunted mice and emitted the sound "meow," we would have a general "cat." But the general "cat" is not any specific cat. Plato argued that this general cat showed the existence of a "universal" cat. It never died. It had no beginning and would have no end. It occupied no time or space. It was eternal.

Figure 4.3 shows the different dimensions of Plato's concept.

This ancient discussion is still very relevant for school leaders today. Leaders must make decisions about all kinds of matters, large and small, enduring and trivial. If, as a leader, you believe there are certain values that are eternal and are not subject to empirical validation, your belief system could be supported only by a corollary belief in the metaphysical (meta = beyond, physical = the five senses). Plato's rationale for the "ideal" as permanent and unchanging lies at the core of Christian theology (Russell, 1955, p. 152). On the other hand, if you are dubious that any value is eternal and that the anvil for decision making is the here and now based on temporary combinations of interests, you have adopted a thoroughly Protagorian outlook. And we should avoid

❖ **Figure 4.3**   Plato's Case for Universals

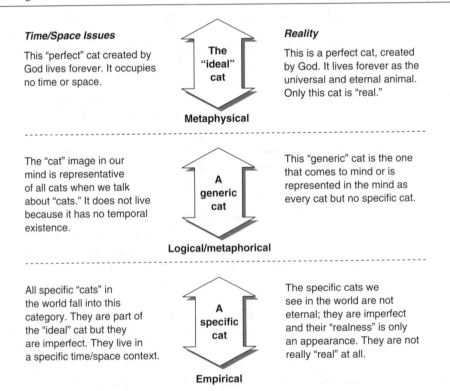

Time/Space Issues

This "perfect" cat created by God lives forever. It occupies no time or space.

The "ideal" cat

Metaphysical

Reality

This is a perfect cat, created by God. It lives forever as the universal and eternal animal. Only this cat is "real."

The "cat" image in our mind is representative of all cats when we talk about "cats." It does not live because it has no temporal existence.

A generic cat

Logical/metaphorical

This "generic" cat is the one that comes to mind or is represented in the mind as every cat but no specific cat.

All specific "cats" in the world fall into this category. They are part of the "ideal" cat but they are imperfect. They live in a specific time/space context.

A specific cat

Empirical

The specific cats we see in the world are not eternal; they are imperfect and their "realness" is only an appearance. They are not really "real" at all.

examining these two antipodes of moral discourse as "correct" or "incorrect" or "right" or "wrong" because they both "work" in the real world.

To illustrate this concept we will examine the lives and value stances of two all-time U.S. moral leaders: Abraham Lincoln (1809–1865), the Protagorian personified; and William Lloyd Garrison (1805–1879), the Platonic man of virtue. Most English speaking persons have heard of Abraham Lincoln, the 16th president of the United States and arguably the greatest. However, William Lloyd Garrison, who knew Abraham Lincoln and was at times a protagonist and political opponent of his, is today not as well known as he was in his own times. Garrison was an abolitionist, a person who worked tirelessly and totally for an immediate and unabridged end to slavery. In the broadest sense he was also an educator. Today William Lloyd Garrison would be called a "Christian fundamentalist," and while he was never "born again," he was from the beginning an evangelical Christian who took the Bible seriously. He defied clergymen who prevaricated and temporized about slavery, he was an avowed pacificist, fought against white supremacy and against the U.S. Constitution because he recognized slavery in its inception, and he accepted and fought for women's suffrage. He was, as his biographer Henry Mayer (1998) pointed out, a professional agitator all his life in the mold of Thomas Paine, although the latter was a deist, but not a Christian (Ayer, 1988, p. 140).

A Man of Unbending Principle
Changes the Center of Gravity of a Nation

William Lloyd Garrison was brought up in the Baptist Church. Max Weber would mark Garrison as a leader who employed "the pathos of distance," which meant he had the "the will to stand alone, the strength to withstand the pressures of the moment, to live for conviction without shirking the demands of action" (Diggins, 1996, p. 131).

Garrison's mother saw religion as an active confrontation with the forces of evil. Garrison absorbed Scripture and family life was a constant attribution to the "rhythms and motifs of the Bible" (Mayer, 1998, p. 17). At an early age he was apprenticed to a printer. He learned to set type and he learned the language. He engaged in a self-education that included reading Shakespeare, Milton, and the poets Robert Burns, Walter Scott, William Wordsworth, and Thomas Moore. He developed a passion for reading and he liked people.

Then came the prophetic moment when Garrison encountered Benjamin Lundy, a harness maker of Quaker belief who denounced slaveholding based on his early life experience in seeing slaves chained in pens. Lundy had established a newspaper devoted to the cause of the abolition of slavery and Garrison became converted to the cause. He began working and preaching. In one of his most remembered speeches he compared the plight of African Americans to that of the colonists urging freedom in the Declaration of Independence. He used such phrases as "They have wedged us into the holds of their floating hells; They have sold us in the market-places like cattle . . . They would destroy our souls" (Mayer, 1998, p. 65). Garrison was not after sympathy, and he did not advocate abolition because of "Christian charity." Rather, he wedged his arguments into the context of the Declaration of Independence. He saw immediate freedom for the slaves as a political guarantee. He said that if the price of keeping the country together under the Constitution was tacit approval of slavery, the price was too high for such a "soul-destroying evil" (Mayer, p. 65). Garrison rejected gradualism against the abolition of slavery because "moderation against sin is an absurdity" (Mayer, p. 70). If slavery was a sin, and indeed Garrison believed it to be so, there could be no gradualism, no moderation. Only the idea of immediacy made any logical sense with this reasoning. And so William Lloyd Garrison espoused the principle that "no valid excuse can be given for the continuance of the evil [of slavery] a single hour" (Mayer, p. 72). While many others recognized that slavery was wrong, they were "realists" that saw that it was so entrenched in American society it could not be abolished overnight. The moral conflict that rose up in Garrison's eyes as a result of these "realists" was an eternal one. He said that "everyone who comes into the world should do something to repair its moral desolation" (Mayer, p. 93).

On January 1, 1831, William Lloyd Garrison published the first issue of *The Liberator,* a newspaper devoted to abolition that had a continuous publication of 35 years. Garrison's motto was that he would speak God's truth. He promised that he would unswervingly speak out harshly and issue no compromises: "I am in earnest— I will not equivocate—I will not excuse—I will not retreat a single inch . . . AND I WILL BE HEARD!" (Mayer, 1998, p. 112).

For the next 3 ½ decades, William Lloyd Garrison worked ceaselessly for the cause of abolition. To reasonable people he was a zealot, a dangerous radical who would dissolve the nation because reasonable people could not see how one could just up and abolish slavery. He treated churchmen who preached gradualism as Satanic agents (Mayer, 1998, p. 214). They, in turn, saw him as a fanatic. Garrison spoke out against laws that justified slavery. He said he would "consult no statute-book than THE BIBLE" (Mayer, p. 224). Garrison's absolutism extended to all facets of the society he was criticizing. He was opposed to the constitutional union because it embraced slavery. He was opposed to racial segregation and supported a boycott of Boston schools because they were segregated. He embraced women's rights to vote and to stand with men and be heard. And he embraced Christian nonresistance (pacifism; Mayer, p. 389).

When William Lloyd Garrison came into contact with the speeches and thoughts of Abraham Lincoln, he found them lacking the moral definitiveness of his own editorial opinions. Lincoln said he was opposed to slavery, but that it had to be left up to the people to decide. The abolitionists found Lincoln's pronouncements lacking in moral certainty and clarity. So Garrison was no fan of Lincoln's. It was only after Lincoln issued the Emancipation Proclamation in 1863 that Garrison finally endorsed him for reelection and he took scornful and sustained criticism from some of his abolitionist friends for it (Mayer, 1998, p. 564).

However, this fundamentalist Christian, the epitome of the Platonic leader who espoused the absolutist moral values embodied in the Bible, who fought the U.S. Constitution as a document of law, and who eschewed elections and politics until the very last, finally met President Lincoln personally. Garrison had once said that he had set out to prove that "the governments of this world . . . in their essential elements, and as it presently administered, . . . are all anti-Christ" (Guelzo, 2004, p. 17), but he was taken back by the candor of the president and he later indicated he had confessed to

Lincoln his own "change of heart" (Mayer, 1998, p. 568).Garrison never indicated in any greater detail the nature of their conversation, but Lincoln is supposed to have remarked to one of his generals following their meeting, "The logic and moral power of Garrison and the antislavery people of the country and the army, have done it all" (Mayer, p. 568).

What is remarkable about William Lloyd Garrison is that he began his work on a platform that never wavered, a platform that he took to its logical conclusion in near-ly all facets of his public and political life. From a political position on the fringe of American politics, his perspective came to be adopted by the entire society and embod-ied in a presidential executive order in which slavery was abolished in the former Confederate territories. At his funeral, William Lloyd Garrison was saluted as an example of "the power of a single soul, alone, to ignite the world with sacred fire" (Mayer, 1998, p. 628). While we are all abolitionists now, when Garrison began, there were only a handful.

A Pragmatic Man of the People Saves the Nation

The similarities of William Lloyd Garrison and Abraham Lincoln were many. Both were born poor. Both struggled in their early lives. Both were very close to their moth-ers. Both were self-educated and loved some of the same writers. All his life Lincoln quoted Shakespeare. He enjoyed reading passages aloud. And, like Garrison, he knew his Bible.

Abraham Lincoln once remarked, "My policy is to have no policy" (Donald, 1995, p. 15). Lincoln was a thoroughly pragmatic frontier politician. He once explained to a friend that in guiding the nation on the path to reconstruction he would follow the practice of navigating boats on the Western rivers in the tradition of point to point. That meant that the boat was set on a course only insofar as the pilot could see the very next place to reset his course.

While familiar with the Bible, Lincoln was ambivalent about formal religion and rejected notions of a tribal God (White, 2002, p. 113). He attended church, but he never joined a church. In his early life he fixed on some values that astound historians today because they are so out of context to his own times. He did not hunt. He did not fish. He did not shoot firearms for pleasure. He never drank, smoked, or chewed tobac-co. He was kind to animals, once giving a lecture on being kind to ants. He fled from all forms of manual labor. He did not embrace anti-Indian attitudes and he rejected slavery throughout his life. In a society that did not value education, he pursued it relentlessly. Lincoln was a social anomaly. But he was extremely affable, told jokes, loved human company, and was popular, not to mention physically strong and fit (see Miller, 2002, pp.3–53).

Lincoln's value framework has been called by Thomas Kenally (2003) "the Doctrine of Necessity" (p. 50). Lincoln believed that his mind was prompted toward actions and by forces over which the mind had no control. Human actions were pro-pelled by motives centered in the self. This view has been called fatalism. From it Lincoln could see that Northerners would act the same as Southerners if they owned slaves. And during the American Civil War he noted that both sides read the same

Bible, prayed to the same God, and asked God to triumph over the other. Lincoln wryly observed, "It may seem strange that any man should dare to ask a just God's assistance in wringing their bread from the sweat of other men's faces" (Miller, 2002, pp. 295–296).

Lincoln was opposed to slavery all his life. It is remarkable that in Kentucky and Illinois, where he spent most of his life, the context of racial relations was marked by anti-Negro sentiment. In the teeth of this culture attitude, Abraham Lincoln consistently opposed "that peculiar institution" but he was never an abolitionist, although he was sometimes accused of being one or being in sympathy with them. Lincoln fully understood that the Constitution had firmly endorsed slavery and that the Negro had been defined as property. Lincoln's "moral opposition to slavery took place within the claims of the Constitution, Union, Law" (Miller, 2002, p. 237). For this reason, Lincoln did not oppose the Fugitive Slave Law. This law provided that in the case of runaway slaves, they could be pursued into nonslavery states, captured, and returned to slave states. While he spoke out that slavery was wrong, he admitted that as long as it was the law of the land, fugitive slaves had to be returned. Others opposed to slavery, such as William Lloyd Garrison, resorted to "higher laws," meaning covenants with the laws of God (a distinctly Platonic view). In this line of reasoning, Lincoln refused to engage (Miller, p. 237). Lincoln saw his opposition to slavery as one involving an argument between men and on principle. In his debates with Stephen A. Douglas, for which he etched his name in history, Lincoln mustered all his ability to shape an argument and follow it with logic and facts. But not once did he resort to any law beyond those constructed by men. In this he was thoroughly Protagorian. Lincoln had the most profound respect for the law and he had ridden circuit for years arguing many cases large and small. He knew all laws were not perfect and he rejected the notion that "from good only good can come." He was keenly aware that sometimes from evil good can come, and if there is doubt about the intent of a law or a policy, one must judge it on the kinds of results it will produce (Miller, p. 196).

Lincoln's personality and his grasp of local context made him a feared opponent in the courtroom. He had worked as a surveyor and served in the state legislature. He had a remarkable gift of memory and could remember names and families. In most cases he knew most of the jurors. He avoided jargon and highly technical language. He had mastered homespun anecdotes, which he used to telling effect. Lincoln confessed he never read any law book deeply. The only part of the law he loved was doing his homework. In this circumstance, the search for precedents was an investigation he relished. He confessed, "When I have a particular case in hand, I love to dig up the question by the roots and hold it up and dry it before the fires of the mind" (Donald, 1995, p. 99).

There is no doubt that if Lincoln had been an abolitionist like Garrison he would not have been electable as president. He walked a narrow line between accepting injustice and trying to change it. As an attorney he respected the law. He had great reverence for the Constitution, although it embraced the evil of slavery. Whereas Garrison vowed to eschew the Constitution because it accepted slavery, Lincoln vowed to defend it. He did so when he became president in taking the oath of office. While both men could be considered moral agents and moral leaders, Lincoln's moral leadership had to be couched in the context of the people and where their minds and hearts were at the moment. Garrison knew he was in a minority. He knew he was reviled, considered a crackpot by many, a fanatic or a lunatic by others. His goal was to keep pressing the issue no matter what. While building a social movement going against the grain, he was prepared to be despised and hated. He was nearly lynched in 1835 by a Boston mob (Mayer, 1998, p. xx). He held no office and ridiculed politicians who did because they had to compromise on issues in which his moral clarity of vision permitted no compromise. While Lincoln chose to work within the system and change it from the inside, Garrison was trying to tear the system down and reconstruct it from the outside. The abolitionists were abhorred by both political parties. Today we would call them "extremists." While Lincoln clearly understood that he could go no further than prevailing public opinion and events permitted him to, Garrison rejected prevailing public opinion for a higher truth, which he believed was supreme, religious truth as revealed in the Bible.

Both Lincoln and Garrison were after "the common good." As a politician, Lincoln had to be constantly looking for the grounds on which to construct "the common good." That meant he had to defend at times a system he knew to be imperfect, even one that embraced evil. This is the special bedevilment of an organizational leader as opposed to an oppositional leader outside an organization. If an organization in its construction has incorporated something that is false (or evil), it may be "beyond the reach of easy correction" (Dunham, 1964, p. 18). One of the first tasks of leadership is to maintain organizational unity. Such an adjustment, says Barrows Dunham, "is not a mere scientific adjustment but a dislocation of the corporate body" (p. 18). The maintenance of unity has to examine issues not merely as "true" or "false," or even "good or evil," but "as conducive to unity or disruptive of it" (Dunham, p. 18). If an idea or a principle is divisive of unity, it becomes by definition a heresy. If it helps unite, it is an orthodoxy. For the organizational leader, this situation, the one that confronted Abraham Lincoln when he came to office in 1861, was in a profound dilemma. Lincoln personally was opposed to slavery. Yet he was sworn by the oath of office to defend it. The same problem had confronted the nation's first president, George Washington, when he had considered publicly rebuking slavery as a practice. He had determined that such a stand would destabilize the nation and so he came down on the side of unity, order, and stability (Burns & Dunn, 2004, p. 156).

Abolitionism as advanced by William Lloyd Garrison, Frederick Douglass, and others was morally correct, yet it was not yet accepted, so the law of the land, the law Lincoln was bound to protect and defend, embraced a fundamentally immoral practice. In the eyes of the abolitionists, Lincoln was a defender of the system that was wicked and morally anathema.

The irony is that as he struggled with the cataclysm of the Civil War, he regrounded the nation on the principles of the Declaration of Independence as opposed to the Constitution in his speech at Gettysburg. On that newly churned and bloody battlefield, Lincoln transformed the Constitution into something different. As observed by Gary Wills (1992), when Lincoln asserted that "all men are created equal" from the Declaration of Independence, he trumped the laborious compromises over slavery that were part and parcel of the Constitution because "if all men are created equal, they cannot be property" (p. 120). So as Wills (1992) observes, while Garrison once publicly burned the Constitution as a demonstration of his rejection of the acceptance of slavery sanctified within it, Lincoln transformed the Constitution by redefining it within the Declaration of Independence (p. 38) in his remarkably brief 272-word speech. At the right time and in the right place, Lincoln refounded the meaning of the war on a principle of equality. In so doing, he laid the foundation to rebuild the nation along the lines sketched out by Garrison in his admonitions and advocacy for an immediate end to slavery and later equal rights for women.

The Creation of a Moral Compass

Whether leaders can be successful transcends the matter of whether the values on which the common good may be anchored are considered a temporary arrangement or connected to "eternal values," often espoused by formal religions. Figure 4.4 lists leaders in U.S. history who represent the perspective of Plato, who affirmed the existence of universal standards and moral values based on his theory of forms, or from Protagoras and the Sophists, who denied there were such forms and insisted "that man is the measure of all things" (Johnson, 1996). Since leadership involves work and discourse in the public arena, even a leader in a totalitarian state cannot be oblivious to public opinion.

Very often Platonic leaders are also religious in their personal beliefs. Plato's ideas were embraced by early Christian scholars as evidence of an eternal God at work. Leo Strauss (2001) observed that "Plato knew that men cannot live and think without a finality of some sort" (p. 5). Such a finality was offered in the concept that while humans were in pursuit of wisdom they would never really truly attain, it was the pursuit of wisdom that mattered. The pursuit of knowledge through reason would reveal the universal standards and moral values (Plato's theory of forms) that should govern human life (recall Figure 4.3).

Most religions proffer that there are universal truths or values that govern human affairs, and it is believed that a divine being, God, stands at the apex of such truths as they can be perceived by humans. Throughout history leaders have prayed to their gods for guidance, deliverance, and succor. In U.S. history, a long line of recognized national leaders have sought refuge and guidance in their religious beliefs, from John Adams; Harriet Tubman; William Lloyd Garrison; George S. Patton, Jr.; and Martin Luther King, Jr.; to Cesar Chavez among others. A person who knew Harriet Tubman (also called Moses by those slaves she led to freedom) said he had "never met with any person, of any color, who had more confidence in the voice of God, as spoken direct to her soul . . . and her faith in a supreme power truly was great" (Larson, 2004, p. 46).

One of the most outstanding U.S. labor leaders, Cesar Chavez, said the following of his leadership in organizing largely poor Mexican field hands in California's agricultural heartland:

> My need for religion has deepened. Today I don't think that I could base my will to struggle on cold economics or on some political doctrine. I don't think there would be enough to sustain me. For me the base must be faith. (Levy, 1975, p. 27)

❖ **Figure 4.4** A Partial List of American Antipodal Leaders From 1706 to 1993

More Protagoran Leaders	More Platonic Leaders
Saul Alinsky (1909–1972)	John Adams (1735–1826)
Clarence Darrow (1857–1938)	Jane Addams (1860–1935)
John Dewey (1859–1952)	Ida Wells Barnett (1862–1931)
Thomas Edison (1847–1931)	Cesar Chavez (1927–1993)
Benjamin Franklin (1706–1790)	William L. Garrison (1805–1879)
William James (1842–1910)	Martin Luther King, Jr. (1929–1968)
Thomas Jefferson (1743–1826)	Robert E. Lee (1807–1870)
Abraham Lincoln (1809–1865)	Malcolm X (1925–1965)
George H. Mead (1863–1931)	Horace Mann (1796–1859)
H. L. Mencken (1880–1956)	George S. Patton, Jr. (1885–1945)
Thomas Paine (1737–1809)	Theodore Roosevelt (1858–1919)
Charles S. Peirce (1838–1914)	Harry S. Truman (1884–1972)
Franklin Roosevelt (1882–1945)	Harriet Tubman (1820–1913)

While admitting that one does not have to have a religion to act selflessly, confessing that he knew some agnostics who were more religious in their own way than some who professed they were believers, Chavez nonetheless observed the following: "To me, religion is a most beautiful thing. And over the years, I have come to realize that all religions are beautiful. Your religion just happens to depend a lot on your upbringing and your culture" (Levy, 1975, p. 27).

A leader who must observe the laws that govern his or her office is often faced with laws that are unjust and unfair, passed by representatives of a mob in a moment of passion or prejudice. Office seekers and holders are beholden to the laws. Leaders who are working to change such laws may have to break or at least ignore them in protest. If they belong to organizations that openly or tacitly support such unjust laws, regardless of the reason, they may be forced, as Frederick Douglass was, to forfeit their membership in them or have their cause compromised.

This is one of the cardinal dilemmas for educational leaders, who are usually serving in state or federal bureaucracies laced with laws, regulations, and rules. Consider the case of Ted Bell.

A Moral Compass in Contentious Times: The Case of Ted Bell

Ted Bell became Secretary of Education in a Republican administration that had pledged itself to abolish the federal agency he was selected to lead. He had been a long-time public school educator, formerly State Superintendent of Public Instruction in Utah. When he became Secretary of Education, he confessed that there could hardly be a lower status in the government than to be "a Republican in the Reagan administration in charge of a department sired by Jimmy Carter, mothered by Congress, delivered by the National Education Association functioning as an active midwife, and publicly designated for abolition" (Bell, 1988, p. 27).

The battles that Ted Bell encountered sorely tested his beliefs in public education, his own party, and his belief in the art of political compromise. He found himself pitted against what he termed "the movement people" (Bell, 1988, p. 39). These were political conservatives who were contemptuous of compromise. They looked at those who did practice the art of political dialogue as "pragmatists" (Bell, p. 39), a derogatory term to designate those who would sell out their beliefs without a fight to the finish. "This group was almost like a secret society," said Bell, "They looked after each other. They shared horror stories about the rest of us, and I knew they had labeled me as philosophically unfit for the high-level position from the day my appointment was announced" (Bell, p. 39).

As Bell began to try to staff his federal department, he found he was in a constant confrontation with the conservatives in the White House. The president's closest advisor, Ed Meese, wanted to put the "movement people" in key roles. Ted Bell wanted educational professionals that would be respected by the academic community. This led to a consistent clash over who would be in his administration, one that dragged out the process of confirmation. Reagan had given his Cabinet appointees veto power and Bell used it to prevent "movement people" from being stuffed into his agency. However, he could not veto everyone proposed, and he found he had to accept some of them for whom he had deep misgivings. In some cases, his fears became unfounded. In others, even individuals he thought he could trust turned on him.

One such case involved the administrator in charge of the National Institute of Education (NIE). This person wrote a memo to the Meese camp in the Reagan administration that recommended abolishing NIE. While the NIE was a subdivision of the Department of Education and only the secretary could actually abolish it, he by-passed his boss and went over his head. He said that somehow he "forgot" to send his boss a copy of the memorandum. This was a clear case of insubordination. Bell moved to fire the NIE chief.

Word came from the Meese camp that perhaps the errant administrator should just be reprimanded, but Bell (1988) was adamant, noting acidly, "In the Washington game of chicken you don't blink" (p. 58). This was an insider's game of hardball. But Bell prevailed by playing one insider against another. Within the president's close circle of advisors he also had James Baker, and Bell learned that Baker and Meese were often at odds with one another over a broad range of policy issues within the Reagan administration. Bell came to depend on Jim Baker in such circumstances. In this case he prevailed with Baker's help.

But Ted Bell's "victory" marked him as an enemy from the "movement people" in the Meese camp. Once again Bell had to compromise in selecting a replacement for his fired NIE chief. He found himself in another uproar in which his choice was opposed by the Meese camp. Rumors were circulated to try to defame Bell's nominee. In these kinds of contests in which press "leaks" are considered tactics both for and against nominees, Bell (1988) observed, "Once the mill starts turning, it feeds on its own momentum, no matter how unwarranted the allegations are. Facts are never relevant in struggles like this" (p. 61).

While Ted Bell's (1988) moral compass was firmly fixed on the values of education and his concern for the less fortunate in the larger society, his weak position in an administration fixed on the demolition of his department meant he was not in a strong position to defend budget cuts to education. When they came from the Office of Management and Budget (OMB), he was stunned: "They were even more formidable than I expected. He [Stockman, director of OMB] intended to reduce the federal role in education to rubble, take away crucial aid to needy college students, and slash financial assistance . . . of the disadvantaged and the poor" (Bell, p. 67). Particularly galling to Ted Bell was that he was going to have to publicly defend them:

> I dreaded the scenes when it came time for appropriation hearings in the House and the Senate. My colleagues in education knew that I knew better. I could read the scorn on their faces. Here was a contemptible little white-haired man acceding to the betrayal of the nation's schools and colleges. (p. 68)

Bell (1988) recounts his internal battles with the OMB. He confessed that he lost so many and so often he considered resigning because he perceived that he was not convincing when he had to testify before Congress to support the OMB (p. 74). And in the matter of "pure" principle, he decidedly was not "pure." Bell had to support decisions in which he did not believe. In his published Cabinet memoir he said contritely, "I had to defend some proposals to Congress that were, in my view, absolutely wrong. I did so after I had either lost the arguments or knew that debate would be futile" (p. 32). There's hardly an experienced school superintendent who could not share a similar perception. School boards sometimes make stupid decisions. The superintendent cannot say publicly that those decisions are stupid if he or she expects to continue to serve in a leadership capacity. So the superintendent may have to publicly defend stupid decisions. While one kind of moral leader might say Ted Bell "sold out" to his principles, others would say he was doing the best he could in the circumstances in which he found himself. School administrators work within large bureaucracies that are constellations of competing centers of ideas and interests.

But perhaps the most telling moment came in the release of one of the most infamous education reports of all time, *A Nation at Risk,* released in 1983 by the National Commission on Excellence in Education, organized by Secretary Bell. The report recommended large-scale changes and greater financial support for education. Bell recognized that the Meese forces in the White House would not find that acceptable.

Despite these reservations, Bell said that the president liked the report. He particularly liked the idea of merit pay for teachers, something he had long advocated. So a full-scale press conference was arranged for the public release of *A Nation at Risk.*

As the date approached, Secretary Bell was warned by an insider that the president was not going to talk about the report specifically, but was going to use the event as a bully pulpit to advocate for school prayer, tuition tax credits, private schools, and the "evils of the NEA" (Bell, 1988, p. 128). Ted Bell immediately called Jim Baker. He was well aware that the press would report what the president said and there was nothing in the report about school prayer or tuition tax credits. When Bell did connect with Jim Baker, he was assured that the offending remarks would be removed. However, just before the press conference, he learned that the president's remarks would be changed back. He was stuck.

As the press conference began, the president was absent. As it went on it became clear he was late. When he finally arrived, he gave his remarks from his familiar note cards and, after a few perfunctory comments about the report, launched into a speech about tuition tax credits and the need for student prayer in schools. Ted Bell had been outflanked. Ed Meese was all smiles (Bell, 1988, pp. 130–131). It was only after the president's remarks that one member of the National Commission said aloud, so reporters could hear, "We have been had" (Holton, 2003, p. B15), and reporters button-holed individual members to find out what this meant. The result was a torrent of publicity about the report and what it really had included. When the Reagan crowd began to realize that *A Nation at Risk* was very favorably received by the public as revealed in the polls, the president gave 51 speeches about the need for the reform of education. According to one commission member, "He stole the issue from Walter Mondale" (Holton, p. B15). Ted Bell found himself in the thick of the 1984 reelection campaign supporting party candidates. His reflections about his work are revealing:

> . . . I found my behavior spurious and my words tainted with a touch of phoniness regardless of my efforts to present an intellectually honest discussion of the issues. . . . This included speaking after a candidate's remarks had extolled the virtues of actions previously taken that were anathema to me, such as slashing funds for the poor, for student aid, and health care for the aged. (Bell, p. 157)

After the election, Ted Bell discovered that Reagan's commitment to education had vanished, and the "movement people" had maneuvered him into a position where he was a political liability. Holton (2003) observed, "In short, Reagan used *A Nation at Risk* as a Trojan horse to help win the election. We [the Commission] had been used" (p. B15). Ted Bell resigned with a sick heart, endured the farewell parties, and felt personally betrayed. It was, he said, "U-Haul time again" back to Utah (1988, p. 162).

Was Ted Bell a moral man in immoral or amoral times? Was he a fool? Or was he the right man for the right job in the wrong times? Here was the nation's top educational leader, the administrator of the centerpiece of the nation's position toward education, reflecting that his personal behavior based on his own morals and values was ajar and less than "pure." It was more than "cognitive dissonance" for Ted Bell. He found his situation profoundly disturbing. He found aspects of politics personally repulsive.

The Case of the Wounded Leader

The student of educational administration and leadership should reflect deeply about the case of former U.S. Secretary of Education Ted Bell. Richard Ackerman and Pat Maslin-Ostrowski (2002) would recognize Dr. Bell as a "wounded leader," something to which they have not only given much thought but studied empirically. The crux of the problem is that "leadership roles often do not support, confirm, or resonate with the psychic needs of the person who becomes a leader" (Ackerman & Maslin-Ostrowski, p. 7). This seems especially the case when a leader is working within a complex and large organization that is especially sensitive to the winds of political change as he was. Leaders working outside organizations, who have organized an oppositional movement, for example, are much less prone to experience the psychic distance between their actions and their true feelings. They may suffer disappointments and setbacks, but they are less likely to experience the demands of the roles they occupy and discover that "they were out of tune with their emotions and growing ever less true to themselves" (Ackerman & Maslin-Ostrowski, p. 8). The gap between the demands of the organizational role and the requirements for a certain amount of "dramatic effectiveness" may result in a leader discerning that he (in this case Ted Bell) has become lost and is in a position in which his moral compass has become confused or points to a false position. "That is the wound," says Ackerman and Maslin-Ostrowski, "It is a daily struggle to allow all sides of oneself to be acknowledged; to be whole is especially difficult during a crisis" (p. 9).

It is clear that Ted Bell was a wounded leader in the sense that Ackerman and Maslin-Ostrowski (2002) have described. The healing process for the wounded leader begins with permitting him or her to tell his or her story. The unfolding of the narrative is itself healthy. One suspects that Bell's book (1988), *The Thirteenth Man*, provided the means for the former U.S. education secretary to rebalance his self-esteem and repair the psychological damage stemming from his wounding in office. Such wounding is not the sign of an inept leader. Ackerman and Maslin-Ostrowski insist that it comes with the territory. It's going to happen. While it may not be spelled out in so many words, it's in your job description. So understand that it's not "if" it happens, it's rather "when" it happens, and more importantly, what you do about it that's really critical.

The wounding process can be an occasion to engage in critical self-reflection and growth. It can be an incentive to peer behind your constructed public image and recast it. It may be a time to rethink how you can work day to day within the value system in which you believe and reset your moral compass. It was most likely your moral compass that caused your wounding in the first place. This is the leader's true dilemma. Whether you are religious and see your values as Platonic, or secular and see your values set more firmly in human affairs as with the Sophists, the admonition "know thyself" is applicable.

Pursuing Learning Extensions of the Chapter

The learning extensions of the chapter involve some of the films now listed. They are intended to illustrate some of the theories about leadership in this chapter and present the ideas of some of the leaders described in the chapter and the ideas that formed their core of beliefs.

Michelangelo: Self Portrait (1989), Color, DVD, I Hour 25 Minutes

Based on Michelango's letters, diaries, and poems, as well as on the biographies of his life by Vasari and Condivi melded together into a compelling narrative by writer Michael Sonnabend, the film shows the artist's masterpiece works and the ideas that were behind them, especially the artist's religious beliefs and struggle to live up to them. Michelango firmly believed in Plato's enduring values as expressed in the legends and stories of the Christian Bible. Michelango's homosexuality is openly discussed.

Thomas Jefferson (2001), Color, DVD, 3 Hours

This is a well-documented film of the life of the third American president, author of the Declaration of Independence, and an owner of slaves himself. The contradictions involved with the life of Jefferson are illustrated in a superb documentary by Ken Burns, which was shown on PBS.

Frida (2002), Color, DVD, Miramax, 2 Hours 3 Minutes

This is an exceptional, academy-award winning film, directed by Julie Taymor, about the unconventional, bisexually liberated, talented, and narcissistic Mexican artist, Frida Kahlo, her passions, hard drinking, pain-wracked existence, and tempestuous twice-married relationship with Mexican muralist Diego Rivera (see Alcantara & Egnolff, n.d.). Although in her life she had few exhibits in her native land, today Kahlo is a national icon in Mexico, perhaps one of the most famous artists in all of the Americas. Her commitment to ideals and her need for socially just causes are amply illustrated in the film. Her modest 140 paintings usually were centered on some strongly held belief. Her artistic work is a combination of passions of the moment, but intertwined with more enduring themes. *The Life and Times of Frida Kahlo,* another film on DVD, was released in 2004 and includes interviews with Kahlo's former students. It is filmed in both color and black and white, and the running time is 90 min. It too is exceptionally well done.

Patton (1976), Color, VHS, CBS/Fox Video, 2 Hours 51 Minutes

The academy-award winning film of the life and generalship of George S. Patton, Jr., centers on the character of the very controversial American warrior called "old blood and guts" by some. Patton came from a Southern family of military men who fought on the side of the Confederacy. He worked his entire life to present a public image of fearlessness and recklessness. He was also an intensely private man, a poet, and a reader of history who believed in reincarnation (D'Este, 1995). His is a portrait of Plato's concept of eternal values as exemplified in the career of a professional soldier.

The Eyes of Tammy Faye (1999), Color, Lions Gate Films, 1 Hour 18 Minutes

This is a sympathetic and intimate portrayal of the controversial fallen TV evangelist before and after her public denouement, along with her husband James Baker, who was involved in fraud and did jail time. Tammy's flamboyant life, her devotion to Jesus Christ, and her makeup (very thick mascara) make for another contemporary film portrayal of hard belief in hard times. She speaks candidly of her life before and after James Baker, as well as the affair of her husband that brought their lives crashing down in public humiliation. While Tammy is unmasked as a mortal woman, she is nonetheless no phony and illustrates great courage in trying to put her life back together, fighting cancer, and repairing her relationship with her children.

Writing in Your Personal Reflective Journal

After this chapter your journal should reflect the kinds of values that comprise your own moral compass. Which values do you hold irrespective of the situation in which you may find yourself? Which values are more likely to be influenced by the situations or contexts in which you may find yourself? Do you consider yourself more Platonic than Sophist, or vice versa?

Enter in your journal whether in the past you have had to publicly endorse a value or a position that you did not personally hold. How did you feel afterward? If you have not had such an experience, can you foresee circumstances in which you may find yourself in a position such as Ted Bell's? If so, how do you think you will react? Have you had to endure the kind of wounding that Ted Bell experienced? If so, how did you overcome it? Were you able to grow from this experience?

Do you consider yourself a good storyteller? This does not mean that you are necessarily good at telling jokes. It means that you can relate anecdotes, personal experiences, or insights, which may or may not be humorous, to relate to a point that you are making in conversation with others. Which leaders that you admire engage in relating stories or narratives? Which kind, if any, do you find most attractive or least compelling?

A Review of Key Chapter Concepts

Use a review of these key concepts as a way to determine your own understanding of the premises, ideas, and main points that were part of this chapter.

a moral compass—This is a metaphor for the cluster of values by which a person's decisions are rendered consistent. Consistency is crucial for a leader to create stability and unity within a followership. The values contained in a moral compass may be considered enduring or temporary, but they serve to anchor a leader's decisions within a logical or empirical narrative or context.

a person of principles—This is an individual working within political or bureaucratic office who finds that the demands of some constituencies are not internally compatible with one another, and has to weigh and balance such interests on a variety of criteria. One "principle" may not be adequate to be able to effectively lead in such an environment, confronting the problem of contradiction and inconsistency. It may take, rather, several principles to do so.

distributed leadership—This is the concept that some of the functions of leadership can be delegated or embedded in other persons or roles in an organization. For distributed leadership to be most effective, organizational stability is a prerequisite so that the leadership is not faced with unique or emergency threats. For distributed leadership to be most effective, those performing the leadership roles or functions must have developed effective means of communicating laterally to coordinate and focus the energies of the organization. Specialization of tasks works against communication by creating specialist language and by creating organizational spaces that are the domain of those grouped to perform specialized tasks. Distributed leadership depends on task routinization so that lateral communication can be focused on the exceptions requiring role/task coordination.

followers create the conditions that enable leaders to rise—When groups of people come to share common circumstances and especially privations, the conditions are often created that find a voice in someone who can give their emotions and feelings a shape and form. This is especially true in the case of charismatic leaders as postulated by Max Weber. Charismatic leaders are identified by followers and not by dint of holding a public office or bureaucratic rank.

leaders compete for followers by trafficking in familiar stories—Howard Gardner's (1995) model of leadership posits that leaders compete for potential followers by engaging them in narratives or stories and that the simpler stories usually are the most potent ones, the ones followers most often remember. Leaders come to understand that they must understand what potential problems or needs followers may have so that they can connect with them. Some leaders are much more effective in doing this than others. Understanding the needs of potential followers does not necessarily mean a leader has to abandon his or her own beliefs. Such an understanding represents a kind of psychic bridge that unites leaders and followers. An example of a profound speech that was only 703 words long, 72% (505 words) of which were monosyllables, Abraham Lincoln's Second Inaugural Address is considered by some experts as his greatest speech, surpassing even the immortal Gettysburg Address (White, 2002).

the common good—This is a concept that a leader's behavior should be directed to accomplishing the most activities or goals for the greatest number of people, especially in a democracy. Sometimes a decision that impacts "the common good" may appear to be negative so that whether any administrative decision or action results in the "common good" being advanced must be determined after some time has passed. In this sense, polls as well as focus groups may be misleading.

the first task of leadership—The first task of leadership is to find oneself in the discourse of the moment. This means that the leader has developed the historical and personal continuity to locate himself or herself somewhere on the continuum of past-present-future. Defining this situation for potential followers is the first task of preparing for leadership.

the Sophists—This is a group of itinerant teachers in ancient Greece that stressed the need to learn to speak well publicly. The Sophists did not establish a coherent doctrine, or a school or academy. They were concerned about ethics, laws, and the relationships to customs. Protagoras of Abdera (490–420 B.C.) was the most famous of the Sophists. Protagoras opined that "humans are the measure of all things" and eschewed the concept of "objective truth," professing that reality is simply what each person believes it to be (see Ide, 1999, pp. 862–864).

the theory of forms—This is the idea advanced by Plato that reality is not perceived directly. Behind what humans see is an "ideal" world made up of what is true and eternal. Only those who were well educated could be counted on to be able to perceive such an ideal world. The great mass of people were largely incapable of doing so and were governed by the passions of the moment. Determining the "common good" therefore had to be left to a few wise men who formed an oligarchy or a republic.

the wounded leader—This is the idea that as leaders work within complex organizations and occupy hierarchical offices, their bosses may require of them the performance of duties, including public utterances, that are contrary or personally repugnant to them. The continued engagement of such behavior leads to self-alienation, self-reproach, and a loss of personal esteem. The disjunction involves a psychic "wound," which can become the locus of a loss of effectiveness. The probability that educational leaders working within public bureaucracies will become "wounded" is very high over their careers, perhaps inevitable (see Ackerman & Maslin-Ostrowski, 2002).

Leadership as Artful Performance

Educational leadership is an applied profession. While educational leaders may have been prepared in a curriculum that was empirically defined by research, the practice of educational leadership is always an art form and it involves storytelling. This chapter identifies how educational leadership is performance and analyzes the rise and fall of one of the most well-known superintendents in the nation, Benjamin Coppage Willis of Chicago, and someone who came along that was more skilled than him in artful performance.

Professional practice is about performance. The application of skills and learned procedures in situations of professional practice is an art. In an applied practice such as educational leadership, artful performance is about assuming a role and acting accordingly. Other applied professions present their practitioners with the same challenge. For example, Klass (1987) describes the routines of medical school in which the constant pressure, lack of sleep, acquisition of a professional vocabulary, and the habitual rounds in a hospital became a way of creating distance from patients and enabling young medical interns to act like doctors and then to "become" doctors. While it isn't recommended for educational leaders, it is the way medical doctors have been traditionally prepared. They learn to "get into" the role of being a doctor and they practice in real situations.

It does not take long for someone to discover that being a doctor or a school leader carries with it certain expectations from those with whom one is interacting. It becomes apparent that other humans are anticipating something from you. They may want directions, assurances, answers to questions large and small, reflection, feedback, friendship, or a variety of forms of personal or professional recognition or affirmation. Such expectations have been bundled around a role, that is, either a designated function or a character that has been assigned or assumed within or without an organizational context.

Outside organizations, leaders are affirmed by followers, especially charismatic leaders (see Samier, 2005a). Inside organizations, leaders are affirmed by being appointed or elected to occupy a formal position. In business, a person assumes the role of chief operations officer (COO) or chief executive officer (CEO). In the military, an individual becomes a commanding officer of some kind, a lieutenant, general, captain, or admiral. In education, persons may become assistant principals, principals (headmasters in the UK and other countries), supervisors, coordinators, directors, or superintendents of schools. In either case, the bundle of expectations of followers serves as a kind of repository of duties or anticipated responses within the larger state of informal or formal human affairs. To use a familiar term, "the bottom line" is that leadership constitutes a role.

Roles Versus Traits: Popular Misconceptions of Leadership

The question has been asked before: "Are leaders born or made?" The popular response to this query is to wonder if you have the traits or personality to lead people. What ought to have become clearer through the chapters in the book so far is that leadership is a "social construction" instead of a genetic capacity (Smith, Miller-Kahn, Heinecke, & Jarvis, 2004, p. 17). It is true that leaders have to develop a kind of inner resiliency. They have to deal with questions regarding the nature and purpose of life and their personal confrontation with mortality. All humans must confront the ultimate abyss of potential personal obliteration in death. Much of the ritual of life is preparing for this inevitability. Religion plays a key role in sustaining human optimism as each of us peers into this eternal abyss (see Weber, 1922/1991). The culture we are born into also embeds us in a rich tapestry of ritual, symbols, and mythology in which we learn to construct (as opposed to "see") the world. Donald Hoffman (1998), a cognitive scientist at the University of California at Irvine, puts it this way: "Everything you see you construct: color, shading, texture, motion, shape, visual objects, and entire visual scenes" (p. 5).

Leadership is a social construct, that is, it is manufactured or fabricated rather than inherited (Duke, 1998; Shapiro, 2006). Peering into the genetic matrix of leaders has revealed very little about it beyond pretty maxims and boy scout mottos (see also Williams, Ricciardi, & Blackbourn, 2006). Howard Gardner (1995) says that he views "leadership as a process that occurs within the minds of individuals who live in a culture—a process that entails the capacities to create stories, to understand and evaluate these stories, and to appreciate the struggle among stories" (p. 22).

The process of leadership, the construction of it socially, is continually made opaque by what Smith et al. (2004) have called "the cult of personality in which social and situational causes are submerged in beliefs about the power of individuals to influence events" (p. 17). Leaders are not born into roles. Nobody is born into a principalship, a superintendency, or a board presidency. Leadership is learned behavior. Leaders are constructed by engaging in "dramaturgical performance emphasizing the traits popularly associated with leadership: forcefulness, responsibility, courage, decency, and so on" (Edelman, 1985, p. 81).

The popular media continually obscure the real nature of leadership by focusing on the personalities of leaders, creating the illusion that leaders are special people who have traits, habits, behaviors, or supernatural qualities that have earmarked them from birth for greatness. This idea, represented in such popular "kitsch management" books (Samier, 2005b) as Stephen Covey's (1990) best-selling text, *The Seven Habits of Highly Effective People,* are representative of the continuing practice of viewing leadership as a kind of "natural endowment" or acquisition of some special traits or habits by faith or ascetic regimen. The important point is that leadership involves a role, and that role is learned, meaning acquired. It "fits" into a larger social order with its own constructions, pretensions, mythologies, conceits, perceptions, and lies. It is culturally defined and centered (Lindle, 2006).

Determining Role Legitimacy as the Basis of Performance

Who pays attention to leaders as they socially engage with others is an important part of determining their legitimacy. By legitimacy is meant determining the source of their power to command or to require obedience from others. The legitimacy of a religious organization is based on claims that extend to the founder, usually a charismatic leader whose original legitimacy was bestowed by others, such as Jesus, Mohammed, Moses, or Buddha. When the charismatic leader dies, followers are in a quandary as to how to continue. According to Max Weber (1968), this problem of transfer can be met by searching for a new charismatic leader who seems to possess the same characteristics as the old one. This was used in selecting a successor to the Dalai Lama in Tibet. A second way that a new leader retains legitimacy is that he or she is chosen by divine judgment or the prophecy of oracles. A third way is that the old leader selects a new leader before he or she dies. As Weber (1968) observes, " . . . legitimacy is acquired through the act of designation" (p. 55).

Leadership can also be transferred by the disciples or "charismatically qualified administrative staff" (Weber, 1968, p. 55) who select a successor, as in the selection of a new Roman Catholic Pope by the bishops. The selection of a Pope also involves the transfer of charisma by ritual in which certain ceremonies and symbols are used to bestow the new Pope with legitimacy. This is also the means of transferring legitimacy with a coronation of a king or queen. In this instance, leadership is transferred via heredity and followed by priestly acts such as the laying on of hands and anointment.

The failure for a charismatic leader to deal with the issue of the transference of legitimacy can provoke a crisis for those followers who require charisma as the connective tissue for leadership to exist in the first place. Weber (1968) points out that if the rise of a leader is due to the bestowal of charisma by his or her followers, there is no way this characteristic can be "learned" or "taught." Rather, it is "awakened" or "tested" (p. 58). So one could not go to the university or a school and earn a degree in charisma and go out and look for a job.

Perhaps the most notable example of the issue of the failure to transfer authority based on charisma and its function as leadership legitimacy occurred in the successor to the Islamic prophet Muhammad (570–632) or Mahomet (see Armstrong, 1992). After Muhammad's death, the Muslim community was in shock. Muhammad had not named a successor and no one thought it possible for anyone to take his place because he had claimed that he was the final prophet (Hill & Awde, 2003, p. 32).

Into this hiatus of ambiguity, Muhammad's followers resorted to the practice of electing four of the prophet's close followers who would take charge in succession. These four were subsequently called "caliphs" or "khalifas," which connotes that they are the "successors" or "deputies" of Muhammad (Hill & Awde, 2003, p. 33). The period that followed has been called the time of the "Rightly Guided Caliphs" and is considered the traditional or orthodox view of how legitimacy was to be properly handled. The people who believed in this transfer of legitimacy were called the Sunnah (Armstrong, 1992, p. 259) or "Sunnis," a name that persists today in the Islamic world. But a challenge was issued to the Sunnah that a significant number of Muslims believed that the fourth Caliph, Ali, was the true and only possible successor to Muhammad. Ali (651–661) was Muhammad's cousin and son-in-law. The people who believed that only Ali was the legitimate heir to the prophet were called Shiah-i-Ali (the party of Ali) and are called Shi'is or Shi'tes (Armstrong, p. 259). Civil strife and wars have marked the differences between these two dominant forms of Islam. While 90% of the worldwide Islamic community is Sunni, the Shi'tes, which are about 14% of the total, dominate Iran and Iraq (Farah, 1994, pp. 170, 173).

The basis of leadership legitimacy in the West, and in much of the remainder of the non-Muslim world, is defined by legal authority. Bureaucracies are organizations normally established within a legal structure in which the power and legitimacy of the leader or official is not found in the personal qualities of the leader bestowed by followers, but by the office itself. A leader "commands" by the norms in place that pertain to the office, not by the nature or volatility of his personal authority. Power is exercised on behalf of the organization of which the leader is but a trustee. "The "area of jurisdiction" is a functionally delimited realm of possible objects for command and thus delimits the sphere of the official's legitimate power (Gerth & Mills, 1970, p. 295). What this means is that the fundamental difference between organizational and nonorganizational legitimacy as a source of power is that a leader inside an organization is acting or leading in an "official sphere" as opposed to a "private sphere" (Gerth & Mills, p. 295).

Max Weber sketched out the importance of this distinction:

> . . . submission under legal authority is based upon an impersonal bond to the generally defined and functional "duty of office." The official duty–like the corresponding right to exercise authority: the "jurisdictional competency"—is fixed by *rationally established norms,* by enactments, decrees, and regulations, in such a manner that the legitimacy of the authority becomes the legality of the general rule which is purposely thought out, enacted, and announced with formal correctness. (Gerth & Mills, 1968, p. 299)

The position of educational leader or school administrator is therefore a formal role, thought out ahead of time, rational, embedded in a larger legal or structural framework. It is designed to embody the overall rules of the organization, to create an official who acts not on his or her personal whims, but as an actor, a person who represents encapsulated authority specifically configured in the overall fabric of purposeful organizational life. This purposeful organizational fabric is socially constructed. It is scripted in advance. It is a kind of theater and as anyone knows who has occupied such roles, it is drama (see Starratt, 1993, pp. 134–149).

Ackerman and Maslin-Ostrowski (2002) reinforce the notion of leadership as acting by noting the following:

> Most school leaders, including those we interviewed, would admit that the role itself requires a certain amount of method acting, a style obliging a performer (leader) to respond as much to his own inner feelings as the requirements of the role. (p. 9)

The reason is that "leadership lives are, for the most part, determined by role expectations" (Ackerman & Maslin-Ostrowski, p. 8).

Is Leadership Acting?

You have probably been to a play or film. You know that what the actors are saying is far from spontaneous. It has been written out beforehand. Actors make the script appear spontaneous. They bring to a play or film the fluidity of real life. They make you feel that you have become part of the ongoing scenes, that you are a silent participant following them in their depictions. In great plays or films, the viewers lose their sense of distance and assume at least a psychological presence inside the drama itself. The "magic" of the play or film is that even as the actors are performing the drama, viewers can move in and out of the scenes. Most are able to assume two stances. The first is that they are "watching" the drama. They are outsiders. The second is that they are insiders, that is, they are silent participants wandering about with the players. A third perspective, more difficult to assume, is that the viewer can peer inward to himself or herself and inquire as to how he or she may be feeling about the players, the play, its purposes, and possible outcome. The most obvious kind of play or film in which all three are often at work simultaneously is a "whodunit," a murder mystery, where the audience is examining each of the characters, trying to assess their culpability, piecing together the plot, and wondering how it may come out at the end. Engaging murder mysteries often have a surprise ending or a plot twist that catches the audience off guard.

Attending a play or a film makes the viewer cognizant that there is more to appearance than what is seen in the outer world. The viewer is aware that there is an inner world too. The inner world represents the construction of the play and the interactions of the players. The viewer knows that the play is a social construction. In really good films, however, the viewer may have to remind himself or herself that "it's only a movie" and not real because his or her emotions are now involved (see Crow & Grogan, 2005). The viewer is also aware that somebody, the playwright or playwrights, had to write the play. Great playwrights, like Shakespeare for example, created a way of enabling a character to share his or her inner feelings with an audience. Shakespeare's greatest tragedies involve key dramatic figures such as the prince in *Hamlet* or Brutus in *Julius Caesar*. In these plays, the characters grope toward an understanding of events of immense and sometimes ghastly proportions. The audience may be only slightly ahead of the character in watching him or her struggle with the meaning of his or her actions. Shakespeare grew to understand that to construct a kind of strategic opacity in his plot for his characters created a dramatic intensity that engrossed audiences (Greenblatt, 2004).

What is engaging about great plays or films is that while we are observant creatures externally, we are often at a loss to confront our own inner selves. The eminent psychiatrist Carl Jung (1958) summarized this dilemma when he said the following: " . . . man is an enigma to himself. This is understandable, seeing that he lacks the means of comparison necessary for self-knowledge" (p. 55). Jung (1958) went on to comment as follows:

> Our psyche, which is primarily responsible for all the historical changes wrought by the hand of man on the face of this planet, remains an insoluble puzzle and an incomprehensible wonder, an objective of abiding perplexity—a feature it shares with all Nature's secrets. (p. 56)

What great plays and films do for us is to sharpen the audiences' questions about universal themes that have puzzled humans across time. It is not the answers, but the questions, that are important. Leaders are humans who have come to grips with some of these issues. As a student of leadership, let us summarize the stance of a viewer of the infinite human drama that is not only ongoing, but into which we will participate in our own time and way. It is shown in Figure 5.1 as a play or film depiction. Figure 5.1 illustrates that there are at least three aspects of such participation. The first is the external world, which comprises the play itself. This world is made up of events represented in the play by "scenes." The construction of scenes enables an audience to see action and decisions in context and time. They give us a sense or proportion and spatiality. They enable us to make judgments about the behaviors and feelings of the actors as they confront the external world they "see." As the actors move within the play and within and across the scenes, the audience then encounters the second layer of the play, that is, the inner world of the characters and how they act and react to the representation of the world. This provides the audience with a representation of the junctures and disjunctures between the following: (a) the reality the audience sees, (b) the reality the characters see, and (c) the actions and thoughts of the characters compared to the reality that the audience sees. The fourth component of this multilayered and complex situation is personal reflection, which occurs only within the audience. It is the resonances and connections that audience members "discover" about themselves as they are involved in the drama. Here, by drama, is meant the "line of action" to which the audience is exposed when it becomes engaged in the play.

With a little adjustment of Figure 5.1, we can see an application to educational leadership. That is represented in Figure 5.2.

The educational leader occupies a position in a formal organization. Like a play, a formal organization refers to "the ways in which human conduct becomes socially organized" (Blau & Scott, 1962, p. 2). The regulation of conduct into roles is determined

❖ **Figure 5.1**   Three Dimensions of Narrative at Work in the Artistry of Leadership

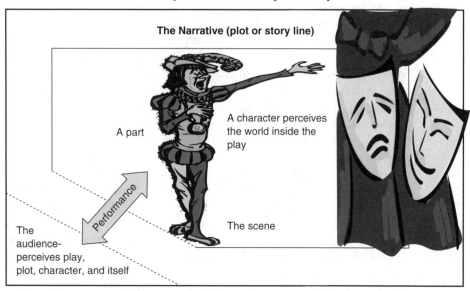

❖ **Figure 5.2**   Three Dimensions of Narrative at Work in the Artistry of
Educational Leadership

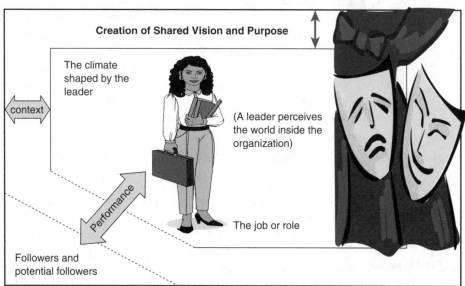

by the structure of social relations within a group or larger organization, and the collective beliefs and norms that govern human relations within that same group or organization. A formal organization is one that has these characteristics but one significant additional factor, that is, the organization has been established for the purpose of realizing certain goals. A formal organization is thus goal-driven.

A play also has goals or purposes. A playwright usually has a purpose in constructing a drama. It too has formal roles and the relationships between the characters in the play are ordered, that is, constructed. They have to "make sense" within a specific culture and context or the audience cannot connect to the portrayed interactions. Leadership is performance and is therefore an art. As John Dewey (1929) observed, leadership, like education, was an art because it was practical. To understand leadership in context and to make sense of its effectiveness means understanding application. It is because educational leadership is inherently practical that it should be considered as a kind of dramaturgy that is, in its own way, theatrical. First, it exists in relationship to other roles. Leadership is therefore interactive. Leadership is cultural, that is, it functions within a specific sea of values and possibilities that take on a range of accepted positions, reactions, and customs. Leadership is communicative. It traffics in the linguistic traditions, symbols, and stories understood by the people who determine to follow or select a person that embodies their values and beliefs. Gardner (1995) has called this quality "linguistic intelligence" (p. 39). Interestingly, research regarding general intelligence indicates that successful leaders are not the brightest persons in a group (Sternberg, 2005, p. 354). In fact, if a person's IQ is too high, he or she is likely to be misunderstood, prompting Simonton (1994) to observe, "Possibly, a person can be too bright to be president" (p. 235). In Shakespeare's greatest tragedies, the heroes are often gullible and dense. Characters such as King Lear, Falstaff, and Othello illustrate remarkable lapses of discernment and insight into their contexts and times. Cuban (1976) similarly illustrates the blind spots of superintendent leadership in his classic work, *Urban School Chiefs Under Fire.*

Cuban (1976) examined conflict and controversies with three urban school superintendents in Chicago, San Francisco, and Washington, DC, and while the case studies he performed were completed over 30 years ago, these same school systems have continued to "churn" superintendents over and over again since that time (see Ayers & Klonsky, 2006; Gewertz, 2006; Hess, 1991). Using Cuban's descriptions and Figure 5.2 as a reference, we turn to a study of the contexts as an example of artful performance of a chief school officer in a real decision-making context.

Real-Life Drama in Chicago: A Portrait of Power Undone

Benjamin Coppage Willis was superintendent of the Chicago Public Schools between 1953 and 1966. As Cuban (1976) notes, Ben Willis built a large number of schools during Chicago's growth as a major U.S. city. He oversaw school construction that averaged $700,000 per week in expenditures. He oversaw the addition of 126,000 new classroom seats. He was a champion of higher teacher salaries and pushed for advancements in English, science, and math long before the Russian sputnik led to the passage of the National Education Defense Act in 1958 (Cunningham & Cordeiro, 2000, p. 35).

Willis was a prolific writer and he was a "media darling" long before the term came into use. He was regularly featured in magazines and newspapers of his times. As for professional honors, he was elected president of the American Association of School Administrators (the AASA), recognition of his leadership among his fellow national superintendents. President Kennedy appointed him to a national educational commission and he was founder and chairman for 10 years of the Great Cities Research Council. Yet this seemingly paragon of professionalism and executive power came up short when he failed to recognize how larger social unrest and shifts in his constituencies would change the basis of the "play." Willis kept reading from the same old script, but the context of the times had shifted. What had been effective performance was now impeding his leadership.

Cuban's (1976) portrait of Ben Willis is one of a rags to riches story line. In education he was the equivalent of Jack Welch, General Electric's CEO of his day (Jenkins, 2006; O'Boyle, 1998). Brought up in rural Maryland, he went to a one-room schoolhouse. In successive jumps he became a school principal and a rural superintendent. He received his doctorate from Teachers College, Columbia University, and quickly moved through superintendencies in Hagerstown, Maryland; Yonkers and Buffalo, New York; to Chicago. Cuban (1976) describes his "leadership style" as filled with "considerable energy, single-mindedness, and towering self-confidence," to the point where he "eats, drinks, sleeps and dreams schools" (p. 3). With subordinates, Willis was equally demanding. He thought nothing of phoning them at odd hours or calling meetings when it was at the end of a normal working day to brainstorm new ideas or chew over new plans.

Coupled with this raw energy was a penchant for detail. He had an uncanny grasp of minutia. Cuban (1976) says Willis knew how much Worcestershire sauce cost the school system annually. He could spew forth volumes of such statistics at a moment's notice and didn't mind using them to intimidate opponents and wow the press. The man had no hobbies and no free time. He was completely absorbed in his job. He had nothing else and he reveled in the detail and exercise of the power of the office.

The downside to Ben Willis was that to some he appeared arrogant, stubborn, and dictatorial. He could bulldoze the opposition with his command of a huge data arsenal and a capacity to memorize and retain colossal chunks of information, and with his board he resorted at times to threats to go to the press and expose its refusal to support his programs. Like some superintendents who want to appear open but are not open to a more democratic approach to educational administration, Willis kept his boards swamped with huge binders of information filled with financial trivia and other matters that focused their attention away from his utilization of power. In frustration one board member is said to have remarked, "I'm not against the superintendent one single, tiny, little bit even when he accuses us of making policy" (*Chicago Daily News,* 1962, as cited in Cuban, 1976, p. 6).

When he turned 60, Ben Willis was president of the AASA, received an honorary degree from Harvard in recognition of his national educational leadership, was offered and declined the superintendency of the New York City public schools, and with a new 4-year contract and a raise offered by his board, became the third highest paid public official in America. He had it made or so he thought.

But as Ben Willis stood on Chicago's stage and continued to "perform" as he always had, the context of his audience was shifting and new demands were escalating. Cuban (1976) notes that in 10 years, from 1953 to 1963, while Chicago's population actually declined by about 70,000 people, the school population increased by 100,000 students and a large percentage of these new children were African Americans. Because of housing segregation, most of the African American children were crammed into the city's South Side. Despite successful bond issues and new construction, the enrollment increases outdistanced the school system's building program. Thousands of African American children remained on double shifts. But in the white-dominated geographical areas of the city, there were empty classrooms and plenty of space. Playgrounds were open and not cluttered with temporary classrooms.

But something began to happen that signaled a shift in how an educational leader like Ben Willis would be judged, and in 2 years his descent to a current footnote in U.S. educational leadership had begun. It occurred at the apogee of his professional rise to prominence, when he was the highest paid public superintendent of schools in the nation, and he failed to grasp its significance. And for once his sense of timing and his command of the facts faltered. What happened was the rise of the U.S. Civil Rights Movement and the redefinition of the nature of "educational quality," which today is still expressed in such national legislation as Public Law 107–110, better known as the No Child Left Behind Act, and which has been aimed at eliminating the achievement gap that was then only dimly perceived (Kronholz, 2003).

And onto the Chicago stage came the Shakespearean figure of Saul Alinsky, a community leader who had a profound grasp of the art of theater in public discourse. Alinsky was to Ben Willis as Iago was to Shakespeare's Othello. Harold Bloom (1998) says that "Othello is a great soul hopelessly outclassed in intellect and drive by Iago" (p. 438). Bloom's description of Othello mirrors Cuban's (1976) description of Ben Willis:

> Othello is a great commander, who knows war and the limits of war but who knows little else, and cannot know what he does not know. His sense of himself is very large, in that its scale is vast, but he sees himself from afar as it were; up close, he hardly confronts the void at his center. (Bloom, 1998, p. 445)

Remember that Ben Willis was totally absorbed in his job. He had no hobbies and no free time. He was "the commander" of the nation's second largest school system. He broached no dissent in his administration. He bullied and he intimidated when he had to. He could and did smother enemies with his remarkable memory and self-confidence in details. But Saul Alinsky, like Shakespeare's diabolic genius Iago, can be summarized as "a great improviser, he works with gusto and mastery of timing, adjusting his plot to openings as they present themselves . . . Iago is an inventor, an experimenter always willing to try modes heretofore unknown" (Bloom, 1998, p. 436).

Let us review Alinsky's methods (1946/1969; 1971) that brought Ben Willis down at the height of his fame. Alinsky's tactics were radical. They were based on his observation that "practically all people live in a world of contradictions. They espouse a morality which they do not practice . . . the vast separation between their moral standards and actual ways of living resolves itself into extraordinary inconsistencies and inner conflict" (Alinsky, 1946/1969, p. 93). Alinsky's tactics took advantage of this "space" or "silence" between words and actions. This was the space to maneuver and to engage in confrontation.

First, Alinsky had to acquire power. Noting, "All life is partisan. There is no dispassionate objectivity" (1971, p. 10), Alinsky wrote the following:"

> It is a world not of angels but of angles, where men speak of moral principles but act on power principles; a world where we are always moral and our enemies always immoral; a world where "reconciliation" means that when one side gets the power and the other side gets reconciled to it, then we have reconciliation. . . . (1971, p. 13)

Alinsky quoted Henry James (1843–1916), the American novelist, as expressing a point of view that matched his own:

> Life is, in fact, a battle. Evil is insolent and strong; beauty enchanting but rare; goodness very apt to be weak; folly very apt to be defiant; wickedness to carry the day; imbeciles to be in great places, people of sense small, and mankind generally unhappy. (as cited in Alinsky, 1971, p. 14)

Saul Alinsky (1971) saw the "real arena" of social action as "corrupt and bloody" (p. 24), and he was unapologetic about pursuing political ends that required unorthodox means, remarking that a change agent could not be picky about such things because there was no "immaculate conception of ends and principles" (p. 24). In a pithy play on words, Alinsky (1971) said, "The means-and-end moralists or non-doers always wind up on their ends without any means" (p. 25).

Saul Alinsky was a master community organizer. A former sociology student at the University of Chicago who had studied street gangs and knew such Chicago mobsters as Frank Nitti, the Capone gang's "enforcer" (Horwitt, 1989, p. 20), Alinsky understood how to build effective street-level community leadership. It was this skill he brought to the table in confronting Ben Willis, the defender of segregated Chicago city public schools, through an organization called TWO (Temporary Woodlawn Organization), a makeshift group of a subsection of Chicago where African Americans had resided for some time and schools were overcrowded, with students on double sessions. Woodlawn became the point of conflict between social activism and the defenders of the status quo. The Alinsky people were clear-eyed about their work. And their leader understood the power of dramaturgy and performance. For starters, when TWO requested data about student populations at the district's schools, Willis and the board "stiff-armed" them, refusing to provide it. They also declined to undertake surveys showing what the real situation was in the schools. Ben Willis claimed there "was no evidence of intentional segregation" (Horwitt, 1989, p. 405).

Alinsky's TWO organized 300 people to attend a board meeting. The board president refused to let them speak. When that occurred, they all marched out to the street protesting double sessions and "double talk public relations" (Horwitt, 1989, p. 405). A short time later, TWO was publicly demanding the resignation of the superintendent. TWO organized their own community meeting, which was attended by more than 700 people. Three teachers draped in sheets took to the stage to talk about the actual conditions in the schools. They disguised themselves to avoid reprimand. This was drama the press ate up.

By 1962 TWO was sending African American parents to school board meetings dressed in black capes to symbolize the "deadly education" being received by their children in overcrowded schools. Most joltingly, TWO sent African American mothers into all-white schools with cameras to take pictures of the empty classrooms there. These "truth squad mothers" were very unnerving to the principals in those schools. When Willis responded to the overcrowding in the schools by purchasing mobile classrooms, TWO branded them "Willis Wagons," a form of ridicule that was trademarked Alinsky. But the theatrical finale was a very successful one-day boycott in May of 1962 in which 1,200 of nearly 1,350 students stayed home from school. The Chicago press had a field day with the pupil boycott (Horwitt, 1989, p. 406).

When Ben Willis finally had to release some statistics, he said that in the entire Chicago public school system there were "only" 14 surplus rooms. The Urban League claimed there were at least 380 (Cuban, 1976, p. 11). Willis's public statements drew howls of disapproval and his carefully built reputation for accurate data was severely tarnished. The fact was that if there were few empty classrooms in all-white schools, African American students could not be transferred there, and Willis's decision to put mobile classrooms in all-black schools was supportable.

The community protests continued. In early 1963, 1,000 African American parents sent a petition to the State Superintendent of Instruction to investigate the Chicago Public Schools. Ben Willis was backed into a corner, where he then publicly defended the policy of neighborhood schools, which was also a defense of racial segregation in the city's schools. Willis was now seen by an increasing number of community groups as a defender of institutionalized racism. In the summer of 1963, a picket line protesting the continued use of mobile classrooms became violent and 170 protesters were subsequently arrested (Cuban, 1976, p. 15). Ben Willis tendered his resignation. But the struggle was not over.

In pure power politics, Willis's supporters got the state chair of the North Central Association of Secondary Schools to write a letter in which he threatened that unless the board and the superintendent reconciled, "accreditation of every single Chicago school would be withdrawn" (Cuban, 1976, p. 19). The board ultimately backed down and Willis was reaffirmed on a 6 to 2 vote.

Then the issue of the school survey resurfaced. Because Willis had refused to provide information to the subpublics in Chicago about the true situation that existed with school enrollment, the board had authorized an external survey. Willis saw in this move an opportunity to assure the public of such a survey. However, Robert Havighurst, a professor at the University of Chicago, was appointed to perform the survey. Havighurst had been a critic of the administration. There ensued a behind-the-scenes struggle in which some board members mouthed Willis's position that a survey should be performed by system insiders because they knew the system best, and other board members who were for a true outsider advocated for a more independent study. It became clear in this struggle that (a) Willis had defined the conflict as a battle between the board and the superintendent over policy, and (b) the superintendent was in full support of the neighborhood school arrangement in the school district.

A compromise was then patched together in which Havighurst, Willis, and a third party, Alonzo Grace, the dean of the school of education at the University of Illinois, were named codirectors for the study. This became a kind of troika, a leadership "team" that on paper offered a solution, but in practice quickly became unworkable. Willis had to supply the data for Havighurst to analyze. Willis appointed working committees inside the school system to gather the data. But Havighurst was not allowed to meet with them. Willis would not authorize a teacher survey that included items regarding race, marital status, and the solicitation of their opinions (Cuban, 1976, p. 26).

A 500-page report was finally issued. At that meeting Willis was present but silent. Neither Havighurst nor Willis spoke to one another. The atmosphere was icy. In the report, Havighurst delineated two fundamental positions regarding how to run a school system. One was clearly Willis's approach, that is, highly economical and professional, with the authority to operate the schools unmistakably in the hands of the "professionals." The other approach involved taking the subpublics and the communities into the equation of administration and working with them to resolve issues and tensions. The report contained some 22 recommendations, and it was Willis who was in charge of their implementation. Willis's lukewarm embrace of the school survey's recommendations continued to polarize Chicago. Although Willis once enjoyed the nearly full support of the board and the business community, the Chicago board was split and once again Willis resigned in 1965. Not wanting to publicly embarrass Willis, the board cut a "deal" in which the superintendent's contract was renewed by a vote of 7 to 4, but it was agreed he would retire in 1 year. Thus, in 1966, Ben Willis left Chicago for good. Once the paragon of power in Chicago and a model of professionalism nationally, this educational Othello had been humbled by his own hubris.

Saul Alinsky (1971) ruminated about the attack on Willis several years later. Alinsky's strategy was to pick a political target and "freeze it." By that he meant that the individual selected as a target tries to shift the blame and get out of the limelight. But the forces for change have to prevent this because he warned, "If an organization permits responsibility to be diffused and distributed in a number of areas, attack becomes impossible" (p. 132). But Alinsky saw that Willis did not try to shift the blame, making himself an easy target. Alinsky (1971) observed the following:

> If we had been confronted with a politically sophisticated school superintendent he could have very well replied, "Look, when I came to Chicago the city school system was following, as it is now, a neighborhood school policy. Chicago's neighborhoods are segregated . . . Why attack me? Why not attack the segregated neighborhoods and change them?" (p. 132)

Alinsky (1971) confessed that if Willis had taken this tack, "I still shiver when I think of this possibility" (p. 132). If that had been done, Alinsky's forces would have been diffused and could not have maintained their focus. The objective in the Alinsky strategy was polarization because as he explained, " . . . all issues must be polarized if action is to follow" (p. 133). And polarization requires a human face because one cannot get angry at an abstraction or a corporation that has "no soul, no identity, or a public school administration, which again is an inanimate system" (Alinsky, 1971, p. 133). For this reason, the forces for change in Chicago had to have a human face on their struggle and it became that of Ben Willis.

Alinsky (1971) further observed that some of the liberals who supported Ben Willis at the time pointed out that he was not 100% bad, that he attended church, and that he was a good family man. He gave generously to charities. Alinsky (1971) brushed those qualifications aside like the calculating Iago:

> Can you imagine in the arena of conflict charging that so-and-so is a racist bastard and then diluting the impact of the attack with qualifying remarks such as "He is a good churchgoing man, generous to charity, and a good husband"? This becomes political idiocy. (p. 134)

What was at stake in the drama of Chicago during the superintendency of Ben Willis was that his theatrical performance was upstaged by someone who understood the politics of performance better than he did and the "stage" of a community organizer such as Saul Alinsky was much larger than the superintendent's. Ben Willis's power was confined to institutional power, power that is almost always vested in organizational relationships. It was "professional power" rooted in hierarchically structured bureaucracies (Friedson, 1986). When confronting community forces over which he had little control, Ben Willis could not rely on professional power and "expert" status conferred by matriculation in a graduate school. Here was the chasm for him. Not only could he not cross over into a purer arena of politics because he had no status there, he was stuck within an organization under attack in which his own source of authority was vested. In addition, he was "captured" by past practices and decisions of his own organization, some of which he had made. This shaped him into a defender of the status quo. In dramatic terms, Willis had a much smaller stage than Alinsky, and his "script" was much more rigid than his opponents' in the larger sociopolitical arena of Chicago. Barrows Dunham (1964) observed the following in his classic work *Heroes and Heretics*:

> Human organizations are founded and built by human beings, and their ideologies have precisely the same human source. It follows that into the ideologies of organizations there creep errors, which may on occasion be gross. Once these errors imbed themselves in doctrine they are beyond the reach of easy correction. They have become part of the source of unity. Their removal is not a mere scientific adjustment, but a dislocation of the corporate body. (pp. 17–18)

In researching the careers of three Latina superintendents, Florida Ida Ortiz (2001) used the lens of "social capital" as a construct to explain their successes and failures. As Ortiz (2001) explains, social capital first became noticed in studies of communities where neighborhood survival was at stake (p. 60). That research found that communities were stronger where trust and cooperation fostered structures of personal relationships and robust interpersonal networks of people. What is of keen importance is that the presence of social capital takes on forms of reciprocal and personal obligations of one member by another. Stanton-Salazar (1997) put it this way: "The value of social capital, as a concept, lies in the fact that it identifies properties (or laws) of social structure that are used by actors to achieve their interests" (p. 8).

Ortiz (2001) differentiated between social capital and "social resources" in her study. The unsuccessful Latina superintendent, like Ben Willis, had developed social resources but not social capital. Social resources are lodged in a structure of relationships that are based on knowledge and technical skill. These are Willis's professional cadre within the school system and certain business leaders in that structure with similar skills. On the other hand, social capital is personal and stems from being embedded in the structure of the community (or in Chicago's case, communities). Social capital is a broader form of power than that based on social resources. Alinsky's groups developed social capital. This was power that could be called on in a social struggle. Ben Willis's social capital was largely confined to the bureaucracy. It had no deep community roots.

As all leaders try to stamp the contexts of their times with their own power, such power is always a two-way street (Russell, 2003). Power is not something possessed by a leader. Power is given to a leader by those who choose to follow. It is the followers who bestow power, especially charisma (see Samier, 2005a). This act of transference is often swallowed up in the emotional conduit that exists between leaders and the led. The applause and adulation that followers sometimes shower on their leaders obscures what has actually been transferred. An actor without an audience is nothing but a solitary voice in a vacuum, no matter how artful may be his or her performance. The strength of a leader lies in the resonances he or she can generate from his or her followers. A leader cannot establish a climate for anything, change or resistance, without trafficking in the symbols, culture, emotions, fears, and aspirations of those with whom contact is made with effective communication.

Howard Gardner (1995) has noted that leaders use "identity stories" (pp. 51–53) to build constituencies. Jacques Lacan (1977) had similarly described the concept of the "identity story" several decades earlier in his idea of "conferred imputation," that is, followers bestow on leaders their "otherness," that is their symbolic world as it identifies with the stories of the leader. In this view, leadership is a kind of mutual dialectic. It is also clear that as in the theater, actors and audiences swim in a sea of language that is in turn embedded in culture and myth. With language as the medium, leadership is dynamic, fluid, and transitory. If charismatic leadership is a flame, it can only be lit by the people who need it (see Lipman-Blumen, 2005; Rost, 1991). As such it is only momentarily "yoked" and must be constantly renewed as it burns. Leadership is an all-consuming fire.

The simple fact is that leaders arise because followers need them. Lipman-Blumen (2005) similarly indicates that followers need leaders for security and certainty, to feel special, and to belong to a human community. They need leaders to combat their fears of social rejection. Such deep-seated psychological needs can also produce what Lipman-Blumen has called "toxic" or "poisonous" leaders who become cynical or corrupt and put their own advancement above that of the well-being of their followers. Toxic leaders have enormous ego needs that lead to arrogance and avarice and to "reckless disregard for the costs of their actions to others as well as to themselves" (Lipman-Blumen, p. 22). Followers with such needs can be deceived and history provides ample evidence of villains, despots, and tyrants who severely abused their own people. The problem with dealing with what Barbara Kellerman (2004) has called "Hitler's ghost" (p.11) is that the same process that produced Abraham Lincoln also produced Richard Nixon (see Gitlin, 2004).

While both presidents were reviled in their times, Nixon remains in a permanent pantheon of duplicity and deceit, the first U.S. president to resign from office before he was impeached. Lincoln's rise continues even into present times (White, 2005).

A study of leadership has to include bad actors as well as good ones. But too often we want to consider "good leaders" only when discussing leadership. Blasé and Blasé (2003) are representative of the very few educational researchers who have put the spotlight on abusive school principals who bully, intimidate, harass, mob (emotionally abuse), and victimize teachers. They document the painful results, the psychic, psychosomatic, and social destructiveness of bad school administrators. So we have to acknowledge the fuse that ignites and connects leaders and the led can be destructive as well as beneficial. It can raise or lower individual and organizational performance. But the connecting tissue is the same.

Robert Starratt (1993) has proposed that leaders become players in their respective schooling dramas. He suggests that part of leadership is being a role model for others. He notes that when leaders becomes players, "they are able to recognize that their own integrity is at stake in the collective moral life of the organization" (p. 138). Starratt also indicates that "leaders need to examine the various scripts they are handed by a variety of groups" (p. 142). It is only when a leader recognizes that there are a multiplicity of scripts at work in schools and that they may work in contradictory fashion to one another that an awareness is constructed of the need to avoid such tensions from destroying the organization. If Ben Willis had been aware of this idea he may have avoided the vilification that was heaped on him in Chicago.

The historical record of those times suggests that Willis's considerable power was stable only as long as the forces outside of the professional bureaucracy accepted his bureaucratic position and authority inside it. While a bureaucracy provides some stability and security, it also enables opponents to "freeze" one in place, and along with it unworkable, unjust, or unpopular practices and beliefs that are embedded in the organization. Once politically cornered as Willis surely was with Alinsky's idea of "freezing him in place" by creating political polarization, his support base was assaulted and eventually eroded where he could not survive as the leader of the system. Ben Willis's dilemma continues to plague superintendents to this day, although the opponents of system change may vary (Gewertz, 2006). The result is that the average length of service by contemporary urban school superintendents is between 26 and 28 months (Snider, 2006).

While these facets of leadership reveal its enormous complexities and applications, the idea that at the core leadership is basically dramaturgical reveals the primacy of language and of artful performance as the centerpiece of the exchange and mutual codependencies involved between actors and audiences, leaders and followers. We now look more closely at this juncture.

How Followers Look to School Leaders for What They Need

Various scholars have indicated that leadership is created as potential followers cast about for someone to satisfy their psychological/sociological needs (Burns, 1978;

Gardner, 1995; Lacan, 1977; Rost, 1991). Jean Lipman-Blumen (2005) describes three such needs as a kind of basic triad of the following: (a) keep us safe, (b) anoint us as special, and (c) provide a seat at a common table for us (p. 29). In a formal organization, there is at least one additional requirement, that is, to tell us why our work is important and what we are about, that is, purpose (Deal & Peterson, 1999). Thus, building a school culture, assembling a vision, and constructing a "mission" for schools is part and parcel of answering some of the requirements from teachers, parents, and students' basic psychological/sociological needs for leadership. Sergiovanni (1996) has called it creating and building a community within a school.

Table 5.1 shows the psychological/sociological needs of followers as identified by Jean Lipman-Blumen (2005). As applied to educational leaders, followers could be teachers in a school, or in the case of the superintendent in a central office, administrators and other support staff. Table 5.1 also illustrates the most positive response from leaders and how the leader's performance is correlative to this expected response. The information in the columns is based on the research of Joe and Jo Blasé (2003), Megan Russell (2003), and the earlier observations of Howard Gardner (1995) and James McGregor Burns (1978) regarding the role of followers being an integral part of the leadership equation. Blasé and Blasé describe in some detail the destructive impact of an educational leader's behavior on teachers. They utilize the research of Davenport, Distler-Schwartz, and Pursell-Elliott (1999) in identifying "the mobbing syndrome" in which a leader engages in a vicious attempt to intimidate and harass someone to force him or her from their workplace position. "Mobbing" involves false accusations, emotional abuse, and engaging in "vulturing," a practice of encouraging others to "gang-up" on the intended victim. They related this to a third and intense level of principal mistreatment of teachers. Level 2 would include such actions as spying, sabotaging a person, and making unreasonable work demands on him or her. Level 1 includes such behaviors as discounting a person's feelings or opinions and withholding opportunities for professional growth.

Since humans are social animals, we require a sense of community for our emotional well-being. We fear ostracism and social isolation. Social death means that we are subjected to extreme isolation in which our connections to the rest of humanity are permanently severed. Lipman-Blumen (2005) recounts the pathetic tale of Covall Russell, an inmate in a California prison, who, facing the prospect of being freed at age 92, requested to remain in prison because all of his friends were there. When this was denied and he was freed, he subsequently jumped off a bridge (p. 71). Effective leaders work to create social unity. Toxic leaders engage in behaviors that lead to disunity. It has long been recognized that group unity represents a key responsibility of organizational leadership throughout history (Dunham, 1964).

Just as a script connects the actors to the audiences, a leader's stories represent a text, a narrative that serves to unite leaders and followers in a common pursuit of goals.

Table 5.1 illustrates the aspects of leadership performance that satisfy basic follower social and emotional needs. Examining what leaders do within organizations and treating it as a kind of storytelling is important in understanding educational leadership in context. Charlotte Linde (2003) observes, "Within the boundaries of an institution, many stories are told daily. Social life is created by, and reproduced by narrative, and life within institutions is no exception" (p. 521). The function of narrative, or storytelling in educational organizations as in other types of institutions, is to assist in getting the work done. In educational settings, narratives relate to the very tasks that comprise the primary function of schooling. The types of stories that tend to reoccur are those that are work related. They are narratives that pertain to "maintaining identity and continuity, negotiating power relations, managing change, and marking membership, as well as transacting the daily business of the organization" (Linde, p. 532).

❖ **Table 5.1**   The Needs of Followers, the Tasks of Leadership, and Leadership Performance

Needs of Followers	Tasks of the Leader	Aspects of Leader's Performance
Need for Security and Certainty	**Engage in Activities/Tasks That Reduce Ambiguity**	**Persona and Role**
Followers may be anxious about expectations for their job performance, about what is an appropriate level of personal commitment to the organization, about how close the supervision (and hence potential interference with their autonomy) is likely to be. They want to know how much "space" there is going to be for them to act and react in the system. They want to know what their work is all about and why it is important and who thinks it is important.	1. Reduce work-related ambiguity by creating vision and mission statements regarding the purpose of the work unit and how the people in it relate their labor to the progress of the whole. 2. Reduce fear of authority and arbitrary actions taken without warning or logic. 3. Sketch out in actions and/or in policy what he/she expects in the way of performance, personal commitment, and why the work is important.	1. Works collaboratively with faculty, students, and parents in creating the vision/mission statements. 2. Shares timelines, adjusts them as necessary to create inclusive climate; welcomes suggestions. Demonstrates willingness to make adjustments. 3. Adheres to contractual/legal processes. Stays within procedural and content boundaries. Is respectful to them. Demonstrates an understanding that their autonomy is important as professionals or as community persons.
The Need to Feel Chosen and Special	**Engage in Activities/Tasks That Earmark the Distinctiveness of the Work Unit and the People in It and Being Served by It**	**Persona and Role**
1. Followers need to know who they are and why they are important. They want to feel special, want to belong to a	1. Identify the unique qualities of the people in the work	1. Values diversity and displays a value orientation of the importance of diversity in feeling chosen and special. Work to reduce or eliminate

Needs of Followers	Tasks of the Leader	Aspects of Leader's Performance
committed group of like-minded people, but also want assurances that their individuality will be respected in decisions that are made for the group or with the group. 2. Followers search for a leader who shares with them stories about the importance of their work, why they are or should be committed to it, and links this purpose to higher ideals and moral purposes. 3. Followers seek an atmosphere of trust where they can be open and grow and where their commitment to the organization is recognized as important and critical to its success.	unit, their aspirations and ideals, as well as the unique characteristics of the community and students in the community. 2. Work the unique qualities identified in No. 1 into the vision and mission statements and make it part of school planning. 3. Delineate special social activities in which the unique aspects of the workforce and the clients can be discussed, displayed, and idealized. 4. Bring in guest speakers from the community to talk about why and how it is special.	comparisons that denigrate others so as to elevate your own work unit or its clients or community. 2. Creates a culture of inclusion where difference is celebrated, valued, and respected. 3. Avoids activities or responses that divide a group with unnecessary competition or recognize individual or subgroup gains at the expense of the whole group (suboptimization). 4. Tells and shares "identity stories" so that group members share a common culture, vocabulary, and outlook in regard to internal/external forces and pressures.
Fear of Ostracism, Isolation, and Social Death 1. Followers are anxious about possible isolation and group ostracism imposed by a leader, that is, the imposition of organizational sanctions against them for a possible wide variety of potential offenses. 2. When things go badly, followers want their leaders to encourage them, to keep up their spirits, and to urge them to remain committed to the overall purposes and ideals of the organization.	**Engage in Activities/Tasks That Eliminate Ostracism, Isolation, and Social Death** 1. Establish formal and informal rules and expectations that social isolation is everyone's job to eliminate. 2. Set up processes and approaches to work that create collaboration and the need to share as opposed to those that lead to individual competitiveness and a "winners" and "losers," dog-eat-dog approach to work.	**Persona and Role** 1. When isolation is observed, move quickly to bring the person back into a subgroup or the entire group. Establish "partners" or "big brothers/ sisters" or "buddies" to mentor younger faculty or students. 2. Avoid behaviors or actions that lead to embarrassment or humiliation when mistakes are made. 3. Avoid any behavior that could be considered "bullying" or be construed as mistreatment or disrespect of individuals.

Crossan (1975) has indicated that stories don't simply reflect the world, they actually create the world. That seems especially important with work-related texts or stories. Human work is artificial in that it does not exist in nature. Human work is constructed. Crossan (1975) examines five different kinds of stories: mythological, apologue, action-centered, satire, and parable. Myths create and structure a world, apologue defends the world, action examines the world, satire assaults the world, but parables undermine the world (Crossan, 1975).

It is important to note that John Dominic Crossan is a professor of biblical studies at DePaul University in Chicago and an internationally recognized Jesus scholar (1992, 1994, 1995). Jesus was a master storyteller. He connected with those who heard him. The stories Jesus told have lived on thousands of years after his death. To understand Jesus as a storyteller, Crossan (1975) focuses on the kinds of stories Jesus told. First, Crossan sees mythological stories and parables as polar opposites. He indicates that the function of myth is to mediate irreducible opposites. Stories about overcoming death through superhuman belief or feats are examples of the function of myth. Such stories reconcile life and death. They bring stability and peace. Parables, on the other hand, function in precisely the opposite way. Parables trade in contradictions. Crossan indicates that whereas myth works at ways followers can be reassured, parables create contradictions and they even challenge the idea that a reconciliation is possible.

Table 5.2 shows the five different kinds of stories leaders tell. To try to understand their differences, applications to education are also shown.

Using the background of the provisions of Public Law 107–110, known as the No Child Left Behind Act, as the backdrop for determining stories leaders tell, the function of myth is to reconcile existing beliefs with practices contained in the law, which may run contrary to those believed by a faculty to promote good education. For example, the installation of increased classroom testing and the reliance of the reward and punishment provisions contained in the idea of "adequate yearly progress" (AYP) can be deeply alienating to teachers who believe that such emphasis is decidedly negative in its impact on children and their work. The principal in this situation creates a myth, that is, a narrative that tries to reconcile such requirements to existing beliefs by perhaps stressing that teachers have always used some sort of criterion to make judgments about their students' progress and that this provision simply formalizes it. The story line may go something like, "We've always done this only we've never given it a name or thought about it this way. All this does is to cast what we've always done into a somewhat different framework."

But as Crossan (1975) points out, the opposite of a myth is parable. The function of a parable is to undermine practice or belief while appearing to defend it. In this situation, the principal might do something like tell a story that the premise of the No Child Left Behind Act is certainly something with which few educators could find fault. But then the principal may indicate that the tests themselves assume that some children will in fact be left behind by defining success in terms of the numbers of children who failed. Without failure children could not be successful. This story borders on irony and initially teachers may take the idea into their minds that no child should be left behind as a laudable outcome. But embedded in the idea also comes the added baggage, which is antithetical and disturbing. How can no child be left behind if some have to be left behind because it's an average score that defines the nature of

❖ Table 5.2   The Five Types of Stories Leaders Tell

Types of Stories	Myth	Apologue	Action	Satire	Parable
Perspective of the Leader to the Context	Trying to reconcile oppositional forces at work in educational systems.	Defending the educational system and the forces within it.	Advocating action to move directly on systemwide problems or issues.	Lampooning the goings-on within the system by attacking the actors or forces in it to show flaws and suggest possible actions or forms of resistance.	To undermine the mechanisms of the system, its rules, laws, customs or operational procedures by appearing to agree but to arouse in others deep reservations.
Educational Example	Attempting to reconcile the increased requirements for testing in the No Child Left Behind Act to constructing a positive classroom learning environment for all children.	Arguing that the school or the system is getting better and that there is no need to create alternatives that will detract from its resources.	Creating a plan to remove the achievement gap in the school or the system through a combination of people and tasks set within a specific timeline.	Telling jokes or mimicking various actors or agencies within or without the system to point out absurdities or contradictions within it.	While advocating adherence to the provisions in the No Child Left Behind Act the leader is engaged in undermining it by calling into question assumptions on which it is based.

"behind"? And indeed in computing an average, somebody has to be below that score. The story being told here is not one of reconciliation, but rather one that undermines the idea of AYP in the first place. This is the power of parable as a form of story. Crossan puts the art of the parable this way:

> It is in the surface structure and texture that the parabler must use consummate skill so that the deep structure of the parable gets into the hearer's consciousness and is only felt in its full force there when it is too late to do much about it. (p. 86)

Crossan (1975) believes that the stories Jesus told that are most remembered were parables. Parables are powerful only if the audience listening to a storyteller is aware of the substantive touches of context and irony that permeate the story itself. A parable contains the unexpected and it springs on the minds and hearts of followers only after they have taken it in. Crossan summarizes this idea when he observed, "They are stories which shatter the deep structure of our accepted world and thereby render clear and evident to us the relativity of story itself" (p. 122).

Educational leaders most often traffic in myth, apologue, and action stories. They are about constructing cohesive working units within schools and school systems. The most common challenges are to eliminate conflict and strive toward reconciliation of oppositional elements or forces in the larger work unit. The function of these kinds of stories is to enable the workforce to attain a greater share of the work goals than would otherwise be possible if there was discord.

On the other hand, if an educational leader is a change agent, he or she may decide to traffic in satire or parable and, by focusing on system contradictions and hidden messages, move a constituency to oppose a set of practices or to form a different response to internal or external challenges than would otherwise be expected.

A Portrait of Two Types of Storytellers as Leaders

Isaiah Berlin (1995) divides leaders into two types. The first kind he calls "the amalgam of simplicity of vision with intense, sometimes fanatical, idealism" (p. 186). This kind of leader reduces conflict to unadorned exemplars of good and evil. They excel in reducing complex issues to pure strains devoid of ambiguity. They usually display purity of character and devotion to a cause. They possess "fewer attributes than the normal compliment, but those larger than life" (Berlin, p. 186). They appeal to potential followers who may be confused by what appears to be overwhelming worldly complexity. The message these leaders provide sweeps such multiplicities aside and helps followers focus on the big picture. These leaders bring followers to their cause by ignoring obstacles and exhibiting utter fearlessness and devotion to a common theme. Berlin (1995) observes that ". . . they create a radiant myth with which they identify themselves, and which their followers bear in their hearts" (p. 187). Examples of this type of leader would be Martin Luther King, Jr., Gandhi, Mother Jones, Joan of Arc, Winston Churchill, or Charles de Gaulle.

The second type of leader Berlin (1995) identifies is one that belongs to ordinary humans who display the full range of humanity to an "almost supernatural degree" (p. 187). Instead of reducing the complexities of the circumstances to simple themes, they have an uncanny capability to integrate "the tiny fragments of which it is composed into some coherent, intelligible pattern" (Berlin, p. 188). These leaders find patterns that include rather than exclude complexity and "then . . . act in accordance with this picture in a sure-footed, morally confident, firm and supremely effective fashion, responsive to the sharpest needs of their time in an infinity of sympathetic ways" (Berlin, p. 188). Into this category Berlin places Abraham Lincoln and Franklin Roosevelt. We could also add Golda Meir and Harriet Tubman.

These men [and women] are regarded not with awe or religious faith—they are not figures surrounded by a kind of unearthly radiance–but with affection, confidence, admiration, sometimes not unmixed with a certain appreciative irony—a delight in their accessibility, their democratic quality, their human failings. (Berlin, 1995, p. 188)

Berlin (1995) does not indicate that one kind of leader is better than another. Throughout history, both kinds of leaders have arisen in response to their times and to the challenges faced by their respective peoples. Likewise, effective school leaders are of both types: the visionary whose stories toward followers create a unitary coherency that sweeps aside compounding variables into manageable themes, and the secondary type who is able to incorporate a dazzling amount of detail into transcendent themes. What is important is to come to some understanding of the type of leader you are and to whom you respond. There are also times when a leader must do both, that is, sweep aside complexities to focus on a few strands to the exclusion of competing stories, and incorporate new detail into ongoing narratives. Equally important is to come to some understanding of the potential of followers and to grasp their expectations for leadership. Followers need leaders to galvanize their actions and to enable them to overcome obstacles. They need leaders to ensure constancy of purpose and to set expectations for the group as a whole.

Educational leaders should understand that even if they obtain their positions by meeting legal and bureaucratic requirements first and those of the followers second, the needs of followers are the only true source of staying power in office. To be able to meet these expectations, leaders must understand that the skill involved in meeting the expectations of their followers is an art and not a science. At the heart of the art is dramatic performance, perhaps not the stuff of a Shakespearean exposition, but dramatic nonetheless.

Pursuing Learning Extensions of the Chapter

The learning extensions of the chapter involve some of the films now listed. They are intended to illustrate some of the theories about leadership described in the chapter and present the ideas of how leaders and followers unite to form a critical connection.

Matewan (1987), Color, VHS, Lorimar Home Video, 1 Hour 40 Minutes

The film is one of the few popular produced ones that feature a labor organizer as the hero. The scene is the famous shootout in Matewan, West Virginia, between the union men and the thugs hired by the mine owners to prevent unions from taking root. Based on historical facts and some actual historical figures, the film superbly demonstrates how the need of the miners for leadership bestows legitimacy on the organizer from the United Mine Workers. In turn, the labor leader, played by Chris Cooper, is able to shape the actions of the followers by appealing to reason and pride.

Mandela: Son of Africa, Father of a Nation (1997), Color, Black and White, VHS, Island Pictures, 1 Hour 58 Minutes

This Oscar-nominated documentary about Nelson Mandela illustrates his rise to power. The need of the African people for leaders in their struggle for freedom and the right to vote in their own country is vividly illustrated. The film features Mandela's return to his birthplace and his commentary about his early years and tribal customs. Later, Mandela returns to Robben Island, the place where he was imprisoned for 27 years, to talk about life behind prison walls (see the Nelson Mandela Foundation, 2005). The film documents Mandela's release and his campaign to become South Africa's first democratically elected president. It also illustrates Mandela's leadership style behind the scenes.

Nixon (1995), Color, VHS, Hollywood Pictures, 3 Hours 18 Minutes

This is a riveting docudrama of the life and turbulent times of Richard Nixon, in which his rise and fall from grace is chronicled by the gifted acting of Anthony Hopkins, following a script written by Stephen Rivele, Christopher Wilkinson, and Oliver Stone (Hamburg, 1995). In this film, there is a telling scene in which Nixon is chatting with China's Chairman Mao. Chairman Mao says he voted for Nixon in the last election. President Nixon responds that he was the lesser of two evils. To this Mao says very seriously, "You're too modest, Nixon. You're as evil as I am. We're both from poor families. But others pay to feed the hunger in us. In my case, millions of reactionaries. In your case, millions of Vietnamese" (Hamburg, p. 235). To this Nixon responds that civil war is the cruelest sort of war. Mao then answers, "The real war is in us. History is a symptom of our disease" (Hamburg, p. 235). This film is the epitome of Jean Lipman-Blumen's (2005) concept of toxic leaders and in the case of Nixon, a democratically elected one. With the recent disclosure that "deep throat" was Marc Feldman, formerly second in command at the FBI, the poignancy of the film takes on deeper meaning.

Writing in Your Personal Reflective Journal

Writing in your personal journal should begin to focus on how leaders and followers satisfy a set of basic psycho-social needs. Too often, leaders were discussed as if it didn't matter what followers desired. So past traditions examined the traits, behaviors, and actions of leaders as if they could be transferred from one context to another and it almost didn't matter what the followers desired. One of the key concepts of this chapter is that leaders are follower dependent and it's the followers who bestow on leadership the "right" to lead.

Think about the leaders you thought were effective and inspired you. You looked to a leader to satisfy your needs. Can you verbalize the needs that you expected a leader to address? What were they? Can you identify the context in which your expectations were mobilized, that is, what events or circumstances were going on at the time in which you became aware of your own expectations from a leader? Can you separate leaders into the two categories identified by Isaiah Berlin? Which one do you think you are?

As a future educational leader, how do you think your experiences in schools so far have prepared you to deal with the needs of potential followers?

A Review of Key Chapter Concepts

followers create leaders—Leaders "rise" from the needs of followers. Leaders are defined by followers. Leader-"ship" includes both leaders and followers. The traditional view of leaders is that they possess some unique characteristic that sets them apart from other human beings. These attributes are bestowed by followers, as is the case with the idea of charisma. Leaders come to understand that followers desire things that can be promised, such as safety, identification of special status, and providing for a "common table" so that all can participate in the affairs of a movement or an organization. Leaders provide meaning to life and labor. They assure followers that their struggles are important and are not in vain in the grand scheme of things.

leadership is a social construct—What constitutes leadership is a dynamic interrelationship between leaders and followers. Leadership is a socially constructed phenomenon. It is not "natural" in the sense that you would observe it in nature. It is peculiar to human affairs and it varies with context and culture. Inside organizations that assume the characteristics of bureaucracy, leadership is proscribed to roles that are arranged in a hierarchical relationship to one another.

leadership is acting or performance—Since leadership includes both leaders and followers, the ways leaders influence followers is through their actions, specifically through forms of narrative or stories. The skill leaders use in telling their stories is the "art" of leadership and it is a form of drama. As in dramatic productions, leadership traffics in the symbols, customs, and linguistic traditions of a specific culture. Both verbal and nonverbal behaviors are cultural forms of communication.

polarization as the focal point for action—This concept by Saul Alinsky entails a leader selecting a target on which his or her followers can focus their actions. Alinsky's tactic was to polarize opinion because the act of polarization created a situation to change things. It creates the "need" for leadership to take followers in a different direction. The same idea is present in the use of the parable as a kind of story that undermines the status quo.

social capital as the basis of leader staying power—Social capital refers to the web of personal relationships between individuals who become embedded within a community's or subcommunity's social structure. By being embedded in that structure, the individual is able to call on others to aid or assist him or her if the need should arise. Educational leaders who are interested in buffeting the winds of change and who cultivate social capital, as opposed to social resources, are more likely to enjoy longer staying power in their jobs.

toxic leadership—Some leaders who are able to satisfy followers' needs have an orientation to power that is destructive or harmful to them. Leaders who use people to further their own ambitions, who engage in bullying dissidents or behaviors that lead to ostracism or social death, abuse the trust that followers have bestowed on them.

Understanding the Landscape of Educational Leadership

The purpose of this chapter is to describe the conceptual landscape of educational leadership, including the major epochs of foundational writings which inform leadership studies in the past and present. By epoch is meant a period of time, sometimes marked with a distinctive event or the publication of a written text that continued along a line of development after publication of the text, sometimes for decades and in other cases perhaps centuries. The demarcation of epochs or eras has also been used by other scholars describing the field of educational leadership.

The major emphasis in educational leadership is its continuing reliance on rationality and efficiency in its models, standards, and approach to preparation. This is partly due to the circumstances in which accountability laws themselves continue to emphasize these same attributes.

Every professional field has major conceptual works that define what professors and practitioners do and think about within that field for specific time periods. To understand why the art of educational leadership has received something less than the emphasis required, one simply has to turn to the intellectual and conceptual markers that have delineated the field historically. The portrayal of the field of educational leadership is shown in Figure 6.1. It illustrates a continuum of epochs of leadership, beginning with Plutarch's *Parallel Lives* in the premodern period and extending through the end of Shakespeare's tragedies. While none of these periods is clearly marked as may be the case with an epoch, the modern period may be said to have arisen with the writings of Rene Descartes (1596–1650), who placed an emphasis on rational thought. Descartes is credited with beginning the scientific revolution (Ross & Francks, 1996, p. 510). Descartes's certainty regarding human reason in approaching all kinds of problems lies at the very heart of modernity and its core tenets in the power of rationality to advance human progress. Descartes stressed the importance of clarity and distinctness as found in geometric proofs. He believed that mathematics was the perfect example of reason and objectivity. His perspective anchors the philosophies of rationalism and empiricism, which are very much alive in contemporary times (Collinson, 1998, p. 60).

Modernism became dominant in "the Enlightenment," which is loosely identified as an epoch in which rational thought, humanism, liberalism, and a belief in scientific progress became crystallized by a stream of thinkers such as Francis Bacon, John Locke, Benedict de Spinoza, Gottfried Leibniz, David Hume, Immanuel Kant, Francoise Voltaire, Charles Montesquieu, John-Jacques Rousseau, and in the United States, Thomas Paine, Thomas Jefferson, and Benjamin Franklin. While modernism is a complex, multilevel set of beliefs and practices that cuts across many fields of human endeavor (Giroux, 1997), what is important is how it continues to dominate thought in education and educational leadership in particular (see Bottery, 2004; Dantley, 2005; Ogawa, 2005).

Central Tenets of Modernism

An examination of Figure 6.1 shows seven epochs (including pseudoscientific works) at work in the modernism period. The reader should not view the three periods (identified as premodern, modern, and postmodern) shown in Figure 6.1 as proceeding along the baseline from left to right. This is in itself a modernistic perspective, that is, conceptualizing human activity proceeding from so-called "primitive" or pre or proto scientific ideas to scientific ones. The perspective that should be adopted is that all three periods are still very much active. For example, key texts are still read in the premodern period as embodied in Plutarch (No. 1 in Figure 6.1), Suetonius (No. 2 in Figure 6.1), Machiavelli (No. 3 in Figure 6.1), Shakespeare (No. 4 in Figure 6.1), and others who still have important messages for modernists and even postmodernists. Figure 6.1 is simply a convenient graphical method to portray a variety of texts still at play in the leadership discourse of contemporary times (Heilbrunn, 1996). What can be said is that the "modern" period is dominant, that is, it is the one in which the largest number of scholars, writers, and researchers remain actively engaged. The recently released National Research Council's (2002) *Scientific Research in Education* and Firestone and Riehl's (2005) *A New Agenda for Research in Educational Leadership* are representative of the continuing influence of the modernistic agenda in education. Nearly all "pop" or "kitsch" management books rest on the modernistic discourse as well (Samier, 2005).

The key beliefs of modernism are that rationality is the best approach to promote insight and understanding of the world "out there." This world is objective and exists apart from human interaction. The second key belief is that the objective of science is

❖ Figure 6.1 Key Texts and Epochs Impacting Leadership Thought on a Continuum of Premodernity and Postmodernity

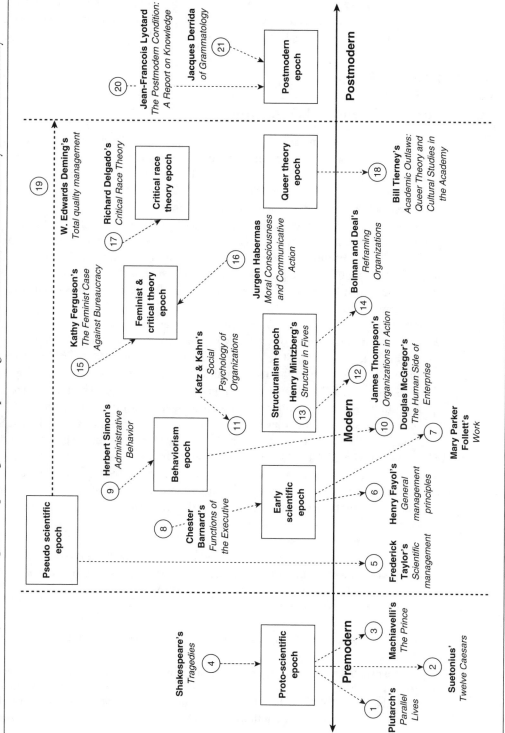

progress, that is, toward a higher plane of living or understanding. The third critical tenet is that modernism is a perspective that is objective and neutral and represents the best lens to conduct investigations into the world and human affairs.

The Pseudoscientific Epoch: Educational Leadership and the Long Shadow of "Scientific Management"

The formal study of educational leadership began with Frederick Winslow Taylor (1856–1915), the nation's first premier management consultant (No. 5 in Figure 6.1). He worked primarily as an engineer in the steel industry and created and introduced a system of work design he termed "scientific management" (1911) based on the idea that there was always "one best way" to do anything.

Taylor's ideas quickly spread into a myriad of related fields and won him international fame. "Scientific management" won praise from such influential thinkers on the political left as Antonio Gramsci of Italy and Vladimir Lenin in the Soviet Union (Kanigel, 1997, p. 505). It was pushed in America by no less than Louis Brandeis, a brilliant Boston attorney who would later be named by President Woodrow Wilson to the U.S. Supreme Court.

Peter Drucker (1974) once observed that Frederick Taylor was one of the first to see the idea that the planning of the work and the doing of the work were separate entities. Notes Drucker (1974), "The planner is needed to supply the doer with direction and measurements, with the tools of analysis and synthesis, with methodology, and with standards" (p. 271). This separation has been called "job de-skilling," where work tasks can be broken down into smaller and smaller pieces until the education levels required to engage in the work are so lowered that labor costs can be reduced. Such work planning has been ruthlessly applied in the fast food restaurant business and lies behind the rise of McDonald's, Burger King, Pizza Hut, and KFC (Kentucky Fried Chicken). Another thing that Frederick Taylor's "scientific management" created was not only the need for planners who were not workers (the "white collar" workforce), but the requirement for absolute authority within management.

Peter Drucker (1974) comments on this requirement:

> One more thing is needed to make responsibility acceptable to the worker: he needs to have the security of a clear authority structure . . . Management has to work out what the task is, what the objectives are, what the standards are. Again, the doers should be used as a source of information. But the job is management's. (p. 272)

Then Drucker (1974) describes the kind of power that is required:

> . . . one man has to make the decision in such a situation, and fast, or everybody is endangered. Who this man is has to be known in advance, or there is chaos. And this man has to be able to say, "This needs to be done; you do it; this way." The survival of the group depends on his unquestioned authority. (p. 272)

Scientific management created the need for professional prepared managers in industry, government, business, and education. Educational administration began in universities to prepare the men (women were not allowed in educational administration programs for a long time; see Blount, 1998) who were now going to "scientifically manage" education (Callahan, 1962). The bottom line for the scientific management of any enterprise was efficiency, that is, making the operation cheaper to enhance profitability. Continuing calls for education to be "run like business" echo the same sentiments today, including the idea that education, as a state monopoly, needs competition to become efficient (Friedman, 1962).

The main thing concerning "scientific management" was that it wasn't scientific. There were no theories being tested. The drive to work faster, harder, and do "more" for less was the mantra of the new "scientific engineers." They had a passionate faith that if they could apply their stopwatches, slide rules, and work tables, productivity would increase. Profits would increase. And the cost of labor, the need for a skilled workforce, would decrease. Not only does Taylor's work continue into the present day because it has been absorbed into the mainstream of American management, but contemporary manifestations include such things as strategic planning and total quality management.

The most recent international application of Taylor's foundational tenets was that of W. Edwards Deming's *total quality management* concept, which, like Taylorism, was all the rage in the 1980s and 1990s (No. 19 in Figure 6.1). Deming's philosophical roots lay in probability theory, a new kind of statistical pseudoscience that insisted that a "fact" had no meaning until and unless it could be located within acceptable control limits (Shewart, 1986). Numbers represent reality, which is ultimately stable in a Platonic universe. Deming's philosopher-ontologist is Clarence Lewis (1929), who held that there is a reality outside of human experience and that "experience does not itself determine what is good or bad . . . nor does it determine what is valid or invalid, or the nature of logical validity" (p. 14). This is the rock not only of modernistic science, but of all pseudoscience doctrines as well.

Foucault's (1972) *The Archaeology of Knowledge and the Discourse on Language* provides the analytical tools to connect Taylor's scientific management and W. Edwards Deming's total quality management. Both are part of the discourse of efficiency. The parallelisms between the two pseudoscientific approaches shown in Figure 6.1 with numbers 5 and 19 can be captured by examining the linguistic analogies, logical identities, and enunciative homogeneities present in both. These are identified in Table 6.1.

The dominant linguistic analogy for both scientific management and total quality management is the assembly line. Frederick Taylor worked with a stopwatch and job task analysis to reduce unnecessary movement and enhance efficiency. W. Edwards Deming employed statistical control charts for the same purpose. Both were primarily aimed at reducing variability, enhancing control, and attaining greater precision. While both professed to enhance worker latitude, democracy, and choice, the opposite conditions actually were at work.

Total quality management (TQM) is the most recent embodiment of scientific management and the language of TQM permeates administrative texts and even extends to the standards for licensing educational leaders (English, 2003). The gospel

❖ **Table 6.1**   A Comparison Between Frederick Taylor's Scientific Management and
W. Edwards Deming's Total Quality Management

Area	Taylor's Scientific Management	Deming's Total Quality Management
Authority	Reinforces top management	Same
Voices legitimated	The expert is external to the system	Same
Major metaphor	The assembly line	Same
Primary data source	Stopwatch–task analysis	Statistical control charts
Primary approach to problem solving	Reduction of variance	Same
Employee motivators	External–piece rate system as defined by management	Internal-"empowerment," but only as defined by management
Implicit objective	Elimination of waste	Same
Major tactic	Didactic–one right way	Same

SOURCE: From F. English, 1994, *Theory in Educational Administration.* New York: HarperCollins, p. 212.

of efficiency that dominates school administration from its inception in scientific management continues into present times.

The Early Scientific Epoch

Figure 6.1 shows that the early scientific epoch was characterized by texts beginning with Henry Fayol (1842–1925; No. 6 in Figure 6.1), a Frenchman who is credited with creating the first "general approach" to administration, as it is understood in human organizations. He has been called the Father of Modern Management Theory (Hodgetts & Kuratiko, 1988, p. 37). Fayol became president of a mining company that was floundering. In exercising management of the company he developed an approach to viewing administration and its functions. He believed that there were five primary functions of administration: planning, organizing, commanding, coordinating, and controlling. In commanding, leadership was exercised.

From these essential functions, Fayol extrapolated 14 principles that dealt with the division of labor, authority and responsibility, discipline, unity of command, unity of management, subordination of individual interests, remuneration, centralization, the hierarchy, order, equity, stability, initiative, and esprit de corps or morale.

In this epoch of early scientific work also fell such texts by Mary Parker Follett (1924), Elton Mayo (1933), Chester Barnard (1938), Lyndall Urwick (1943), and Luther Gulick (1948). These pioneers were trained in political science, psychology, and philosophy, and were not merely engineers in the vein of Frederick Taylor or his disciples, Lillian and Frank Gilbreth. They brought experiences from many disciplines, government, and industry. Their thoughts roamed far beyond efficiency, and confronted the full range of issues facing leaders in organizations.

Mary Parker Follett (1868–1933; No. 7 in Figure 6.1) developed ideas in management far ahead of her time (Tonn, 2003). In fact, they are just beginning to be appreciated for their depth and complexity today (Massie, 1965, p. 395). One concept she developed was called *the law of the situation*. Follett saw that authority was not solely determined by the administrative hierarchy, but by the situation itself, and by the person who could exercise competence and leadership in that situation. This insight was developed around an assumption that people were not simply motivated by personal gain, but by what was "good" for the group as well (Hodgetts & Kuratiko, 1988, p. 38). Follett believed that the leadership skills necessary for "unifying" or "integrating" multiple ideas would revolutionize the world (Rusch, 2006, p. 402).

Follett believed that there were four primary principles of organization. All of them revolved around the idea of *coordination* because management was a social process. She developed the idea of conflict management because she recognized that conflict was inherent in all of management's work. She advised three methods for dealing with conflict: (a) domination, (b) compromise, or (c) integration. Follett argued for integration as the preferred method of resolving organizational disputes by bringing the differences between parties into the open (Massie, 1965, p. 395). In this respect, Mary Parker Follett laid the groundwork for much of what today is called *organization development* (French & Bell, 1973).

Another seminal thinker in this early scientific epoch was Chester Barnard (1886–1961; No. 8 in Figure 6.1). Barnard was the Bill Gates of his day, leaving Harvard before graduation, becoming president of New Jersey Bell and later the Rockefeller Foundation. In 1937 he was engaged to lecture on administration at Boston's Lowell Institute. His talks were later published in *The Functions of the Executive* (1938). Barnard believed in three indispensable functions of the executive, the first of which to create a purpose as a requisite for unifying an organization (Shapiro, 2006, p. 68). Second, the executive had to establish effective communications to enable all in the organization to understand its mission. The final attribute of the executive was to create a place where all could and would participate and cooperate together. Barnard (1938) insisted that for a subordinate to accept a superior's communication as legitimate, it had to contain four things: (a) be understandable, (b) be consistent with the subordinate's understanding of the purpose of the organization, (c) be consistent with the individual's own personal purposes, and (d) be able to be carried out by the individual (Shapiro, 2006, p. 68). Barnard (1938) also recognized that organizations were comprised of informal subgroups and characterized by a concern with efficiency as cost-cutting and effectiveness as goal attainment. These basic distinctions remain firmly ensconced in managerial thinking today.

The Behaviorism Epoch

The next epoch shown in Figure 6.1 is that of behaviorism. This epoch is anchored by the work of Herbert Simon (No. 9 in Figure 6.1), whose book *Administrative Behavior* (1945) is the watermark text on behaviorism/logical positivism in administration.

Behaviorism was primarily the offspring of Edward Thorndike, John Watson, and B. F. Skinner. As a perspective, it centers on the phenomenon of observable and measurable actions that are believed to be under the conscious control of an individual who is responding to stimuli in a specific situation. Behaviorism fit nicely into the ideology of scientific management and total quality management (Blackbourn, 2006, p. 71).

Logical positivism, also known as scientific empiricism or logical empiricism, placed great emphasis on a "scientific attitude and on co-operation; hence emphasis on intersubjective language and unity of science" (Runes, 1984, p. 302). Logical positivists believed that for something to be true, it had to be verifiable by experience, chiefly observation. The foundational epistemology of the logical positivists rested "ultimately on beliefs that are non-inferentially justified" (Fumerton, 1999, p. 515).

Simon blended together the perspectives on human relations and decision making of Follett (1924), Roethlisberger and Dickson (1939), Roethlisberger (1941), and Mayo (1945), and coupled these perspectives from the previous epoch with a new emphasis on scientific behaviorism, which reflected the social psychology of Talcott Parsons (1951), to attack the old "principles" as "unscientific" and to offer the new as again "truly scientific."

Simon (1945) utilized the criterion of efficiency as the most important of all principles in developing an adequate theory of administration. Despite taking pains to dissociate himself from the work of Frederick Taylor, he defined efficiency as "the ratio between input and output" (Simon, p. 180) and one in which "to be efficient means to take the shortest path, the cheapest means, towards the attainment of the desired goals" (Simon, p. 14). Efficiency for Simon involved the metaphor of the balance sheet and conceded that "the criterion of efficiency is most easily understood in its application to commercial organizations that are largely guided by the profit objective" (Simon, pp. 172–173).

In this scenario, what is most efficient is simply the cheapest route because the attainment of goals is about maximizing profit. In this economic model, the means and the ends match. The less money spent up front on costs, the more money one has at the end, or as Simon (1945) put it, "In practice, of course, the maximization of income and the minimization of cost must be considered simultaneously—that is, what is really to be maximized is the difference between these two" (p. 173).

Simon's (1945) theoretical base is derived from this model of efficiency. From it, he defines *rational organizational behavior* on the part of management: "The efficiency of a behavior is the ratio of the results obtainable from that behavior to the maximum of results obtainable from the behaviors which are alternative behavior to the given behavior" (Simon, p. 179).

The implicit value that underscores this identification of efficient behavior is that of scarcity of resources. Administrative behavior is rational if it maximizes results at the lowest cost. To do this, Simon (1945) casts out the human dimension of his proffered theory of administration. He eliminates personality as a domain outside of his notion of science, and ethics along with it. He engages in a false bit of posturing when he declares that a science of business has no ethical content. The statement "Alternative A will lead to maximum profit" is a scientific statement, he asserts. However, he insists that the statement "To maximize profit is good . . . has no place in any science" (Simon, p. 250). By defining the maximization of profit as the "best" alternative because it maximizes results (profits) with the lowest possible cost, the outcome is the same, that is, what is good is the greatest profit. In this self-deceptive tautological stratagem, what is ethical (nonscience) is subsumed under a rational alternative that is stipulated as factual without the so-called ethical component being present. Simon's approach has simply suppressed the ethical component instead of eliminating it. The logic becomes "what is cheap will maximize profit." The greatest profit is the highest goal of a commercial organization. It is therefore the "best" of all possible alternatives. By default, it is the greatest good to be desired by the organization and its management.

Despite its many shortcomings, Simon's (1945) work has left a lasting imprint on administrative studies in educational, public, and business administration. Simon's focus on decision making in organizations centered on an economic focus in which decisions led to "satisficing," that is, since decision makers could never know all of the variables involved in any given decision, their world was "bounded" and rational only within those boundaries. Decisions could never represent some ultimate known universe because there would always be unknowns involved. Human decisions, therefore, would rarely represent an "optimal solution" (Nelson, 2006, p. 897).

The concept of rationality within an organization was simply where one was "concerned with the selection of preferred behavioral alternatives in terms of some system of values whereby the consequences of behavior can be evaluated" (Simon, 1945, p. 75). Simon's work was expanded by those analyzing the behavior of a person within a human organization, motivating employees to work, and participating in the work of the organization. Much of contingency theory, as exemplified in school climate studies (which are really individual/group interactive behavioral patterns—such as Halpin's [1966] work on bomber pilots and later school principals), is distinctively behavioral in focus. Halpin's work was preceded by the best-selling book *The Human Side of Enterprise*, by Douglas McGregor (1960; No. 10 in Figure 6.1), who examined management's influence and control through two views, which he labeled "theory X and theory Y." These two theories were based on an analysis of manager behaviors in business in the 1950s (Skidmore, 2006). The pursuit of these different paths in management created a psychological "climate." McGregor said the following:

> The climate is more significant than the type of leadership or the personal "style" of the superior. The boss can be autocratic or democratic, warm and outgoing or remote and introverted, easy or tough, but these personal characteristics are of less significance than the deeper attitudes to which his subordinates respond. (p. 134)

Fiedler's (1967) concept of *style,* based on a leader's disposition to emphasize people or work tasks leading to an interpersonal setting that could be identified, is Simonian in nature as well. A leader's "position power" was the result of the interaction of a leader's style with the group.

Any study of organizations in which individuals and their behaviors are the focus of the work is usually an example of the behavioral epoch in operation. Behaviorism abhors the "subjective," the feelings, emotions, cultural leanings, and predispositions of humans. These are neither objective nor directly observable. Behaviorism is steeped in logical positivism and the concept of verification by observation. If at all possible, the necessary behaviors are reduced to numerical equivalents so as to display their "objectivity" (Cyert & March, 1963).

Another example of the behavioral epoch in action is the intervention method of Chris Argyris (1970). The intervention method described by Argyris is not used with individuals, but with organizations. Individuals in the organization are referred to as "clients" (an impersonal term), and the organization as the "client system." Argyris also employs the concept of "open" and "closed" systems as composite categories within an organization. Closed systems are seen as those in which, at lower hierarchical levels, client systems are characterized by "fighting, withdrawal, apathy, indifference, goldbricking, distorting information sent upwards, and developing internal defensive establishments" (1970, p. 136). Open systems are those in which the strategy is "reaching out, learning, and becoming competent in controlling the external and internal environment so that its objectives are achieved and its members continue to learn" (1970, p. 136).

Modern adaptations of behaviorism using Argyris's notion of an open system are exemplified in Peter Senge's (1990) text, *The Fifth Discipline*. Senge characterizes an effective organization of the future as a "learning organization" that is the result (like climate) of an interaction between patterns of behavior and systemic structure (p. 52). Another recent example is the work of Kouzes and Posner (2002).

The Epoch of Structuralism

The next epoch shown in Figure 6.1 is that of structuralism. Once the perspective of analysis shifts from the behaviors of the people within an organization to the organization itself, the result is the epoch centered on organizational structure in which a person must work. Structuralism is based on the premise that a study of whole units or structures represents the key to understanding individual phenomena (behaviors). It is like turning a sock inside-out. Instead of using behaviors to predict impact on the organization or structure, one begins with the structure and assumes it impacts behaviors. Thus, behaviorism fits neatly within a structural epoch and is mutually reinforcing and supporting of it.

One of the important transition texts between behaviorism and structuralism is Katz and Kahn's (1966) book (No. 11 in Figure 6.1), *The Social Psychology of Organizations*. This important text combines the view of psychologists and that of sociologists (the latter influenced by Marxian concepts of social class), and attempts to build superorganic sociological models as exemplified in the works of Emile Durkheim (1858–1917) who proposed the idea of the "group mind," and Talcott Parsons (1902–1979), who worked to integrate findings from economics, anthropology, and sociology into one systematic approach. Another prolific writer-researcher in the structuralist tradition is Rensis Likert (1961), who worked at the Institute for Social Research at the University of Michigan.

Perhaps the most influential of disciplines in the field of educational leadership as it revolves around structuralism was general systems theory. General systems theory is derived from biology, and the writings of Ludwig von Bertalanffy (1968). He has defined a system as "a set of interacting units with relationships among them" (p. 3). A system can be understood only as the sum of its parts. This emphasis on wholes emanates from a study of human languages, specifically the work of Ferdinand de Saussure (1857–1913; Gadet, 1986).

A controversial text that combines the behavioral view of humans within organizations as "situations" is that of Cohen and March (1974). These two authors examined the college presidency and found that a president works within an "organized anarchy." The latter situation exists when there are problematic goals, unclear technology, and fluid participation (Cohen & March, p. 3). Cohen and March called the role of the college president an example of "garbage can leadership," in which the major job of the president was to sort problems into the right "garbage cans" (p. 211).

The purely structural epoch is represented by James Thompson's (1967; No. 12 in Figure 6.1) book, *Organizations in Action;* Henry Mintzberg's text (1983; No. 13 in Figure 6.1), *Structure in Fives;* and Bolman and Deal's (1991) work (No. 14 in Figure 6.1), *Reframing Organizations.* These works can be clustered together around the idea of organizational theory(ies).

The Bolman and Deal (1991) text centers on the idea not of finding the one right organizational pattern, but knowing how to select the correct perspective or "frame" to view problems. This is what they choose to call "frame theory." Bolman and Deal (1991) offer four basic organizational frames from which to select: the structural frame, the human resource frame, the political frame, and the symbolic frame. The job of the leader is to select the right frame for his or her organization and to ride the waves of change somewhat like surfers.

Bolman and Deal (1991) do not break out of the epoch of structuralism because they see organizations as "organic forms in which needs, roles, power, and symbols must be combined to provide direction and shape behavior" (p. 450). Such wholes are structure or complete systems. It is assumed that they possess a unity that subsumes their respective parts. Thus, even while the Bolman and Deal frame theory model appears to be selective, it is in reality a rationale for knowing what structural lens will yield what results when imposing it on an organization. The choices are limited to purely structural alternatives. Boleman and Deal never postulate the essential immutability of the wholes governing and directing the parts—an idea in language called logocentrism (Lefkovitz, 1989, p. 63). Frame theory's logocentrism is never disputed or questioned.

Texts in this epoch epitomize the structuralism essence, that is, they deal with behavior of organizations, not the individuals in them. They are centered on matters of organizational design, that is, how organizations, as wholes, can be restructured internally to become more effective and efficient.

The Feminist/Critical Theory Epoch

Feminist critique and critical theory are close allies in the next epoch shown in Figure 6.1. As a modern movement, feminism is said to have begun with Betty Friedan's (1963) text, *The Feminist Mystique.* Yet history records much earlier protests against the subservience of women, as for example Mary Wollstonecraft's (1989) tract, *A Vindication of the Rights of Women,* in which she asserted "that the sexual distinction which men have so warmly insisted upon, is arbitrary" (p. 205).

The voice and intensity of feminist thought has waxed and waned since the early 1960s, and has undergone various transformations. For example, Bem (1993) notes that for a brief period, feminists advocated androgyny as a solution to the inequality between the sexes. This inequality produced the rigid sexual polarization that existed in Western society. The idea was that androgyny incorporated aspects that were masculine and feminine, thereby becoming a genderless ideal for equality between the sexes.

The idea of androgyny was quickly discarded, however, because historically the male was enhanced by providing him with certain desirable female characteristics such as enriched emotionality, and therefore it did not really provide equality between the sexes. Another reason for discarding androgyny was that it failed the political test by not dealing with institutionalized androcentrism. It placed the problem on the personal level where it could be solved, but it left socioeconomic male hegemony untouched. Finally, it accepted gender polarization, that is, male/female exclusivity, as a given, thus privileging heterosexuality (see Bem, 1993, pp. 123–124).Homosexuality was given a name in 1870 and as Foucault (1990) notes, it was moved from "a temporary aberration . . . [to] a species" (p. 43). Positivistic science, with its proclivity to categorize reality, created scales of degradation/abnormality with zoophiles, auto-monosexualists, mixoverts, gynecomasts, presbyophiles, sexoesthetics, and dyspareunist women (Foucault, 1990, p. 43). Once categorized, these differences in sexual preferences became real, a stunning example of how reality is preshaped prior to observation or the collecting of data. Feminist thought today includes the concepts not only of attacking the socioeconomic-political strongholds of androcentrism but of assaulting the very idea of gender polarization and exclusivity that results in the oppression of homosexuality as "unnatural." What is important to note is how feminist critical inquiry struggled to find a name for itself. Then, it reacted against the hegemony of androcentrism, worked to find alternatives, abandoned those that did not eliminate socioeconomic-political oppression, and finally turned again on the linguistic and ontological categories that had shaped its own thought patterns about equalization that did not liberate.

A key text that has impacted business, public, and educational administration is Kathy Ferguson's (1984) *The Feminist Case Against Bureaucracy* (No.15 in Figure 6.1). In this text, Ferguson makes a case for understanding power as enshrined in a bureaucracy, because without such understanding, feminists cannot construct an "adequate theory of domination and liberation" (p. 5). As Ferguson points out, bureaucracies are both structures and processes. They include formal roles and informal expectations. Bureaucracies are hierarchical. They order and arrange people. They set up rules to be obeyed. Penalties and punishments are established for those who violate such rules. And bureaucracies maintain silences about some things, shrouding their actions as politically neutral. As Ferguson notes, the "myth of administration" is that it claims it is "the non-ideological instrument of technical progress . . . [and] clothes itself in the guise of science and renders itself ideologically invisible" (p. 16).

Ferguson (1984) advocates using feminist discourse as the fulcrum for constructing a nonbureaucratic way of life and for exposing bureaucratic and male-dominated norms: "The goal of feminist discourse is to articulate the relations between women's experiences, the forms of speech that can adequately convey these experiences, and the forms of institutions that can encourage and legitimate them" (p. 29).

In formulating an alternative to both bureaucratic discourse and socializing processes, Ferguson (1984) reminds her readers that ". . . real people cannot be collapsed into their organizational identities" (p. 37). Because women have been culturally conditioned to be in the weaker social position, they have learned certain ways of coping with their status as being politically powerless. These attributes have come to be called "feminine" when applied to women as a class. But the paradox is that resistance to bureaucratic oppression can be initiated within the organization that survives on oppression. Feminization in a bureaucracy is not a biological process, but a political one. Using the idea of the "subjugation of knowledge," in which the special language and experiences of women can become a potent source of organized resistance to bureaucracy, Ferguson stresses that women should not act like men, and they should not engage in playing games or participate in their own subjugation within bureaucracies. She criticizes programs of equal opportunity and affirmative action because they provide the equivalent of a bureaucratic safety valve, "a place where the outsiders—women of all colors, blacks, and Hispanics of both genders, and others—fight over the crumbs" (Ferguson, p. 195). Women must organize their own organizations and act collectively in everyone's best interest to create antibureaucratic organizations. Ferguson is quite bleak in insisting that women in groups cannot change bureaucracies from the inside.

Kellner (1992) posits that critical theory began as essentially a "Marxian critique of capitalist modernity, and then progressively moved away from orthodox Marxian positions . . ." (p. 1). Kellner also notes that critical theory has been the center of deep concerns regarding the modern epoch. It has proffered a "critical diagnosis of some of the latter's limitations, pathologies and destructive effects—while providing defenses of some of its progressive elements" (Kellner, p. 3).

An anchor text in this epoch is Jurgen Habermas's (1990) *Moral Consciousness and Communicative Action*. Habermas was part of the Institute for Social Research, sometimes called the Frankfurt School, in the 1920s. Critical theory was the title of the approach given to a study of society from 1930 to 1970 (Barbour, 2006). Critical theory had its philosophical roots in the works of Hegel and Marx. However, the critical theorists eschewed notions of absolute truth that were deterministic and made humans subservient to impersonal social forces, although they recognized that confronting those forces was a formidable challenge. Habermas posited that for equality to exist within social groups, class distinctions and those connoting hierarchical social positions related to privilege and freedom to speak had to be uncoerced and given without fear of retribution. He referred to this context as an "ideal speech situation" (Habermas, pp. 201–202). Only in this situation could the necessary conditions of freedom and mutuality exist by which power and money could be equalized. The overlap between many of the arguments advanced by Habermas (1990) and Ferguson (1984) are rather remarkable. Other writers from the Frankfurt School included Max Horkheimer, Theodor Adorno, and Herbert Marcuse.

The Critical Race Theory Epoch

Closely aligned to critical theory is critical race theory. For there to be a critical theory of race, Omi and Winant (2005) indicate it must be "explicitly historicist; it must recognize the importance of historical context and contingency in the framing of racial categories and the social construction of racially defined experiences" (p. 7). Such a theory must also apply to contemporary politics, include a global context, and apply across historical time. Villalpando (2006) indicates that critical race theory (CRT) is centered on the notion that racism is endemic in American life and exists in educational institutions in a myriad of forms, despite majoritarian claims that educational practices are neutral and work in meritocratic ways. Racism is not individualistic, but rather located in the very institutional structure of a large number of social agencies, among them schools. CRT takes into account the lived experiences and views of persons of color who tell "counterstories" to those that are dominant and believed to be true. The purpose of CRT is to end racial inequality and oppression of persons of color. Key texts of CRT are Richard Delgado's (1995) *Critical Race Theory: The Cutting Edge* and Gloria Ladson-Billings and William Tate's (1995) "Toward a Critical Race Theory of Education," which appeared in the *Teachers College Record.*

The Queer Theory Epoch

Another related development to critical theory and CRT is queer theory. Queer theory attempts to expose the binary in sexuality and sexual identity. Blount (2006) has pointed out the difference between gender and sexual orientation. Gender is about social relations and how men and women define each other as masculine or feminine. Gender is a process that is negotiated over time and varies by historical period and culture, while sexual orientation involves who a person desires sexually.

Queer theory challenges the social system's construction of sexual identities, which are usually straight, gay, lesbian, bisexual, and transgendered individuals. Queer theory seeks to expose such categories as invalid and not reliable or accurate descriptors (Koschoreck, 2006).

Queer theory advances five perspectives. First, it seeks to come to terms with sexual identity over time. Second, it works to deconstruct sexual norms and accompanying practices in institutional life. Third, it is confrontational. Fourth, it sees sexual identity as more than sexuality. And finally, it views society and its culture as inherently political and cultural (Tierney, 1997, as quoted in Young & Lopez, 2005, p. 344).

As Koschoreck and Slattery (2006) indicate, the stringent normativity of heterosexism at work in schools places some children at a decided risk, and often in physical danger. Koschoreck and Slattery (2006) report the research of John Ashton (2001) in which gay or lesbian students were exposed to sexual slurs over 20 times per day and that 69% of these students experienced harassment or violence in school. Queer theory is a form of sexual identity de-construction, a postmodern tactic to be discussed in the postmodern epoch.

The Postmodern Epoch

Unlike modernity, which has a core set of beliefs around which various epochs have clustered, postmodernity has no coherent theme, except perhaps in what it chooses to reject. So postmodernity is known for what it isn't as opposed to what it is. Best and Kellner (1991) indicate that postmodernity is "undertheorized" (p. 2). And as it is true with the other epochs shown in Figure 6.1, there are no clean "breaks" between them.

Postmodernity posits that there are no realities outside of a person's culture and experience. Reality is constructed, multidimensional, and multitheoretical. Science is not the be all and end all of human inquiry, and it is not "neutral." Science is merely one kind of language game. Science has to use nonscientific language to describe itself. As Lyotard (1997; No. 20 in Figure 6.1) has observed, "Who decides the conditions of truth?"

> . . . the rules of the game of science, are immanent in that game, that they can only be established within the bonds of a debate that is already scientific in nature, and that there is no other proof that the rules are good than the consensus extended to them by the experts. (Lyotard, p. 29)

Postmodernism does not accept that the knower and known are separable from one another or that it is possible to test reality at all. Postmodernists see "truth" as relational and circular and not independent. Science cannot be an arbiter for truth because it is a kind of tradition in itself (English, 2003b).

As if to provide a linkage from modernism to postmodernism, Lyotard (1997) sees postmodernism as a kind of premodernism: "A work can become modern only if it is first postmodern. Postmodernism thus understood is not modernism at its end but in the nascent state, and this state is constant" (p. 79).

What Lyotard (1997) is trying to express is a state where in formulating rules there are, in fact, no rules. He calls this "putting forward the unpresentable in presentation itself" (p. 81). There is still another expression of this notion advanced by Lyotard (1984): ". . . it must be clear that it is our business not to supply reality but to invent illusions to the conceivable which cannot be presented" (p. 81).

Despite Lyotard's (1997) descriptions of the postmodern, Figure 6.1 shows postmodernism "after" modernism. The reason is that postmodernists deny the "reality" that anchors modernism. To traffic in Lyotard's description for a moment, the "presentable" cannot be constructed and stand apart from the presenter. That would amount to a double illusion. A postmodernist prefers to work in only one illusion.

Any discussion about postmodernism has to include the enigmatic figure of a French Algerian, Jacques Derrida (1930–2004). Derrida sent the American academic world into a tailspin when in 1954 he spoke at a conference at Johns Hopkins University and laid out the anatomy of de-construction, a way to take apart textual passages. Critchley (1992) indicates that de-construction is a double-reading of a text. The first reading is simply to interpret the passage as most people would construe it. The second reading is to look for contradictions, hidden silences, binaries, and circularities in the text itself. Nearly all texts have them. This "second text" may, if reconstructed after exposing them in de-construction, offer a very different reading of what most people think the text is about. Texts are not only about what is said, but about what is not said. De-construction focuses on both. De-construction has been used in education long before Derrida gave it a name. For example, Boyd

Bode may be said to have de-constructed the logic and contradictions in Franklin Bobbitt's (1918/1971) approach to curriculum engineering when he wrote *Modern Educational Theories* in 1930. Bode found paradoxes and contradictions in Bobbitt's theories, which were very popular at the time. He exposed them. He was after what he called the "absolutes." His biographer says, "With Bode there would be no preexistence to tap and surely no preordained truths at the end of the process" (Winetrout, 1996, p. 71).

Another example of de-construction comes from feminist critique. In discussing *homosociality*, the practice of how men bond together, Lorber (1996) observes how men cluster together and go off to a sporting event such as golf or go hunting or fishing. The role of the women was to listen to the men, prepare food, urge them to have a good time, but not to join them. In staying behind, the women colluded in their own subjugation. The men built their superior social status by excluding their wives and girlfriends from their space. In so doing, they never have to treat them as equals or competitors. This observation represents a de-construction of a social practice that sustains gender superiority.

De-construction makes it possible for postmodernists to expose the flaws and assumptions in modernism as irrational. Yet postmodernism does not offer any alternative because to do so would be to center something in its place. This, postmodernists refuse to do, except as a very temporary measure. The postmodern epoch is still very new on the scene. The implications for educational leadership are still being explored.

Kitsch Management Texts and Educational Leadership

Educational leadership is an applied field. The intellectual/epistemological foci for much of the content of theory and operations of schools and school systems are also common to public and business administration. There is a whole list of largely popular business texts that are cited from time to time in educational leadership books and which many students in education have read. Virtually none of them appear in Figure 6.1. The reason is that very few are research based and the few that claim to be engage in a highly reductionistic and oversimplified list of generalities that require complex organizational situations to be de-contextualized, that is, "dumbed down" for them to fit. Some that claim to be research based are not. For example, the popular and hugely influential text *In Search of Excellence* (1982) by Peters and Waterman used "faked data" to support its oversimplified advice to business leaders (Lieberman, 2001). Stephen Covey's (1990) bestseller, *The Seven Habits of Highly Effective People,* offers research claims but never reports any data to support them (English, 2002b). These examples belong to a cluster of popular texts that Eugenie Samier (2005) has called "kitsch management" [kitschmensch], a sort of "pulp fiction" of the world of management.

"Kitsch" or "kitschy" is a slang term that means "rubbish or trash" (Partridge, 2002, p. 651). Synonyms for kitsch include words such as "cheap, crass, vulgar, saccharine, gaudy, ersatz or pseudo-art, and indicative of bad taste" (Samier, 2005, p. 36). Management "kitsch" produces works that have high emotional appeal—usually sentimentality (Samier, 2005, p. 37):

Kitsch requires no knowledge, understanding, critique, or analysis; it is predigested and pre-packaged, sparing effort and providing a short-cut to pleasure . . . [it] satisfies an immediate desire, does not disturb or challenge basic sentiments and beliefs, does not question socio-political reality or vested interests, it reinforces our prejudices, avoids unpleasant conflicts, and promises a happy ending. (Samier, 2005, p. 38)

A partial list of some of the most popular kitsch management texts, which are to be found in many airport bookstores, is shown in Table 6.2.

❖ **Table 6.2** A Partial List of Popular "Kitsch" Books on Management and Business

Author	Title	Publication date	Publisher	Sales figures
Ken Blanchard and Spencer Johnson	*One-Minute Manager*	1981	William Morrow	3.5 million copies
Lee Bolman and Terrence Deal	*Leading with Soul*	1995	Jossey-Bass	unspecified
Donna Brooks and Lynn Brooks	*Ten Secrets of Successful Leaders*	2005	McGraw-Hill	unspecified
Richard Carlson	*Don't Sweat the Small Stuff and It's All Small Stuff*	1997	Hyperion	bestseller
Subhir Chowdhury	*The Ice Cream Maker*	2005	Doubleday	unspecified
Jim Collins	*Good to Great*	2001	HarperCollins	2 million copies
Pat Croce	*Lead or Get off the Pot: 7 Secrets of a Self-Made Leader*	2004	Simon & Schuster	unspecified
Stephen Covey	*The Seven Habits of Highly Effective People*	1990	Simon & Schuster	10 million copies
Bill Diffendorffer	*The Samurai Leader*	2005	Source Books	unspecified
Hans Fenzel	*The Top Ten Mistakes Leaders Make*	2004	Cook Communications Industries	unspecified
Jeffrey Fox	*How to Become a Rainmaker*	2000	Hyperion	bestseller

(Continued)

❖ **Table 6.2**   (Continued)

Author	Title	Publication date	Publisher	Sales figures
Keven and Jackie Freiberg	*GUTS! Companies That Blow the Doors Off Business As Usual*	2004	Doubleday	unspecified
Craig Galbraith and Oliver Galbraith	*The Benedictine Rule of Leadership*	2004	Adams Media	unspecified
Louis Gerstner, Jr.	*Who Says Elephants Can't Dance?*	2002	HarperCollins	unspecified
Malcolm Gladwell	*The Tipping Point*	2000, 2002	Little Brown Company	unspecified
Judith Glaser	*The DNA of Leadership*	2006	Platinum Press	unspecified
Robert Hagstrom	*The Essential Buffet*	2001	John Wiley	unspecified
Phillip Van Hooser	*Willie's Way: 6 Secrets for Wooing, Wowing & Winning Customers & Their Loyalty*	2005	John Wiley	unspecified
Joseph Jawarski	*Synchronicity: The Inner Path of Leadership*	1998	Berrett-Koehler Publishers	unspecified
Jason Jennings	*Think Big Act Small*	2005	Portfolio	unspecified
Spencer Johnson	*Who Moved My Cheese?*	1998, 2002	G.P. Putnam & Sons	21 million copies
Laurie Beth Jones	*Jesus, CEO: Using Ancient Wisdom for Visionary Leadership*	1995	Hyperion	unspecified
Larry Julian	*GOD Is My CEO*	2001, 2002	Adams Media	unspecified
Donald Krause	*The Art of War for Executives*	2005	Penguin	unspecified
Dean Lundell	*Sun Tzu's Art of War for Traders and Investors*	1997	McGraw-Hill	unspecified

Author	Title	Publication date	Publisher	Sales figures
John Maxwell	*The 360 Degree Leader*	2005	Thomas Nelson, Inc.	unspecified
John Maxwell	*The 21 Irrefutable Laws of Leadership*	1998	Thomas Nelson	unspecified
Justin Menkes	*Executive Intelligence*	2005	HarperCollins	unspecified
Geoffrey Moore	*Dealing With Darwin: How Great Companies Innovate at Every Phase of Their Evolution*	2005	Portfolio	unspecified
Frank Pacetta	*Don't Fire Them, Fire Them Up!*	1994	Simon & Schuster	unspecified
Tom Rath and Donald Clifton	*How Full Is Your Bucket?*	2004	Gallup Press	500,000 copies in print
Wolk Rinke	*Don't Oil the Squeaky Wheel*	2004	McGraw-Hill	unspecified
Lance Secretan	*Inspire: What Great Leaders Do*	2004	John Wiley	unspecified
Susan Steinbrecker and Joel Bennett	*Heart-Centered Leadership*	2003	Black Pants Publishing	unspecified
Jack and Suzy Welch	*Winning*	2005	HarperCollins	unspecified
Spencer Tillman	*Scoring in the Red Zone*	2005	Thomas Nelson	unspecified
Dave Ulrich and Norm Smallwood	*How Leaders Build Value*	2003	John Wiley	unspecified
Pat Williams	*The Paradox of Power*	2002	Warner	unspecified
Marie Wilson	*Closing the Leadership Gap*	2004	Penguin	unspecified
John Wooden and Steve Jamison	*Wooden on Leadership*	2005	McGraw-Hill	unspecified

All of these kitsch texts promise what Samier (2005) has labeled as "pre-digested, prepackaged" works that present a variety of predigested nostrums "sold as largely unproblematic activities with a barely disguised 'how-to' training guide intent" (p. 39). These texts oversimplify reality and promise a rationality that does not exist in the real world. Because they avoid dealing with managerial subtleties and erase situational complexities and conflicts, they are at their base ideologies being passed off as codified wisdom. A large number of the authors are managerial consultants who are peddling their wares in training sessions, videos, CDs, and spin-off books. They use cutesy "pop" titles for their books such as Pat Croce's (2004) *Lead or Get Off the Pot!*; military models like Dean Lundell's (1997) *Sun Tzu's Art of War for Traders and Investors,* or Bill Diffendorffer's (2005) *The Samurai Leader;* sports situations such as Spencer Tillman's (2005) *Scoring in the Red Zone;* or offer coaching icons as models for leaders in John Wooden and Steve Jamison's (2005) *Wooden on Leadership.* Other kitsch management books appeal to religious themes, such as Laurie Beth Jones's (1995) *Jesus, CEO,* or Larry Julian's (2002) *GOD is my CEO.* Other kitsch titles attempt to capitalize on scientific themes, such as Geoffrey Moore's (2005) *Dealing With Darwin: How Great Companies Innovate at Every Turn of Their Evolution,* or Judith Glaser's (2006) *The DNA of Leadership.*

The politics of "kitsch" are decidedly conservative. Kitsch texts offer only a superficial view of the world or the managerial situation. For folksy homilies to make sense, situational ambiguities have to be erased. Kitsch advice assumes a kind of internal organizational stability that at least for educators does not exist. Educational organizations are rife with organizational contradictions, conflicting value orientations of members, power struggles based on real differences of perception, and highly charged political externalities. Educational environments are complex and multifaceted. Kitschy one-liners that offer nothing more than vanilla humor contain what Carter and Jackson (2000) warn are "the intellectual equivalent of sentimentality, laying the foundation for excessive power, leadership idolatry, and eventually the suppression of divergent beliefs and values ... the asymmetry inherent in the general normal experience of organizational life" (p. 39).

The key word in understanding the downside of kitsch managerial texts is the "asymmetry" in organizational life. Not all values, perceptions, loyalties, and morals run parallel with one another, especially in democratic organizations that create forums to express such differences and that include the idea of divergence as healthy rather than threatening.

To these contentious and multifaceted issues, kitsch management offers little to no help because the context in which their proffered simplicities don't really exist in public school administration. So the student of educational leadership will not find the kind of understanding that has the potential of working in a contested environment filled with the inevitable conflicts in public policy and operations receptive to the magic elixirs proffered by the quick fixes of the management consultants to be anything but an amusing read on a short plane route.

Another popular contemporary management text is Jim Collins's (2001) *Good to Great.* This work is fraught with warmed-over TQM concepts. Collins is famous for his consultant "managementspeak," which included advising companies to develop BHAGs, which stood for "big hairy audacious goals" (Hymowitz, 2006).

In trying to take his ideas for business into the nonprofit sector, Collins (2005) wrote a short monograph to build such a bridge. Like Stephen Covey (1990) and other management consultants such as John Maxwell (1998), Collins claims that his work is about constructing "a framework of greatness, articulating timeless principles . . ." (2005, p. 2). Consultants advocating change based on "eternal" or "timeless" principles appeal to a reader's need for absolute certainty. With "timeless principles," no thought has to be given to doubting the methods to be employed for the ends desired. With "timeless principles" at work, a kind of fantasyland can be created that absolves leaders from the moral consequences of their actions as they pursue a utopia in which human flaws become obstacles to be erased (see Mohawk, 2000). Using "timeless principles" makes it easier to make some decisions without having to think about them very much (O'Shea & Madigan, 1997, p. 301).

For example, one of Collins's (2005) admonitions about working toward greatness is "to get the right people on the bus, the wrong people off the bus, and the right people into the right seats" (p. 14). This simple analogy is filled with assumptions about hiring, about motivation, and about who are the "right" people. Collins (2005) advises that the "right people" are "those who are productively neurotic" (p. 15). Such persons ". . . wake up every day, compulsively driven . . . because it is simply part of their DNA" (Collins, 2005, p. 15).

Collins's (2005) view about humans is that such qualities are inborn like traits. When building a "great" organization, one has to get rid of the noncompulsive neurotics because being "great" isn't in their genes. The idea that "greatness" is about heredity can be traced back to the works of Francis Galton (1822–1911) and the birth of the eugenics movement (Kevles, 1999).

In Collins's (2005) model of greatness, there is no need for an organization to develop talent or to be concerned about fostering human growth. The responsibilities for management to create the kind of organization that optimizes human abilities is unnecessary. If people don't have greatness in their DNA, they are the wrong people. They should be ordered off the bus or fired. Collins's (2005) approach is a kind of managerial social Darwinism packaged into bumper sticker homilies. The Collins model of greatness is testimony to the continuing influence of social Darwinism at work in the world of for-profit organizations and a rationale for the kind of ruthlessness that is often found there.

One function served by managerial kitsch is to rationalize predatory thinking and behavior fueled by calls for managerial perfectionism centered in utopian schemes. Collins's (2005) portrait of a successful leader is "ambitious first and foremost for the cause, the organization, the work . . . a fierce resolve to do whatever it takes to make good on that ambition" (p. 34). This kind of ideology imbues Collins's (2005) work with what Mohawk (2000) has called an "insurmountable dilemma" (p. 156):

> They [ideologues such as Collins] may not compromise their ideals or they will betray the very concept that frames their identity. They may not negotiate their articles of belief with nonbelievers, because the beliefs . . . are absolute and not negotiable [Collins' timeless principles]. Since the beliefs represent perfection, agreeing to something else [less than "great" in Collins' binary] betrays the ideal itself [these organizations are simply "good"]. (p. 156)

Students of educational leadership should view such texts as oversimplified, watered-down solutions to the pressure-packed conundrums of contemporary educational leadership today.

Pursuing Learning Extensions of the Chapter

The learning extensions of the chapter involve some of the films now listed. They are intended to illustrate some of the ideas about leadership described in the chapter and present concepts of how critical texts have led to epochs of leadership.

The Magician (1959), Black and White, VHS, California Video Distributors, 1 Hour 41 Minutes

This is one of Ingmar Bergman's very successful films and it was originally called "The Face" (Bergman, 1990, pp.161–172). This is a film that contrasts the ways of science and the ways of faith and magic. The plot involves a magician who is travelling with his wife and other companions who is stopped by police and must demonstrate his supernatural powers. The magician, played by Max Von Sydow, is humiliated by the police chief and a health official, Vergerus, a doctor who epitomizes early positivistic scientific attitudes toward anything that cannot be logically explained. Vergerus says to the magician's wife, " . . . you represent what I hate most of all: that which cannot be explained" (Bergman, 1990, p. 167). In the final scene in the film, the magician corners Vergerus in the attic and quickly surrounds him with fear, revealing his scientific faith to be quite shallow. There is much science cannot explain. This is a wonderful film to explore the many meanings of perception and truth.

The War Room (2004), Color, DVD, Universal Studios, 1 Hour 37 Minutes

This film is an intimate documentary of the first Clinton campaign to win the U.S. presidency. It centers on two main characters, James Carville and George Stephanopoulos, who work the Clinton campaign center. It includes the controversy over Gennifer Flowers through the Democratic National Convention. One sees the day-to-day strategies, maneuvering, and "spins" given by Carville and Stephanopoulos to fast-moving events. The film is a superb testimony to a postmodern world. The "center" rapidly shifts in keeping with events. In fact, the center is often any tack that will put the opposition on the defensive. The importance of context is continually emphasized over static principles as the decision makers work to put their candidate in the best possible light and work to shield him from his own weaknesses and foibles.

Serving in Silence: The Margarethe Cammermeyer Story (1998), Color, VHS, Columbia, Tristar, 1 Hour 32 Minutes

The film focuses on the true story of Margarethe Cammermeyer, a decorated Army colonel who contested the U.S. military's antigay policy. Produced by Barbra Streisand and Glenn Close, the film focuses on how homosexuality has been defined in purely negative terms by the dominant heterosexual norms of society. The film would be a good companion to a class discussion of queer theory.

Malcolm X (1992), Color, VHS, *Warner Brothers, 3 Hours 35 Minutes*

This is Spike Lee's masterpiece of the life of Malcolm Little, aka, Malcolm X (1925–1965), with Denzel Washington as an amazing look-alike for the former hipster, drug dealer, and small-time hustler who was transformed in prison into an electric, charismatic leader of the Nation of Islam, Temple No. 11 in Boston, Massachusetts, and later national spokesperson for the Nation of Islam. The film can be teamed with a reading of the widely read autobiography of Malcolm X co-authored with Alex Haley in 1964. Various leadership epochs can be represented in the film, both critical theory and CRT being the most obvious.

Writing in Your Personal Reflective Journal

After becoming acquainted with the various epochs of leadership described in the chapter, position your own beliefs about leadership in the one you believe was domi-nant for you prior to encountering an explanation of all of them. Indicate if any of the alternatives appeal to you and why. Remember that all of the epochs are still being used, although some have been renamed in the process, the most obvious being texts and thinking along the lines of scientific management. Indicate if you have read any of the books listed in the "kitsch" management section and if they appealed to you. Has the discussion in the chapter shed any new light about their value as guides for educa-tional leadership?

A Review of Key Chapter Concepts

behaviorism—This is a view of human action that stresses that a scientific study of human behavior involves observable and ultimately measurable motions that are under the conscious control of a person who is responding to environmental demands or stimuli. Behaviorists eschew speculating about human motives that are not observ-able. Behaviorists stress the importance of changing environmental stimuli, which will lead to changes in human responses. Both scientific management and total quality management are deeply rooted in behaviorism (Blackbourn, 2006).

critical race theory (CRT)—As defined by Villalpando (2006), critical race theory is "an analytical framework that offers a race-based epistemological and methodological approach to study racial inequality in the field of educational leadership" (p. 236). CRT is based on the assumption that racism is endemic to American life and that includes institutions of education. Any claim that educational politics and practices are race neutral are simply false. CRT uses "counterstories" by persons of marginalized groups to combat the dominant false themes spread by those who profess that educational institutions are not racially privileged places for whites.

critical theory—Bohman (1999) indicates that the term *critical theory* can be applied to "any social theory that is at the same time explanatory, normative, practical, and self-reflexive" (p. 195). The term *critical* is applied to negative assessments of current social or educational practices and it includes feminism and queer theory. The underlying rationality is that critical theorists want to remove barriers to human suffering and obstacles to human expression. Critical theory often attacks positivism, empiricism, and relativism (postmodernism). It espouses scientific procedures and includes historical analysis as one of its approaches to creating alternative epistemologies.

de-construction—A major analytical tool of postmodern critique, de-construction involves the reading of a text in which the critique involves "a demonstration of the incompleteness of incoherence of a philosophical position using concepts and principles of argument whose meaning and use is legitimated only by that philosophical position" (Wheeler, 1999, p. 209). De-construction does not allow the reviewer the luxury of reverting to meanings that rest on language that is uncontaminated by philosophy. What this means is that the de-constructionist cannot rely on anything but the words in a text and their connections to other words. There are no ultimate meanings apart from the words and their usage in analyzed passages. When passages are shorn of their connections to uncontaminated logic, then they cease to have foundations that differentiate among them, such as Plato's theory of forms. From this view there is no difference; ideas that separate metaphorical, literal, rhetorical, or logical have no additional foundations other than common words and their meanings.

epochs of leadership—An epoch is a unit of time initiated with a critical event or text that subsequently spawns more texts and leads to the centralization of ideas or tenets, which serve as a conceptual or intellectual anchor around which major concepts are advanced.

feminism—According to Dentith, Brady, and Hammett (2006), there are three broad categories of feminist theory: liberal, radical, and postmodern (p. 384). The liberal perspectives work within traditional Western ideas of rationality and logic. Notions of legal equality, removing barriers to women such as affirmative action and working to place more women in the "pipeline," will increase their representation in educational leadership positions. Critics such as Blount (1998) indicate that the liberal notion of feminism is not the problem. Rather, it is the nature of a patriarchal social structure reproduced in educational administration that is the culprit. The oppression of women is part and parcel of that structure and nibbling at the edges simply won't change the current situation. Patriarchal values embedded in institutional culture have to be exposed and replaced. Postmodern feminists reject both these approaches and prefer a more multiple perspectival view that envisions gender as only one constructed social identity that has to be de-constructed along with race, class, and sexuality.

inductive method—This is an approach to the study of things that dictates that an observer should begin with no preconceived ideas of how things are and observe and derive explanations/theories from the data that is gathered, rather than formulating generalizations and then going out to gather the data that supports those generalizations. Induction is from the Latin *in* and *ducere*, meaning *to lead in* (Runes, 1984, p. 161). The approach dictates that conclusions "fit" but do not go beyond the data gathered. Advocates of this method were Francis Bacon (1561–1626) and John Stuart Mill (1806–1873), among others. The inductive method has largely been discredited. As Karl Popper (1979) observed, "All knowledge is theory-impregnated, including our observations" (p. 71).

kitsch texts/kitsch management—Something can be labeled "kitsch" when it is crass, cheap, vulgarized, unduly saccharine, and serves to stir up sentimentality instead of presenting the full complexity of real life. According to Samier (2005), the function of kitsch is to oversimplify reality, usually to apply simple, ready-made solutions. Kitsch management texts, especially those proffered by management consultants, are extensions of their homely and "common sense" antidotes to nagging or novel organizational issues. They reduce the requirement to engage in any deep analysis or tough thinking, and they do not disturb conventional wisdom and values or question prevailing sociopolitical realities or vested political interests. Kitsch management texts explicitly or implicitly promise happy endings to managerial problems.

logical positivism—Also known as positivism, this was a philosophical movement that began in the 1920s and was dominant for nearly three decades. Positivists held that true statements were only those that could be conclusively confirmed by experience or observation. This principle was called "the verifiability criterion of meaning" (Fumerton, 1999, p. 514). One of the dilemmas of the positivists was their belief that all justified beliefs rested on principles that were "self-evident," that is, tautologies. Positivists also eschewed ideas that emanated from religious or moral perspectives as "metaphysics" (Fumerton, p. 514).

modernism—This is the rise of a perspective rooted in the rationalism of the renaissance and the triumph of scientific empiricism as a dominant and totalizing metanarrative regarding how inquiry and thought are to be regarded that is ostensibly believed to be "neutral" and "objective" about phenomena observed and researched. Lyotard (1997) describes modernism as

> any science that legitimates itself with a reference to a metadiscourse . . . making an explicit appeal to some grand narrative, such as the dialectics of Spirit, the hermeneutics of meaning, the emancipation the rational or working subject, or the creation of wealth. (p. xxiii)

Education and educational leadership are still in the thrall of modernism. The tenets of modernism have been recently advanced as superior by the National Research Council's (2002) text, *Scientific Research in Education*.

parsimony—This is the notion that the best explanations or theories are also the simplest and the shortest among alternatives. This is sometimes called "Ockham's razor" after William of Ockham (1285–1349).

postmodernism—Postmodernism is neither a unitary view of the world nor a coherent doctrine about it. Postmodernity is chiefly identifiable by what it isn't and what it rejects (Usher & Edwards, 1996). Postmodernism pans the idea that there is an underlying unity to the world that is divine or secular, and that any certainty about such matters centers some values, de-centering others, and marginalizing persons whose identity and views are automatically dubbed inferior. Historically these have been women and persons of color, and those whose sexual identities were categorized as abnormal according to pseudoscientific norms established in Victorian times. According to Bauman (1992), "postmodernism is marked by a view of the human world as irreducibly and irrevocably pluralistic, split into a multitude of sovereign units and sites of authority, with no horizontal or vertical order, either in actuality or in potency" (p. 35). Postmodernism is about the breaking down of barriers, calling into question and disrepute the binaries on which culture and social stratification have been based that privilege a class, gender, sexual identity, and race-based social/cultural differentiated structure. One of its principal weapons is textual de-construction.

progress—This is the idea that tomorrow will be better than today and that with faith in reason, humankind is advancing toward an improved life on earth. The concept of *progress* is essentially religious and can be traced to early Christianity. As Nesbit (1970) has observed, the concept of progress is neither "empirically or logically verified" (p. 6). It is an article of faith. There are modern manifestations of progress built into managerial thinking. For example, the concept of "continuous improvement" is essentially the concept of progress repackaged (English, 2003b, pp. 127–129).

queer theory—Queer theory is a strategy to question one's assigned social sexual identity. It seeks to bring into focus the many categories that have been used to marginalize and oppress persons who have been identified as "not normal" as it pertains to their gender identity and sexual orientation. Hall (2003) posits that there is no singular queer theory, but many queer theories in which there are many voices and perspectives at work. He insists that "queer" analysis "help[s] us understand the lived realities and day-to-day activities of diverse individuals today, whatever their sexual identity may be" (Hall, 2003, p. 5). Queer theories de-construct and critique the categories that are used to keep people in their place and to assign adjectives that degrade them. Sexual identity is socially constructed and queer theories work to undercut those identities as stable, divine, singular, or scientific.

scientific management (job de-skilling)—Developed by Frederick Taylor (1856–1915), this is an approach to the study of work tasks that began with the notion that there was one best way to do any kind of task. This one best way was derived by observing a variety of workmen doing the task and selecting the one who could outperform the others. This "best" worker's approach was then studied and copied and made the norm for all workers thereafter. The calculation of the one best way was the amount of output a worker could produce within any given time period. Taylor's assumptions have been later repudiated as pseudoscientific and rooted in arbitrary rules and not science. The idea of breaking work tasks into smaller units and hiring less skilled workers to do those tasks and lower rates of pay has been called "job de-skilling" and is still used today in the fast food industry (Schlosser, 2001).

structuralism—This is the umbrella term given to a wide category of research regnant between 1950 and 1970, primarily in France. A broad range of disciplines were involved, including anthropology, philosophy, literary theory, psychoanalysis, political science, and mathematics. The nexus of structuralism begins with the work of Ferdinand de Saussure (1857–1913), who was a Swiss linguist. Saussure's thoughts were collected by his students and published in a *Course in General Linguistics* (Gadet, 1986) after his death. Saussure posited that language systems were arbitrary collections of signs and sounds and that meaning was determined by the syntax of the language itself. Words had meaning only when related to other words. The rules of language had to be accepted as a system specific to any given human culture or community (Allison, 1999). Saussure's ideas were given modern currency in the works of Claude Levi-Strauss (1908–). Strauss advanced the idea that social structures could be examined through their substructures. Each society was composed of a kind of social rationality open to investigation stemming from observable empirical information and proceeding via inference and deduction (Allison, p. 883). Social substructures contain models of specific relations within any given social structure. Strauss's work paved the way for other kinds of structural analysis, including the work of Noam Chomsky in the United States and Roberto Eco in Italy.

total quality management (TQM)—This is an approach to management credited to W. Edwards Deming (1900–1993) that employed many of the assumptions of scientific management warmed over with some concepts from Elton Mayo's (1945) human relations principles. Deming's ideas captured the imagination of American management in the 1980s and such terms as *continuous improvement, 100% perfection, and doing it right the first time and every time* are still found in popular managerial texts, such as Jim Collins's (2001) *Good to Great* bestseller two decades later.

7

Balancing Performance and Accountability

Educational leadership as a performing art draws its inspiration from the humanities, not the sciences, especially drama, literature, history, and philosophy. But the overwhelming emphasis on learning how to lead has been centered on models of machine efficiency adapted from popular business literature. Such a stance has been reinforced by hegemonic social science research methods, which also dominate the field, along with organizational sociology, which erases the human variable and with it human agency. This chapter delves into the dilemma of recentering educational leadership in the humanities, where the art of performance can reemerge as the guide to actually improve the practice of educational leadership in the schools.

John Wiens (2006), a veteran Canadian school administrator for over 30 years, remarked that when examining notions of leadership,

> The fact that the educational leadership literature basically matched or emulated the popular business management literature (with its emphasis on excellence, changer, effective "habits," total quality and the like) did little to squelch my unease. . . . (p. 215)

Wiens (2006) felt that this literature was "not only counterintuitive but also too prescriptive and too presumptive, generalizing to the point of meaninglessness . . ." (p. 215).

Much of this literature has the veneer of social science, but not the substance. But even if social science approaches are followed rigorously, there are inherent limitations to the kinds of results that can be expected. For the most part, such research studies also remove human interiority as anything of importance. A social scientist observes actions, but not the beliefs that prompt the actions. Human emotion and intuition, matters of action, are in a different realm, however. Perhaps Mahatma Gandhi said it best: " . . . I have come to this fundamental conclusion that if you want something really important to be done, you must not merely satisfy the reason, you must move the heart also" (Ayer, 1973, p. 287). Samier (2005b) summarized the strength of the humanities over typical social science research performed in educational administration and business when she explained, "Positivistic and structural functional approaches to administration are simply not equipped to deal with questions of freedom, authenticity, responsibility and individual action . . . and is obscured in the current fad of 'leadership training'" (p. 126).

Unlocking the mysteries of leadership using social science methods has posed innumerable difficulties for scholars and practitioners ever since leadership studies became "scientific" at the turn of the last century. Positivistic and neo-positivistic science, with its rules about avoiding subjectivities and unscientific speculation, has concentrated on the actions and consequences of decisions made by leaders largely in organizational settings. The emphasis on observable and measurable actions in theorizing about leadership has led to the dominance of organizational sociological theories and approaches intertwined with behavioral research in coming to grips with the phenomenon of human leadership.

Even when current methods and approaches are augmented with qualitative methods such as ethnographies (Ribbins, 2003) or biographies (Gronn & Ribbins, 1996), the underlying assumption is that institutional life, culture, and context can at least be summarized into coherent or recurrent patterns (i.e., "steady state conditions;" Ribbins, 2000, p. 3).

The purpose of "discovering" or "recognizing" such patterns or career paths could become the focus for improved programs of leadership preparation because it would be possible to engage in some prediction of what to expect in school leadership situations, and one would have a better idea of who might be successful under specific similar circumstances (see Kochan, Jackson, & Duke, 1999). But what if this assumption is invalid?

Michael Mann (2003) proffers such a perspective in his study of the history of social power when he says that history does not repeat itself: "Precisely the opposite: World history develops. Through historical comparison we can see that the most significant problems of our own time are novel. That is why they are difficult to solve" (p. 32).

It is time to reinsert "life" into school administration by expanding the content of what constitutes appropriate texts in the preparation of educational leaders by examining life writing in its various forms, not so much in pursuing patterns, commonalities, cycles, or career roads based on assumptions of regularities being present or absent that are enduring or "steady state," but that the value of examining life writing is critical because only it contains the full range of human actions.

This is a decidedly postmodern perspective because the value of life writing is not what it reveals regarding the continuities involved in leadership, but rather it is the discontinuities, the ruptures, and the dissimilarities that are of most importance because that is where solutions to the novel problems of times may be found (English, 2003, pp. 40–41). Mann (2003) summarizes it this way: "History seems just one damned thing after another. If the damned things are patterned, it is only because real men and women impose patterns" (p. 532).

As Ribbins (2000) and Gronn and Ribbins (1996) make clear, understanding the context in which leadership is exercised is of critical importance. Other countries, such as the United Kingdom, have made greater progress than their U.S. counterparts (see Erben, 1998; Ribbins, 2003) in moving away from continued "management science" approaches. Unfortunately, the recent release of the National Research Council's *Scientific Research in Education* (Shavelson & Towne, 2003) in the United States has all but relegated life writing to the near "fiction" category of what the government should fund as "scientific research."

One example in which an analysis of leadership superbly demonstrates Michael Mann's contention that the most significant problems of the times are novel is the British-led Gallipoli campaign of World War I. Gallipoli became a disaster that Winston Churchill had to live down for decades (Keegan, 2002, p. 86). Approached traditionally, the measurement of the campaign is not difficult, that is, a calculation of British and French warships gathering in the Dardanelles Straits, the minefields, the Turkish guns and forts, and the ensuing battles, ship sinkings, and human and material losses over a definitive time period. Both actions and outcomes were measurable. What is much more difficult to determine is the question of British leadership. Particularly vexing is understanding how Churchill, whose uncanny ability to detect weaknesses in a potential enemy, and whose intuition was so right about grand strategy in two world wars, was so wrong about Gallipoli. But while Churchill paid the political price of a failed campaign in the Dardanelles, history and biography have combined to show that his sense of strategy was as good as ever.

At this point in World War I, the Western front was at a stalemate. Casualties were staggering. War weariness was pervasive. The strategy of the Dardanelles thrust was about breaking the deadlock on the Western front by driving a wedge into Turkey and creating a new Eastern front. It could have been won with more capable local admirals and generals in command (see Massie, 2003, pp. 426–471). However, until one understands Churchill's intentions and the political and military contexts in which he worked, his decisions appear as a huge miscalculation, a failure on a grand scale.

A closer look, however, reveals a more complex situation and Churchill's leadership requires a second appraisal. While behavioral/structural variables exercise a parsimonious hold for a so-called "objective" analysis, the serious researcher of leadership comes to recognize that all situations and outcomes are polyvalent, that is, they have many meanings that are open to multiple interpretations.

Understanding leadership involves more than a simple calculus of behaviors or results of recurrent themes based on surveys. They are too limited to provide much more than a mechanical narrative, however statistically accurate or patterned. In the United States, educational leadership has popularly been replaced with management studies that are much more aligned with sociological/behavioral rules and reduce contextual complexities to axioms, best practices, or "principles." The irony is that in a quest for parsimony and statistically significant results within the locus of numeracy, the leadership quotient is much reduced, for as Michael Mann (2003) has trenchantly observed, "No laws are possible in sociology . . . for the number of cases is far smaller than the number of variables affecting the outcome" (p. 341).

To affect any improved understanding of leadership as a field of study, what must be restored to it are the lives, intentions, interactions, and contexts in which leaders labor and an understanding of the objectives they were pursuing. In this respect, Stephen Skowronek's (1997) biographical work, *The Politics Presidents Make,* is path breaking and predictive. In it Skowronek (1997) observes the following: "Notwithstanding the limitations of method, simple periodization schemes and modern-traditional dichotomies structure most of what we think and write about presidential leadership today" (p. 6). Rejecting a quest for one pattern over another, Skowronek (1997) offers a fresh perspective:

> Some rather ordinary men have wielded extraordinary authority, and some of great repu-
> tation have failed miserably. Political wizards have self-destructed and successful incum-
> bents have not always had the most salutary effects. The characters and talents of the
> incumbents themselves tell us so little about the political impact of presidential leadership
> precisely because leadership has not been a standard test in which each in his turn is given
> an equal opportunity to secure his place in history. (p. 19)

The polyvalencies and contradictions involving leadership cannot be reduced to formulas. To engage in a search for standardized or patterned contexts amounts to a form of reductionism aimed at eliminating the novel. What we may have erased is what we engaged in the research to find. Jung (1958) proffered that while statistical methods provided an "ideal average," this creation did not similarly provide an "empirical reality" (p. 17):

> . . . the real picture consists of nothing but exceptions to the rule, and that, in consequence,
> absolute reality has predominantly the character of irregularity . . . There is and can be no
> self-knowledge based on theoretical assumptions, for the object of self-knowledge is an
> individual—a relative exception and an irregular phenomenon. (p. 17)

The perspective in this book is that the primary function of forms of life writing is to deal with the exceptions, the irregular—the individual. Samier (2005) has called it the restoration of "individual agency" (p. 24). The forms of life writing that are available all in some way accomplish this task, some in greater detail than others.

A Review of the Many Forms of Life Writing

There are at least 12 forms of life writing that may serve as sources for approaching a study of leaders. They are shown in Figure 7.1. The 12 types of life writing are divided into first person and third person forms, and positioned on two axes, life span scope (birth to death) and contextual density (environmental depth). The latter dimension involves a metaphor of what geologists call *ground truth.* Ground truth

❖ **Figure 7.1** Locating First and Third Person Life Writing Forms on Indexes of Contextual Density and Life Span Scope

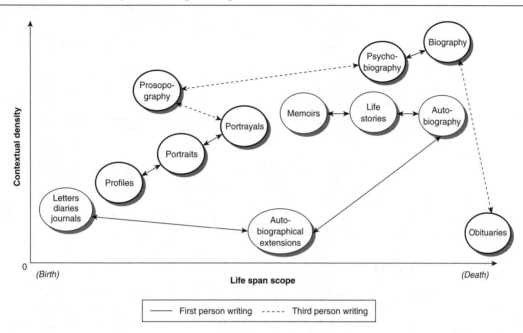

Evokes the dust-on-boots conclusions that arise from personally grabbing samples of rock, walking formations, and exposing fresh stone. Generations of geologists have placed their literal, bedrock faith in ground truth. Ground truth gives scientists the confidence to interpret wide stretches of geography seen from afar. (Petit, 2005, pp. 60, 71)

The concept of ground truth applies almost exclusively to third person forms of life writing. These forms are now briefly explained.

Third Person Forms of Life Writing

Biography

The equivalent of ground truth in biography, for example, is to walk the same ground as the subject. David McCullough (1986), for example, the awards-winning biographer of Harry Truman (1992) and later John Adams (2001), wrote the following:

> You have to know enough so that as you're writing, everything is second nature. And you have to know a great deal that you can't get from books—especially from other people's books on the same subject, or even from printed records, such as letters, diaries, and contemporary newspaper accounts. You have to know the territory. You have to go to the place. (p. 29)

Well-written and intensively researched biography provides the contextual richness essential for understanding how to interpret the actions of a leader because it provides the keys to glimpsing what the leader thought he or she was about in decision making, and the guideposts to how those thoughts were anchored in their core beliefs and perceptions about the world. McCullough (1986) remarks the following about Truman:

> He lived almost ninety years. But at heart he remained a nineteenth-century man. He is from nineteenth-century America. He was never really happy with our twentieth century. He didn't like daylight saving time. He didn't like air conditioning. He didn't like the telephone at all; he would use his pen, or pencil. He would far sooner write a letter than use the telephone. . . . (p. 33)

Robert Caro (1986), a similar Pulitzer Prize winning biographer of Robert Moses (1974) and Lyndon Johnson (1990), determined that to understand the Texan president, he had to actually move to Johnson's Hill Country outside Austin. There, he and his wife resided for 3 years as he visited the people and learned about the former president who had both a light and dark side to his life.

Psychobiography and Theater

Biography is perhaps only equaled as a tool for locating a leader in context by theater, a form of psychobiography. Shakespeare's *Hamlet* is not only an example of an intense psychodrama, but one in which the interiorities of a character are revealed in his own thought processes. Bloom (1998) has called Hamlet a "hero-villain" divulged to himself as he listens to his out-loud thoughts strained through a technique Greenblatt (2004) has called "strategic opacity" (p. 47), in which Shakespeare probed the "dark side" of human interiority.

Another example of psychobiography is Sigmund Freud's (1964) work on Leonardo da Vinci. Freud explored da Vinci's past through the lens of his psychoanalytical theories regarding psychosexual development. While it was an attempt to explain da Vinci's form of homosexuality, it also tried to explain da Vinci's artistic work, and remains, while flawed, a portrait of human narcissism (Strachey, 1961, p. 7).

Prosopography

Prosopography is a biography of a group of persons who lived in the same time period. Some examples include Ribbins and Marland's (1994) *Headship Matters;* Ribbins's (1997) *Leaders and Leadership in the School, Colleges and University;* Pascal and Ribbins's (1998) *Understanding Primary Headteachers;* and Tomlinson, Gunter, and Smith's (1999) *Living Headship: Voices, Values and Vision.*

Another example of prosopography is the personal and moving account of the relationship between Helen Keller and her teacher Anne Sullivan Macy called *Helen and Teacher* by Lash (1980), which was also made into the Broadway play *The Miracle Worker.*

Portraits, Portrayals, and Profiles

Portraits, portrayals, and profiles are examples of third person life writing involving shorter forms than full-length, "ground truth" biography, although they may contain birth–death chronology. When Sara Lawrence-Lightfoot wrote *The Good High School* in 1983, she called her depictions of high school principals "portraits of character and culture." They were sketches of the actions and contexts of six principals in public and private secondary schools. Since then, "portraiture" has become one of the many qualitative research tools in describing the dimensions of educational leadership in doctoral studies at several U.S. universities (see Lawrence-Lightfoot & Hoffman Davis, 1997). The emphasis on portraits and profiles is usually confined to a few contexts or one major context. On the other hand, portrayals usually tend to be more biographical and more advanced on the birth–death axis (see Figure 7.2) but are still not as detailed as a full-length biography.

An educational example of portrayals is Larry Cuban's (1976) *Urban School Chiefs Under Fire,* in which the Stanford professor and former urban school chief sketches out several critical incidents involving big city superintendents. He discusses external pressures in Chicago and Washington, DC, to de-segregate the schools, which caught the superintendents in community-wide controversy, and in San Francisco, a curriculum conflict erupted over so-called "progressive education" with the two teacher unions. Cuban then reviewed the kind of leadership models and implied leadership roles that were at work in each of his portrayals. Cuban (1976) indicated that each of the models tested the limits of leadership. A recent portrayal of the lives and careers of education secretaries in the UK was published by Ribbins and Sherratt in 1997.

Obituaries

The most common form of third person life writing is the obituary. While in most cases obituaries are fairly staid examples formulaic expression, in some publications they have become almost art forms, as those that have been published in *The New York Times.* One of the issues with nearly all third person forms of life writing is a dependence on chronology, of which the obituary is usually the least elegant example. Robert Caro (1986) was once asked whether he thought it was necessary for a biographer to stick to chronology in crafting biography. His response is instructive:

> In the case of the two men I've been writing about—first Robert Moses and now Lyndon Johnson—I think it's absolutely vital to stick to strict chronology because they were so devious. Things they did that you can't understand if you try to take them as isolated decisions suddenly become clear if you just make yourself take one thing after another. Then you see what the person was doing. Dumas Malone wrote the definitive explanation of that in connection with Jefferson—about how Jefferson's mystery falls away if you'll just follow him through life the way he went through life—chronologically. (Caro, 1986, p. 230)

First Person Forms of Life Writing

Autobiography

First person life writing forms consist of autobiography, autobiographical treatises, life stories, memoirs, diaries, letters, and journals. First person accounts always suffer from the inevitable issues of memory loss, selective emphasis and biases, both hidden and deliberate. Hidden biases are those that are caused by cultural eccentricities and blinders. Deliberate biases are due to the author's inattention to aspects of his or her life that are not deemed important or are intentionally omitted. For example, in his autobiography,

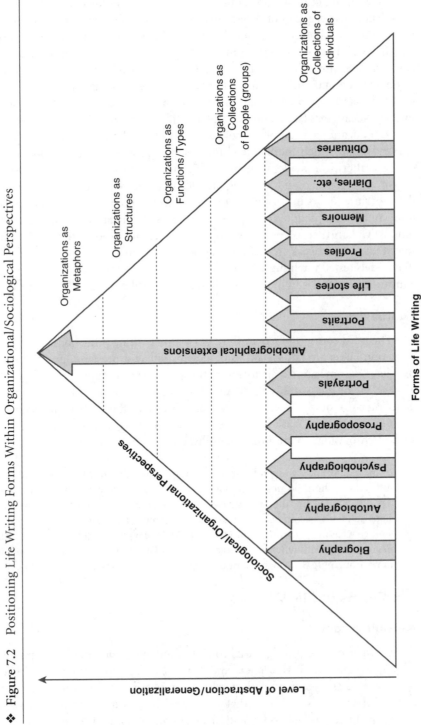

❖ Figure 7.2   Positioning Life Writing Forms Within Organizational/Sociological Perspectives

President Theodore Roosevelt never mentioned his first wife. David McCullough (1986) indicated that when reading autobiographies, one should note that what the person leaves out is revealing. McCullough, who authored a biography of Theodore Roosevelt, said that Roosevelt's autobiographical omission regarding his first wife occurred because "it was too painful" (1986, p. 50). Roosevelt's mother died on the same night as his first wife and it was an overwhelming loss he could hardly bear. McCullough (1986) notes that he reads with some suspicion autobiographies after a person has become famous. There is a natural tendency for humans to want to put a gloss on terribly unpleasant or embarrassing episodes in their lives or to avoid them altogether.

Autobiographical Extensions

Autobiographical extensions represent intellectual/artistic or other writings by people who have also written autobiographies or had biographies written about them. Such extensions apply to such figures as Maria Montessori's (1965/1917) *Spontaneous Activity in Education* or Franklyn's (1974) *My Brilliant Career.*

Life Stories, Memoirs, Diaries, Letters, and Journals

Life stories and memoirs are very closely aligned, often with very little difference between them, although life stories may rank slightly more on the axes of life span scope than memoirs. One example of a memoir covering a 4-year period is Peter McLaren's "Crises From the Corridor: Teaching in the Suburban Ghetto," in his book *Life in Schools,* in which he describes his 4-year stint as an inner-city elementary schoolteacher in Toronto, Canada.

Gauging the Possibilities of Life Writing to Understand Leadership

The possibilities of understanding leadership from the 12 forms of life writing reviewed in this book depend on how the reader views them. If the reader believes that such forms are not scientific and are not very reliable (although perhaps interesting), life writing will offer very little in the way of improved insights or understanding of leadership. Such a perspective will concentrate on continuing to approach leadership through behavioral/structural lenses because they are most congruent with the tools at hand. The scholarship produced by these perspectives will continue to look like that of Kouzes and Posner's (2002) best-selling book, *The Leadership Challenge.* This work offers five practices for leadership: (a) model the way, (b) inspire a shared vision, (c) challenge the process, (d) enable others to act, and (e) encourage the heart (Kouzes & Posner, p. 22). Such generic nostrums are platitudes proffered without any sensitivity to context.

If this is the kind of "research" that a person believes will lead to improvement in leadership, then forms of life writing as important sources to divulge an enhanced understanding of leadership are nearly superfluous. Life writing is about context and the interaction between a perceiving human being and his or her context. The purpose of the research by Kouzes and Posner (2002) is to minimize context.

In this sense the research by Kouzes and Posner (2002) follows a line of studies that are interested in context-free generalizations about an abstracted set of laws that are good for all times and places. As John Keegan (1987) has observed, it was the same idea that propelled the establishment of military academies such as Sandhurst and West Point in the 19th century. As is the case with Kouzes and Posner's (2002) work, Keegan indicates that such studies like theirs are the methods of social scientists and, as will all social science, "condemn those who practise them to the agony of making universal and general what is stubbornly local and particular . . . the generalship of one age and place may not at all resemble that of another (p. 1) [because context] is all" (p. 3).

The forms of life writing reviewed in this book begin to introduce to the study of leadership increasingly denser forms of context ("ground truth"; see Petit, 2005) across the life span of the leader (see Figure 7.2). The richness of context is a necessary ingredient to begin differentiating forms of leadership, not in an attempt to derive universal laws and erase the contexts, but to begin to match the variety of contexts with various arrays of decisions and subsequent actions and outcomes that follow within them. The more complex the leadership situation the more likely that Michael Mann's (2003) admonition may be relevant, that is, that no laws are possible in sociology because the number of variables exceeds the number of cases. The use of various forms of life writing may well underscore Mann's point. To make sense of a leader's actions one must come to understand the context in which the leader was working. Then one must also try to make sense of the interaction between all of the various personality factors at work within that context, such as the leader's world view, character, and working style as he or she functions within a climate of expectations and various forms of existing power relationships (see Barber, 1985).

The continued proliferation of studies of leadership such as the Kouzes and Posner (2002) variety offer very little to leaders in general and to educational leaders specifically. Cuban's (1976) study of large city school superintendents is instructive: "The times, the local political context, and the dominant conception of leadership may well determine whether a schoolman can do an effective job or not. There are fall, summer, spring, and winter superintendents—but none for all seasons" (p. 170).

Cuban (1976) proffers that there exists a very slim margin of leadership actually available to superintendents as chief executive officers (CEOs) of "massive organizations" by which they "will be able to parlay the multiple, conflicting roles into a leadership constellation that delivers both symbolic and real gains" (p. 171). The primacy of coming to grips with the decision-making context is the locus for such a constellation.

Table 7.1 illustrates how the continuing utilization of organizational sociology (organizational theory) obliterates forms of life writing as viable sources of information about leadership.

Early organizational forms concentrating on leadership examined it as collections of individuals. For example, Frederick Taylor's (1967/1911) seminal work on scientific management consisted of looking at individual workers in industrial settings. It was assumed that as individual workers became more productive, the organization as a whole became more productive. In the last decade, John Gardner's (1991) book *On Leadership* or Gary Wills's (1994) *Certain Trumpets: The Nature of Leaders,* assume the same perspective.

School climate studies assume that organizations are groups of people. In education, climate studies involve one person, the principal or headmaster, the faculty, and the nature of the interactions between them. Climate studies began with the research of Andrew Halpin (1966), who worked for the U.S. Air Force gauging the performance

❖ Table 7.1 Definitions and Examples of 12 Life Writing Forms

Life Writing Form	Definition	Exemplars
1. Biography	A written narrative of one person by another, most often historical/chronological in form, that attempts to offer a verbal picture of some depth of an individual of importance or notoriety.	– Jacqueline Goggin's *Carter G. Woodson* – Kurt Leidecker's *Yankee Teacher* – Robert Caro's *The Power Broker* – David McCullough's *Truman* – Johnathan Messerli's *Horace Mann*
2. Psycho-biography/theater	A written narrative of one person by another that attempts to explain that person's life preferences and choices from a psychological perspective based on an implicit or explicit psychological theory or theory of morals or a moral code, written or unwritten. Many of Shakespeare's tragedies are biographies or portrayals of figures in dramatic context.	– Sigmund Freud's *Leonardo da Vinci and a Memory of His Childhood* – Mary Francis Berry's *Reflecting a Tarnished America* – Peter Gronn's *Psychobiography on the Couch: Character, Biography and the Comparative Study of Leaders* – In theater, Shakespeare's tragedies, *Hamlet, Julius Caesar, King Lear, Macbeth, Antony and Cleopatra*
3. Autobiography	A written interpretation and presentation of one's own life, often in chronological order, that tries to explain the forces that shaped one's perspectives and actions in the world.	– Ida B. Wells's *Crusade for Justice* – Jesse Stuart's *To Teach, To Love* – Sandra Dean's *Hearts and Minds, a Public School Miracle*
4. Life stories	A form of autobiography, often with a thematic centering.	– Helen Keller's *The Story of My life* – Clarence Darrow's *The Story of My life*
5. Autobiographical treatises/extensions	A form of life writing that presents a point of view distinctly autobiographical, which may be intellectual, political, military, theological, and from which glimpses of a person's life, values, and perspectives may be derived.	– John Gardner's *On Leadership* – M. Franklyn's *My Brilliant Career* – Maria Montessori's *Spontaneous Activity in Education* – Deborah Meier's *The Power of Their Ideas*
6. Portraits	Fairly detailed biographical/anecdotal verbal renderings of personages of fame or renown that are not full-blown/in-depth biographies.	– Socrates as noted in Plato's *Dialogues* – *Plutarch's Parallel Lives* – Merle Curti's *The Black Man's Place: Booker T. Washington* – Sarah Lawrence Lightfoot's *The Good High School*

(Continued)

❖ **Table 7.1** (Continued)

Life Writing Form	Definition	Exemplars
7. Portrayals	A written and detailed account of a specific episode or event in a person's or persons', life/lives.	– Peter Ribbins and Brian Sherratt's *Radical Educational Policies and Conservative Secretaries of State* – Larry Cuban's *Urban School Chiefs Under Fire* – Harry Wolcott's *The Man in the Principal's Office: An Ethnography*
8. Profiles	Written snippets of famous or revered personages that provide a glimpse of their personalities, characters, or eccentricities.	– Glen and Joan Smith's *Lives in Education* – Craig Kridel's *Teachers and Mentors: Profiles of Distinguished Twentieth-Century Professors of Education* – Peter Gronn's *The Boyhood, Schooling and Early Career of J.R. Darling*
9. Memoirs	Written recollections in narrative, chronological form that highlight what an individual believes are important events or people in his/her life. A form of autobiography.	– Terrel Bell's *The Thirteenth Man: A Reagan Cabinet Memoir* – Gerald Grant's *The World We Created at Hamilton High*
10. Diaries, letters, and journals	Short, written passages that may be culled and woven into a larger narrative fabric usually governed by the rule of chronology and periodization.	– Peter McLaren's *Life in Schools* – Michael B. Katz's *School Reform: Past and Present*
11. Prosopography	A form of group biography usually identified within a specific time period or event.	– Peter Ribbins and M. Marland's *Headship Matters: Conversations With Seven Secondary School Headteachers* – Smith, Kleine, Prunty, and Dwyer's *Educational Innovators: Then and Now* – Joseph Lash's *Helen and Teacher*
12. Obituary	The most common form of biography, usually a compacted narrative regarding birth and death of famous persons or celebrities with a few highlights of their lives or careers.	Obituary columns in *The Economist* or *The New York Times*

of B-29 bomber crews over Korean targets and the number of them destroyed (pp. 91–92). This "outcome-based" research was related to crew morale and the group's relationship to the bomber's captain.

Max Weber differentiated between leaders by types (Gerth & Mills, 1970). From this point, leaders as individuals began to be erased until they became "actors" and were marginalized in importance as social science research began to abstract humans into more and more faceless functions (Hall, 1972). As the focus shifted to systems and away from humans with values, emotions, and needs, social science became concerned with predictability of activities and behavior was to be rational, perhaps best epitomized in the concept of "bounded rationality" (March & Simon, 1966).

As forms of organizational sociology/theory became more abstracted with works by Mintzberg (1983), which focused on horizontal and vertical job specialization and the various "pulls" between subconfigurations within the total organizational structure, or Nadler and Tushman's (1988) structural decisions triggered by strategic shifts in the environment, the individual human was totally effaced as an important variable, or in the words of Argyris (1972), "the variable human seems to be minimally variable and minimally human" (p. 33). Finally, the approach taken by Morgan (1986) is to envision organizations simply as metaphors. If, for example, the dominant metaphors of an organization are mechanistic, then the processes of the organization are about determining which repetitive actions will lead to the greatest efficiencies.

It can be seen in Table 7.1 that nearly all forms of life writing would be confined to the lowest level of organizational abstraction. Exceptions would be prosopography, the study of individuals as a group or class of persons, and autobiographical extensions. This latter category permits an examination of a person from his or her position on a variety of subjects. For example, Deborah Meier's (1995) *The Power of Their Ideas* is not only a work about her success at Central Park East in Harlem, but it contains a good bit about her views on leadership and the challenges she faced in innovating in the nation's largest public school bureaucracy.

The continued dominance of organizational theory in educational leadership preparation programs works to marginalize the importance not only of leaders as individuals, but of all humans in educational organizations. Logically, and as a corollary, the importance of life writing is similarly marginalized. Life writing is not important as long as lives are not important, or as Carr (1985) has noted, "Life that is not some kind of story is unthinkable—or more precisely, unlivable" (p. 120).

A full consideration of the benefits of biography and life writing as important sources in understanding leadership will involve a serious reconsideration of how leadership has been reduced to a select set of social science variables and finally earmarked as unnecessary at all in the grand scheme of things, a position recently advocated by Lakomski (2005).

The intellectual countermovement to such a "final erasure" of the human leader is to reposition leadership as acts of theater and performance, and to recast leading as artful because it involves forms of drama (see Starratt, 1993). In this turning, biography and life writing forms will have much to say about leadership, as they have since Plato and Plutarch, and there is something innately human about great persons that is both fascinating and enduring (see Rost, 1991, pp. 70–75).

BIOGRAPHY BOX 7.1

Septima Poinsette Clark (1898–1987)

Fearless Schoolteacher Who Developed Civil Rights Leaders

She began teaching on Johns Island, South Carolina, in a school that had no glass windows and was heated by a wood fireplace. She had one coteacher and 132 students. For her work she was paid $60 while a white teacher who had three students on the island was paid $85. Septima was fired from her job in 1956 because she belonged to the National Association for the Advancement of Colored People (NAACP; Clark, 1986). Thereafter for almost 20 years she took up her work as a civil rights leader, involving herself with the Highlander Folk School in Monteagle, Tennessee, where Clark worked on the development of training African Americans in literacy and methods for active political participation to promote social justice. She eventually returned to Johns Island and opened a school for citizenship participation that was a model all across the South (Murtadha, 2006, p. 142).

Clark traveled all over the South working to register African Americans to vote and empowering them to take political control of their lives. She had a knack for selecting those who could be future leaders. She also had to struggle within the African American community to convince the male leadership that women could be and should be on the forefront of the fight for civil rights. One person who she was unable to convince was her own husband, who thought a woman should stay in the home. She later said, "Women need to grab the men by the collar and do more . . . We still have a hard time getting them to see what it means to vote" (Clark, 1986).

In an ironic twist of fate, Clark also became the first black woman to serve on the Charleston Public School Board of Education, from 1978 to 1983. She worked all her life to equalize pay between African American and white schoolteachers. She recounted that her mother was reared in Haiti and had learned English very well. Her mother also was fearless and proud as well as very strict with her children.

Clark recounted that in Haitian the name "Septima" means "sufficient" and that her aunt in Haiti was named "Septima Peace," connoting "sufficient peace" (Lanker, 1989, p. 168). However, Clark recalled that she was never "sufficient" and had never been very peaceful.

Recalling that her life was about fostering social change, she reminisced that she had a "great belief . . . that whenever there is chaos, it creates wonderful thinking. I consider chaos a gift" (Lanker, 1989, p. 168). Clark felt very differently about change than most educational leaders who fear social upheaval. She had been part of one of the nation's greatest social upheavals in its history as African Americans once again demanded and this time gained full rights to citizenship. African American women such as Clark were on the forefront of that conflict when it happened.

Confronting the Myopia of "the Field"

Too many educational leaders see themselves as continuing the legacy of efficiency in systems theory and refurbished total quality management. Educational leaders have not been agents of moral leadership. Both schools and society continue to be plagued with issues of racism, sexism, poverty, and homophobia. Continuing to look for possible solutions inside behavioral-structural models offers no solutions to intense moral issues. However, the myopia of the field has precluded both practitioners and professors from expanding its borders to the arts, where moral dilemmas have been the topic of discussion and debate for thousands of years. It is not an accident that the neoconservative domination of politics and political thought in the United States has its foundation in the humanities and not the sciences. A key thinker who has served as a focal point for neoconservative doctrine was Leo Strauss (1899–1973), a professor at the University of Chicago, who had earlier fled Europe when the Nazis came to power in Germany. Strauss's writings (2001) were not based on "management science" or "social science research based investigations" as advanced by the National Research Council's *Scientific Research in Education* (2002) and subsequently published in peer reviewed business, educational, or technical journals, but rather "long and dense interpretive essays on Plato, Thucydides, Alfarabi, Maimonides, Machiavelli, Hobbes and other philosophers" (Fukuyama, 2006, p. 22). The world of action in leadership must be grounded in a thorough understanding of the moral dilemmas facing schools, society, and the world, and not a technical subset of those issues stripped of the "subjectivities" that are messy and do not lend themselves easily, if at all, to the strictures of social science.

Before we reduce educational leadership to a collection of organizational abstractions completely devoid of the human variable, we ought to pause and reflect if our quest for a science of leadership hasn't led us to the ultimate Weberian "iron cage" where "economic man" works "without regard to the person . . . without hate and therefore without love" (Gerth & Mills, 1970, p. 334). In this respect, biography and life writing are not only the antidote, but the raison d'etre leaders and leadership still matter, not only for schools, but in human societies everywhere.

Servant Leadership: The Mind and the Heart as One

The antithesis of an exemplar of leadership, which often lies behind the concept of the modern business CEO, is the work of Robert K. Greenleaf. Greenleaf came from industry, but he was not the archetype of the CEO. He lived and worked in AT&T's management echelon that was responsible for leadership development. He created an approach to leadership and leadership development that began with the notion that leaders were not extraordinary people, or simply the product of their position, education, income, religion, or ethnicity (Frick, 2004, p. 254), but rather, ordinary people who learned how to be leaders. Greenleaf, a Quaker by choice, believed in an approach to leadership that was noncoercive, and nonmanipulative. Much of what motivated Robert Greenleaf were Quaker beliefs in which all persons were equal before God, and a person did not speak among a congregation until the spirit within prompted him or her to do so. Quakers have no formal roles or clerical hierarchy. They practiced the art of consensus decision making, constructed meetings so that everyone could participate, and believed not in what they had found, but rather piety was about "seeking" to know, waiting on the "light within" to shine. They referred to themselves as "seekers" (Frick, 2004, p. 126). Bob Greenleaf's "hero" was George Fox, the founder of the Quakers.

When Robert Greenleaf began organizing leadership development for AT&T, he went to the humanities for his curriculum and not the business school. His courses included logic, music, art, American civilization, architecture, city planning, philosophy, law, economic thought, social history, and literature (Frick, 2004, p. 157). Greenleaf defined leadership in the corporate world as follows: "Management ability is the ability to state a goal and reach it, through the efforts of other people, and satisfy those whose judgment must be respected, under conditions of stress" (Frick, 2004, p. 154). It is instructive that Greenleaf's evaluation of the success of his leadership development was not in how much money he made or if stockholder shares increased in value: "The only objective for manager education which seemed dependable for the future was that of inculcating a research and experimental attitude toward work and a sustaining interest in personal growth" (Frick, 2004, p. 158).

Greenleaf proffered that a leader was a servant. He was concerned that there was too much of a tendency to deal with unresolved social issues of the day through system approaches, ideologies, and other types of movements. His second concern was "for the individual as a serving person and the tendency to deny wholeness in oneself by failing to lead when one can lead, or by not choosing with discrimination when it is more appropriate to follow" (Greenleaf, 1978, pp. 3–4). Greenleaf's writings became more popular and widespread. One of his readers was a medical doctor named Patch Adams who thought that humor played a large role in the healing process. Adams's story was later the subject of a film in which the doctor was played by Robin Williams. Greenleaf recognized that more and more social issues were being handled by institutions. Leaders in these institutions had to care deeply about people and believe that if a better society was going to be built it had to be done through organizations such as schools. Greenleaf's proposal was to turn the usual hierarchical, pyramidal organization chart into a circle akin to a Quaker meeting. Greenleaf also recognized that when the times were short and drastic action was called for, one couldn't always call for a meeting of all participants. But when such an approach was practiced in good times, it made the tough times easier to handle. There was better understanding and trust among the participants. Greenleaf observed, "I think it is possible to be strong without being tough and that one doesn't have to lose her or his gentleness just because some apparent hurtful action has to be taken" (Frick, 2004, p. 289). The notion of the effective servant leader began with listening, very hard listening. And it included personal reflection and introspection. Above all else, it was hard work, but a very different kind of leadership work than typically envisioned by today's business or education executive. Servant leadership is about empowerment. It isn't giving power to people. Rather it is enabling people to become powerful, finding the leaders in themselves. While it is practical and patient, it is also very spiritual, not so much in any religious sense, but in the way it cares for the interiority of human beings and respects differences and believes in the possibility of human growth. A servant leader first wants to serve and second wants to lead to serve. Greenleaf observed, "Everything begins with the individual— 'in here, not out there!'" (Frick, 2004, p. 348).

Pursuing Learning Extensions of the Chapter

The learning extensions of the chapter involve some of the films now listed. They are intended to illustrate some of the ideas about leadership described in the chapter and present models of leadership.

Mandela: Son of Africa, Father of a Nation (1996), Color and Black and White, DVD, Palm Pictures, 1 Hour 58 Minutes

This documentary about the life of Nelson Mandela was an Oscar nominee for best documentary in 1996. It is expertly edited, and contains trips by Mandela to his childhood home, where he recounts his upbringing and where he learned about his tribal heritage. It contains footage of Mandela's sojourn back to Robben Island, where he spent over two decades in prison and where he explains prison routines and how he and his fellow revolutionaries kept alive while the apartheid regime sought to break them. Mandela's work ethic, his "leadership style," is amply illustrated with actual videos of his meetings and with his election to the first president of South Africa in which Africans were allowed to vote. Mandela says about retaining these events that " . . . memory is of fundamental importance. It is the fabric of identity . . . The struggle against apartheid can be typified as the pitting of remembering against forgetting" (Mandela, 2006, p. 9). This is an inspiring film in which leadership, communication, context, and culture come together in "real time" sequences.

The Fog of War (2004), Color and Black and White, DVD, Sony Pictures Classic, 1 Hour 47 Minutes

Winner of the best documentary feature award by several film critics associations, this film features former Defense Secretary Robert M. McNamara in a candid, autobiographical portrait in which he recounts the fateful decisions that triggered the Vietnam War. He acknowledges that he was wrong and that American leaders completely misread what the Vietnamese War was all about, that is, a civil war as opposed to a war of liberation. Actual newsreel footage is shown of meetings in Washington, DC, and tapes of President Lyndon Johnson in telephone conversations with McNamara, which are revealing of the deep misgivings of the war's progress as time went on and there was no American victory. The film highlights McNamara's "10 lessons" about leadership, especially in war, many of which echo in the writings of Machiavelli. One of the aspects of the film that is superbly illustrated is how leaders can be misled, even when they believe they are acting logically and rationally. No social science research study could have produced this stunning testimony to the fragility of human leadership.

Elizabeth (1998), Color, VHS, Poly Graham, 2 Hours 4 Minutes

This film chronicles the rise to power of Elizabeth 1 (1533–1603), daughter of Henry VIII and Anne Boleyn, his second wife to be Queen of England. Superbly played by Golden Globe winner Cate Blanchett for best actress, the young queen shrewdly negotiates her way to consolidate her authority in divided land between Catholics and Protestants. The film is a great display of nearly all of Niccolo Machiavelli's warnings and admonitions about ruling and amply demonstrates the notion of executive (root word *execute*) and secretary (root word *secret*) as the modern day forerunner of the CEO.

Heart of the Country (1998), Color, VHS, Alaska Center for Documentary Film, University of Alaska, 1 Hour

This is an award-winning film (from the National Education Association) about Shinichi Yasutomo, an extraordinary elementary school principal in Hokkaido, Japan, which exemplifies many of the ideas of Robert Greenleaf as a servant-leader who inspires by example and by listening. Yasutomo expertly shows how deep caring, loyalty, and sensitivity to the students, teachers, and the community create the kind of school climate and culture that lead to commitment and achievement. The film uses English subtitles.

Writing in Your Personal Reflective Journal

This chapter was concerned with re-inserting whole lives into a study of leadership, not simply reading a "research study" about the characteristics of leaders. Reflect on the leaders you admire the most. What do you actually know about them? Consult Internet site reviews in search of information about your favorite leaders. What are the characteristics that stand out in your mind about them? What did the leaders actually do to merit being a leader? Who followed them? What did they expect? What did they desire? How did the goals of the leaders and followers mesh? What types of contexts did your leaders encounter and how did they display the capacity to inspire others?

A Review of Key Chapter Concepts

ground truth—This is the idea that to understand the true nature of things, a researcher or a biographer has to tread the ground the subject actually walked on, and stand in the places seen by the object of study to really grasp what was perceived as "true" by those being described. Ground truth is centered in first-hand knowledge gathered directly in the environment being written about.

individual agency—This is the idea that individual persons are powerful, can act independently of their environments, and act in ways that can change their organizations. Too many studies in administration minimize the importance of the individual human in the amalgam of structural components and variables. In such studies, the importance of morality and moral decision making is subjugated to the organization. While schools are forms of organizations, to lose sight of individual students, teachers, and leaders is to de-humanize the entire enterprise.

life writing—This refers to a broad variety of forms of writing in which a person's entire life or part of his or her life is the subject of the writing. Life writing is usually in the first or third person. The most inclusive third person form is the full-length biography. The most comprehensive form of the first person life writing is the autobiography. Shorter forms of life writing include memoirs, diaries, letters, and journals.

8

Artful Performance and National Standards

The main focus of this book has been on attempting to balance artful performance with accountability within educational leadership. This has not been an easy task.

The current national standards for the preparation of school leaders focus heavily on marketing efficiency metaphors and concepts. Such standards have a long history in the field, tracing their origin to scientific management and later total quality management. Currently the national standards for evaluating preparation programs for educational leaders focus on accountability and assessment strategies that are not reflective of the actual practice of educational leadership. They have little to do with artful performance as outlined in this book. This chapter reviews the challenges facing the profession in correcting the imbalance.

Sections of this chapter first appeared in F. English (2003e), *Leadership and Policy in Schools*, 2(1), pp. 27–46, and are reprinted with permission from the publisher, Taylor and Francis.

The movement for the creation of national standards for school leaders gained momentum in the United States when in 1988 the National Policy Board for Educational Administration (NPBEA) was formed. This organization was comprised of the University Council of Educational Administration (UCEA), as well as practitioner associations such as the American Association of School Administrators (AASA), the National Association of Secondary School Administrators (NASSP), and others. From this effort came a host of standards for principals and superintendents advanced by the national practitioner associations that had the purpose of establishing a baseline for assessing job performance, creating staff development programs, guiding graduate study projects, and serving as possible benchmarks for degree and licensure exams as well as the basis for examining the content of university preparation courses and programs.

This movement was given more serious import when in 1994 the Council for Chief State School Officers created the Interstate School Leaders Licensure Consortium (ISLLC; Murphy & Shipman, 2002, p. 4). The ISLLC has been adopted by nearly 30 states and has become the basis for a national exam known as the School Leaders Licensure Assessment (SLLA). In addition, the National Council for the Accreditation of Teacher Education (NCATE) adopted the ISLLC standards in judging the efficacy of preparation programs at the university and college levels. In some states, accreditation is required by state regulation, or university programs can be shut down. In a final step, NCATE subcontracted the review of university programs to the Educational Leadership Constituent Council (ELCC), which is comprised of five national administrative associations who pay a membership fee to review and judge university/college programs.

The National Leadership Standards

The ISLLC-ELCC standards were adopted by NCATE in January of 2002. They are shown in Table 8.1.

It is instructive to review the "framing principles" of the ISLLC standards because here we see the instrumentality and indexes of efficiency clearly at work. The standards are silent about what might constitute "artful performance." The ISLLC framing principles with commentary are shown in Table 8.2.

Foucault's Concept of Apparatus

The perceptive analyses of Michel Foucault (see Gordon, 1980, p. 119) regarding the nature of a political apparatus takes shape when a group of institutions develop an interlocking agenda around what they consider to be the essential "facts" or truth about something. This "regime of truth" is a system where "truth is to be understood as a system of ordered procedures for the production, regulation, distribution, circulation and operation of statements" (Gordon, 1980, p. 133). As Foucault (1979) makes clear in his classic work, *Discipline and Punish,* a regime of truth is an expression of power knowledge that not only includes the authority to repress and engage in denial and rejection, but produces forms of knowledge and creates its own discursive practice (see Fairclough, 1992). We see this regime of truth expressed in the ELCC standards. What is extremely disturbing is that the knowledge constructed and produced by the ELCC standards embraces the doctrine of efficiency, namely, standardization. The ELCC knowledge base has been cleansed of variance (difference). Variance is always a fundamental problem when efficiency is its own end, or a teleology. Variance is also a problem in extending control and in being responsive to appeals based on decisions in which variance has caused different interpretations being simultaneously offered for legitimacy. In an environment in which agencies must work to extend their power because none exercise it over the entire arena of discourse, the contestation of power being applied rests on unambiguous interpretation. NCATE has already been criticized

❖ **Table 8.1**   The Interstate School Leaders Licensure Consortium (ISLLC) Standards for the Preparation and Licensure of Educational Leaders

Standard	Area
1	A school administrator is an educational leader who promotes the success of all students by facilitating the development, articulation, implementation, and stewardship of a vision of learning that is shared and supported by the school community.
2	A school administrator is an educational leader who promotes the success of all students by advocating, nurturing, and sustaining a school culture and instructional program conducive to student learning and staff professional growth.
3	A school administrator is an educational leader who promotes the success of all students by ensuring management of the organization, operations, and resources for a safe, efficient, and effective learning environment.
4	A school administrator is an educational leader who promotes the success of all students by collaborating with families and community members, responding to diverse community interests and needs, and mobilizing community resources.
5	A school administrator is an educational leader who promotes the success of all students by acting with integrity, with fairness, and in an ethical manner.
6	A school administrator is an educational leader who promotes the success of all students by understanding, responding to, and influencing the larger political, social, economic, legal, and cultural contexts.

on the problem of ambiguity (see Seidel, 2002, p. 10). The importance of power knowledge is that it "always points away from power towards 'objective' measurement of what is there 'naturally.' Assessment is therefore carried out against 'objective' criteria which subjects have to accept (because not to do so would be irrational and deviant)" (Usher & Edwards, 1996, p. 103).

We see with the ELCC standards all of the trappings of the use of power over a contested terrain, and the creation of interagency collaboration to engage in the policing function. To do so unambiguously and retain the facade of neutrality, the knowledge base issue has been sanitized and reframed in the language of technical efficiency or what Ball (1991) has called "management as moral technology" (p. 157) and Sergiovanni (2000) has called "one best way thinking" (p. viii).

Problems With the Knowledge Base: Producing an Unequivocal Platform for the Normalizing Gaze and the Policing Function

To engage in this kind of political policing actions, a platform is required to shroud them in a discourse that is acceptable to those who may be disciplined. For sanctions

❖ **Table 8.2** Major Metaphors of the Interstate School Leaders Licensure Consortium (ISLLC) Framing Principles

Framing principle	Commentary
Standards should reflect the centrality of student learning.	This is not related to artful performance by the educational leader. There are no descriptors for performance. The metaphor is the "black box" of inputs/outputs in simple economic models.
Standards should acknowledge the changing role of school leadership.	This principle is not related to the performance of the educational leader. Role changes and performance in the role are two separate things.
Standards should recognize the collaborative nature of school leadership.	A "recognition" of the need for collaboration says nothing about the performance required to collaborate.
Standards should be high, upgrading the quality of the profession.	This refers to entry requirements to the profession and has little to do with performance once within the profession.
Standards should inform performance-based systems of assessment and evaluation for school leaders.	The framing principle is silent about the nature of what constitutes "performance" except to indicate a system would be "performance based."
Standards should be integrated and coherent.	Standards can be both and not indicate artful performance.
Standards should be predicated on the concepts of access, opportunity, and empowerment for all members of the school community.	Standards may have all of these components and have nothing to do with artful performance, meaning they don't define good practice.

SOURCE: From *A Framework for School Leaders: Linking the ISLLC Standards to Practice,* by Hessel and Holloway, 2002. Princeton, NJ: Educational Testing Service, p. 6

to work, those who can be disciplined must consent to the process. For such possibilities to be acceptable, the actions have to be perceived as unambiguous, nonpolitical, and fairly applied. The exercise of surveillance inherent in policing depends on a norm "that works by excluding; it defines a standard and criteria of judgment thus identifying all those who do not meet the standard" (Usher & Edwards, 1996, p. 103). Foucault (1979) describes this idea as "the normalizing gaze" and its significance is that "it appears to be neutral" (Usher & Edwards, 1996, p. 103). This is extremely difficult to do when the knowledge base is actually ambiguous, multidimensional, highly subjective, nonempirical, and filled with huge epistemological holes (see Anderson, 2001; Dantley & Rogers, 2001; English, 2000; 2002a; Furman & English, 2002; Littrell & Foster, 1995; Marshall & McCarthy, 2002).

To engage in actions that may potentially disbar preparation programs from continuing, the knowledge base on the which the ELCC standards rest has to be portrayed as the following: (a) unequivocal and unidimensional, (b) possess the veneer of objectivity and scientificity, and (c) be supported by forms of political consensus that minimize the dissent that will emerge when policing actions result in disbarment. In short, the frailties, complexities, contradictions, and discontinuities embedded in the knowledge base must be simplified (Murphy, Yff, & Shipman, 2000) or obscured or denied (Murphy, 2000), and alternatives denigrated or ridiculed as unworthy of serious consideration (see Murphy, 1999, p. 48). Many of these conversations and tensions already dot the landscape in the emerging literature (see Capper, 1995; Gronn, 2002; Larson & Murtadha, 2002; Scheurich, 1995).

Retracing the Steps in the Developmental Process

The steps by which the ISLLC-ELCC standards were created are as follows: (a) eliminating the full scope of an administrator's responsibilities to a "core" (Murphy et al., 2000, pp. 23–24); (b) developing generic standards that are good for all school levels irrespective of locality, student mix, or even school specific objectives (the elimination of context; see Anderson, 2001, p. 207); (c) the marginalization of any research or questioning of the efficacy of the standards by defining and confining acceptable research to the standards themselves (NPBEA, 2002, p. 16); and (d) the installation of a regime of truth by linking the standards to program accreditation (Gordon, 1980, p. 119; English, 2003b, p. 131; English, 2006).

Step 1: Reductionism, Rationality, and Core Technologies

The ISLLC-ELCC standards were created by de-limiting the previous work that had been done in the field to map "the existing leadership terrain" (Murphy et al., 2000, p. 24). Step 1 was to severely de-limit the terrain to a "core technology" (Murphy et al., 2000, p. 23) defined on ideological grounds. The process of de-limitation of a school administrator's job was bolstered by a belief or a tenet rather than a set of empirical or theoretical constraints. First, the proponents were afraid that what they "privileged" (placed in the most important position) in the administrator's job was learning and teaching and that this value would be displaced if all aspects of the job were considered. They also confessed the following: "Also, those dimensions of the job that traditionally have not been tightly linked to learning and teaching were recast in the service of school improvement and student performance" (Murphy et al., 2000, p. 23).

The need for tight linkages between functions in schools has long been sought by those trying to reform schools (Eisner, 2003; Wise, 1979, pp. 55–56). It represents a push for a highly rational organization in which means and ends are connected and can be subjected to cost–benefit analyses. Art Wise (1979) noted the following:

> Two mechanisms which couple some non-school organizations are "technical core"—an automobile factory is coupled by its technical core as embodied in its assembly line, for example—and "authority in office"—a military organization is coupled by its authority of office as embodied in the chain-of-command. The school may be coupled by neither of these mechanisms. (p. 93)

Three things are accomplished by de-limiting the range of tasks of the school administrator. The first is that the necessary rationality required to link administrative actions to outcomes (tight means–ends relationships) can be accomplished when the potential range is narrowed. This is a requirement of most state-imposed accountability schemes (see Wise, 1979, pp. 58–61). The second is that context as an important variable in the job is eliminated. Such elimination was accomplished by a belief that "there is a single set of standards that applies to all leadership positions" (Murphy et al., 2000, p. 23). A third result is that by de-complexifying the job via standardization of the work tasks, the costs of administrative preparation can be similarly reduced and educational administration programs removed from the university campus to the Internet and to other agencies that will prepare administrators for profit (English, 2003c). A uniform set of standards that is not contextually contingent and that is theoretically simple greatly assists in such a transfer. Uniform standards that also eliminate the importance of the university's research function open the doors to not only lateral entry by candidates who might not otherwise quality for university admission, but competition from former agencies that had no chance to engage in such efforts before with any legitimacy.

Thus, job standardization eliminates or severely erodes the primacy of professional preparation in a university setting. It also eliminates any unique university approach to professional preparation. For example, those university programs now deeply concerned about social justice (which are not reflected in the ISLLC standards) are no longer relevant in the preparation of school administrators when the content knowledge is acquired via the Internet and licensure guaranteed with passage of the School Leaders Licensure Assessment (SLLA).

Step 2: The Erasure of Context So One Size Fits All

The erasure of the importance of context in shaping job tasks accomplished by assumption in the ISLLC-ELCC standards conforms to the need for a high degree of rationality to connect means and ends (inputs and outputs) and to accomplish job de-skilling. When the administrator's job can be simplified and narrowed, a generic test can be employed to assess a candidate's "competence." But as Anderson (2001) notes about the SLLA, it is an instrument that not only rewards glibness and superficiality, but "enforces administration as a systematic exercise in the legitimation of the status quo that favours certain social groups over others" (p. 214).

Standardization as a strategy depends on the elimination of variation. When it comes to defining work tasks, the strategy of Frederick Taylor, who has been described as a "thoroughgoing rationalist" (Kanigel, 1997, p. 397), prevails to this day, whether it be for the administrative leadership of schools or for the de-skilling of short order cooks, which was one of the secrets of the rise of McDonald's fast food outlets (Schlosser, 2001, p. 20).

When a common set of standards applies to not only all principalships, but all formal leadership positions as averred by Murphy and Shipman (2002, p. 4), then administrators become interchangeable parts, and "jobs that have been 'de-skilled' can be filled cheaply. The need to retain any individual worker is greatly reduced by the ease with which he or she can be replaced" (Schlosser, 2001, p. 70).

Another downside regarding the loss of context in shaping generic standards is that professional practice is considered apart from the situation in which it is embedded. What is lost is what has been described as "circumstance contingent," in which outcomes will vary because of situational differences (Christensen & Raynor, 2003, p. 71). It isn't just defining the nature of a "core" that is important, but rather answering the question "Under what circumstances will staying close to the core help me sustain superior returns and when will it be critical to set the forces of creative destruction to work?" (Christensen & Raynor, p. 71). It is the circumstances or context that is crucial to success. In this respect, the ISLLC standards are framed on a static model of school improvement supposedly good for all times and all places. Claims that standards apply to virtually all positions irrespective of context should be considered skeptically. In considering such claims in the world of business, Christensen and Raynor comment as follows:

> If the authors imply that their findings apply to all companies in all situations, don't trust them. Usually things are the way they are for pretty good reasons. We need to know not only where, when, and why things must change, but also what should stay the same. (p. 73)

Step 3: Stifling Research Dissent by the Vicious Circle Principle (V.C.P.)

The national standards work to blunt the possibility of refutation and silence critics by carefully defining scholarship within the accreditation process in the following manner:

> Describe the scholarly productivity of faculty by documenting their current understanding of teaching about, use of, and contribution to the knowledge base in educational leadership (e.g. publications, citations, external funds secured, editorships of journals, etc.). (NPBEA, 2002, p. 16)

Since the ISLLC/ELCC standards have been developed with a narrow view of the role of the administrator, the standards are the definition of "the knowledge base," one is synonymous with the other, or as claimed by Murphy and Shipman (2002), " . . . those topics that formed the heart and soul of effective leadership" (p. 4) and " . . . are scaffolded on the knowledge base that connects the work of school leaders . . . to more effective organizational performance . . ." (p. 6).

The NPBEA has made it clear in its standards, which inform the specialized review of educational administration programs, that the only scholarship that will count for accreditation is that which is confined to this knowledge base defined in the standards. The potential impact of contrary research, or research that questions this base, will not count for accreditation review. Thus, the installation of the NPBEA standards within the accreditation process has silenced any potential criticism of them. The words that describe what is acceptable are ". . . documenting their [the faculty] current understanding of teaching about, use of and contribution to the knowledge base . . ." excludes any other type of "scholarly productivity" (NPBEA, 2002, p. 16).

In reality, the definition of "scholarly productivity" is a subset of "the knowledge base," which is synonymous with the ELCC standards. This is an example of the V.C.P. as enumerated by Bertrand Russell (1908). The definition of "scholarly productivity" is circular and solely contained with the larger subset. Also called "Russell's paradox" (1908), it was stated as follows: "If, provided a certain collection had a total, it would have members only definable in terms of that total, then the said collection has no total" (p. 63).

Clearly the NPBEA places no value on the independence of scholarship that would question the standards. This is an interesting posture since implicit in the Murphy and Shipman (2002) knowledge base is a model of schooling that Arthur Wise (1979) identified over 20 years ago as "hyperrational," that is, a process that causes more bureaucratic overlap without attaining the intended policy objectives (p. 48). One of the consequences of hyperrationalization identified by Wise was a danger to institutional autonomy in higher education (p. 211). Wise went on to say that the forces of hyperrationalization menace a number of educational traditions: ". . . They threaten teacher professionalism in schools and collegial governance in colleges. They threaten the independence of private education at all levels . . . They threaten liberal education and the belief that education is important as an end in itself . . ." (p. 211).

The national accreditation process headed by NCATE welds the enforcement of the ISLLC/ELCC standards into a confluence of agencies, each of which erodes the autonomy of every preparation program in the nation by insisting on an approach of uniformity. Interlocking agencies focused on the same confluence of concepts and propositions amount to a "regime of truth," a political agenda that is repressive to all other possibilities and alternatives (Gordon, 1980, p. 119).

Since Arthur Wise is the executive director of NCATE, these are unusually prophetic words, especially this sentence near the end of his book:

> The most tragic loss will be to the students who are cast as objects being prepared to assume their place in society. Lastly, our society will be the worst loser, for it is the tendency of educational policies to cast the welfare of the individual as subordinate to the welfare of the state. (Wise, 1979, p. 212)

Wise's (1979) words have come true in the embodiment of a model of rationality and bureaucracy in the NPBEA/ELCC standards and the assumptions that support them (pp. 57, 89).

The Metaphors of Efficiency in the ISLLC Standards

Wise (1979) proffered a definition of efficiency as "maximizing output for a given level of input " or "achieving a given level of output at least cost" (p. 3). Concerns regarding efficiency are connected to the notion that the "schools are not performing as effectively as they might—that they are not attaining the goals or objectives that they should" (p. 3). Such language regarding the failure of schools is replete in the rationale for the ISLLC standards (Murphy et al., 2000, pp. 17–23).

Efficiency in operating schools requires tight connectivity between means and ends, inputs and outputs. Murphy (1999) has indicated the following: "School management and the preparation of school administrators need to be vigorously redirected toward the enhancement of the outcomes of schooling for children" (p. 53). The same rationale undergirds the ISLLC standards (see Hessel & Holloway, 2002, pp. 21–23).

Hyperrationalization occurs when those attempting to reform schools use the rationalistic model of change as advanced by Corwin (1975). Each of the five criteria defining a rationalistic model of bureaucracy are shown with citations from the ISLLC standards showing how they are embedded in the licensure process for future school administrators. The presence of the rationalistic assumptions in the ISLLC standards belie any claim that they will not lead to further organizational bureaucracy and hierarchy and indeed represent something "new" or a "reform" of school bureaucracy with caring communities as alleged by its advocates (see Murphy & Shipman, 2002, p. 6). What follows are the assumptions of the rationalistic model in use and quotations from Hessel and Holloway (2002) that are illustrative of those assumptions.

Rationalistic Model Assumption No. 1—Organizations have clear-cut goals that are understood and subscribed to by the members: "The leader then assumes that learning goals that speak to the vision and mission of the school are developed . . ." (Hessel & Holloway, 2002, p. 34).

Rationalistic Model Assumption No. 2—Activities are planned: ". . . the school leader implements a strategic plan" (Hessel & Holloway, 2002, p. 39).

Rationalistic Model Assumption No. 3—Activities are closely coordinated: "The implementation plan consists of a series of connected strategies that identify what needs to be done . . . , define how to accomplish it, identify the needed resources, outline the timeframe and benchmark measures" (Hessel & Holloway, 2002, p. 39).

Rationalistic Model Assumption No. 4—The necessary information is available for making the informed decisions necessary to achieve the goals: "The school leader is committed to doing the work necessary . . . continuously using information about student performance to guide improvements" (Hessel & Holloway, 2002, p. 39).

Rationalistic Model Assumption No. 5—Officials have sufficient control over the organization to ensure compliance with long-range plans: "Staff development meetings, parent meetings, faculty meetings, student assemblies, and community informal meetings all focus on these priorities" (Hessel & Holloway, 2002, p. 36).

When the rationalistic model is combined with organizational characteristics such as subordination, a division of labor, goal consensus, power centralization, office holding based on expertise, and "close-knit coordination and extensive planning" (Corwin, 1975, p. 253; see also Silver, 1983, pp. 73–94), a bureaucracy is reinforced. All of these characteristics are exemplified in the ISLLC standards for educational leaders.

Wise (1979) indicates that behind the hyperrationalization of schools lies a theory of education that includes several key rationalistic (bureaucratic) assumptions. These are now listed with citations from the ISLLC standards where they are similarly expressed.

Theory of Education: Assumption No. 1— The Child is Pliable: "At the very core of the leader's mission is the development of a vision. This vision shapes all educational programs, plans, activities . . . Chief among these is the school leader's commitment to the educability of all children and adherence to high expectations for their success" (Hessel & Holloway, 2002, p. 33). This statement places children as means to the leader's mission and vision. Children must "fit in" as the leader's vision exerts itself on everything, including their success.

Theory of Education: Assumption No. 2—The teacher is pliable and will modify his or her behavior to comply: "The leader then assumes that learning goals that speak to the vision and mission of the school are developed . . . and that all individual teachers, teams, and departments align their goals and individual growth and improvement plans with the school goals" (Hessel & Holloway, 2002, p. 34). Not only must teachers align what they do to the leader's goals, but they must also align their own professional growth to be congruent as well.

Theory of Education: Assumption No. 3—A science of education exists that yields treatments that can be applied by teacher to student: "Management decisions are made based on complete knowledge of learning, teaching and student development. The school leader must use knowledge of organizations to create an effective learning environment that enhances the success of every student" (Hessel & Holloway, 2002, p. 59). Decision making, which links the environment together, is based on "complete knowledge" and that such data will yield "success for every student."

Theory of Education: Assumption No. 4—If shown, people will prefer cost-effective behavior over behavior that is not cost effective: "Effective administrators define job roles, assign tasks, delegate appropriately, and *require accountability*" (Hessel & Holloway, 2002, p. 59). The leader will take action to structure work, which will lead to accountability, which is cost effective results. Accountability is not only about results, it is about costs.

Over 20 years have passed since Art Wise (1979) wrote about hyperrationalization. The ISLLC standards and accompanying trends have become all too real on the educational scene. Wise noted that the belief that the implementation of such standards will lead to improved results "remains to be proved" (p. 57). And while the so-called "effective schools" research provides some evidence, it has not been shown to be predictive (English, 1994, p. 51). So Wise is still correct. It remains to be proved.

The ISLLC standards are shot-through with the phrase *continuous improvement,* a term with an enormous amount of baggage from Deming's total quality management and that pertains to organizational efficiency, that is, cost (English, 2000, pp. 161–162). Here is an example: "This framework for school leaders is organized around the core proposition that the most critical aspect of a school leader's work is the continuous improvement of student learning" (Hessel & Holloway, 2002, p. 2).

Continuous improvement is not centered on goal attainment or goal expansion. It is, rather, centered on cost reduction. Let us see how Deming (1986) described the idea of continuous improvement. First, continuous improvement is the result of establishing statistical control over a process, in most cases a process related to manufacturing. After establishing statistical control, those causes that are special, that is, unique, are identified and removed ("controlled"). This means that, according to Deming's doctrine, system stability is established via statistical control and it "has a definable identity and a definable capability" (p. 321; meaning "capacity"). Once all unique sources of variation are identified and removed, one then turns to common courses of variation. It is at this point that "improvement of the process can be pushed effectively" (Deming, p. 59). These "common causes" are ones of "trouble and of variation" caused by "errors . . . mistakes, of low production, of low sales . . . poor sales may stem from a faulty product, or from high price" (Deming, p. 322).

Deming (1986) then goes on to the discuss job specifications that will lead to "continuous improvement":

> The production worker's job description should therefore, for best economy, help him to achieve statistical control of his work. His job, therefore, is to reach an economic level of the distribution of his quality-characteristic, and to continually reduce its variation. Under this system, his output will meet the specifications and in fact leave them beyond the horizon, reducing costs in subsequent operations, and elevating the quality of the final product. Workers that are in statistical control but whose output is unsatisfactory can be transferred and trained in other work. (p. 335)

The idea of applying "continuous improvement" to schools is an inherently conservative doctrine rooted in the status quo. It cannot be "leverage for reform" but rather leverage for refinement. It is not a doctrine to establish "the profession around learner-centered leadership" (Murphy & Shipman, 2002, p. 9) but rather the establishment of leadership aimed at reducing variation and reducing costs. It is a profound process of goal reduction in which an instrumentality described by Wise (1979) becomes dominant. Such an instrumentality posits that education is not an end in itself but is preparation for the world of work.

The translation to the policy making process to produce goal reduction was presciently sketched out by Wise (1979) as follows: "Neither colleges nor schools are viewed . . . as institutions for the generation or transmission of the cultural heritage . . . nor does [it] view education as an end in itself—as the means to increase individual enlightenment and social welfare" (p. 60). Elliot Eisner (2003) echoed the same sentiments as Wise when he said the following: "I would argue that the major aim of schooling is to enable students to become the architects of their own education so that they can invent themselves during the course of their lives" (p. 652).

Instead, the ISLLC standards and the NCATE processes that police them have reduced university preparation programs to extremely narrow and instrumental programs in which what is rewarded is the systematic elimination of variation as the key to the reduction of costs in a recursive process that reinforces the bureaucracy it strove to change. It continues the tragedy cited by Raymond Callahan (1962) in his classic work *Education and the Cult of Efficiency*. The ISLLC standards are simply the latest version of a continuing infatuation with manufacturing and business concepts and the cult of reductionism in continuing guises.

Portin's (2003) study of the principalship in which 150 interviews were conducted in 21 schools of all different types ended with this admonition:

> One-size-fits-all generalizations about what principals "need to know and be able to do"—no matter how carefully crafted—ultimately misrepresent the situation in many schools. Making sense of what goes on in schools and helping principals do their jobs better requires more than an inventory of things for the ideal principal to oversee. (p. 2)

We will not prepare better principals either by simplifying the context in which they work or by de-skilling the jobs they are required to do. Standardization works only when everything else can be standardized. The only way standardization works in schools is to ensure that they are all the same. Then every principal will fit after completing a standardized preparation program. But this is a dangerous and dysfunctional utopia. We ought to rethink the agenda for national standards by rejecting the erasure of context and the seduction of job simplification as prerequisites to thinking about applying new or "higher" standards in preparing school administrators.

The National Debate on Educational Leadership Preparation

The function of leadership depends on the often unstated assumptions and implicit theories carried in the heads of those who agitate for change. Such assumptions need to be made explicit to separate the issues and agendas of those involved with preparing educational leaders. To initiate the discussion, four current "scenarios" to the problems of educational leaders are shown in Figure 8.1. There are two axes involved. The first (horizontal) is the adequacy/inadequacy of leadership preparation practices and the programs that prepare them. The second (vertical) axis is the assumption made regarding schools and schooling. If schools as they are presently constituted are considered adequate, then the role of school leaders is simply to run them well. Leadership preparation is about training future school leaders to perform the functions of administration in perpetuating schools as they are understood to work. Innovation is not necessary, at least in relation to the functions of leadership per se, although there might be some attention to preparing future leaders via the Internet or using technology in other ways in the process.

Cell A—The "Pipeline" Scenario: Not "Enough" Quality Leaders for the Schools

If schools as they exist are considered adequate and no change in what schools do is envisioned, then there is no need to alter preparation programs. Good preparation programs duplicate the conditions principals and superintendents will be expected to

❖ **Figure 8.1**   The Major Perspectives of Leadership Preparation

Leadership Preparation Practices

	Adequate	Inadequate
Adequate (Schools as They Currently Exist)	**A** The major issue is the "pipeline." There's not enough "quality leaders" for the schools in the future. Do away with current "License to lead" regulations. Open schools to noneducators.	**B** The major issue is more "real world" experience for future educational leaders. Too much "theory." More stress on internships. A "craft knowledge" approach.
Inadequate (Schools as They Currently Exist)	**C** Leaders are needed to "fix" the schools using national standards and accreditation compliance. Success is judged by standardized test scores.	**D** New leaders are needed to change schools to be more socially responsive. Emphasis on "social justice"—transformative leadership.

face and make sure that successful candidates acquire the skills to confront them. The major issue with these assumptions is that there is not enough of them, that is, the numbers in the "pipeline" are not enough to meet the projected demand. The "pipeline" problem is met by offering incentives to increase the supply, creating programmatic alternatives to standard programs, and reducing the requirements and experiences currently deemed necessary to become a principal or a superintendent. Sometimes proposals to increase the numbers of candidates involve lifting the need for licensure or previous kinds of experiences school leaders are believed to need. This notion has been a favorite attack by right wing think tanks such as the American Enterprise Institute (see Hess, 2003; Hess & Kelly, 2005). A proposal advanced by the Broad Foundation and Thomas B. Fordham Institute (2003) involves erasing the requirement for school leaders to have had prior classroom teaching experience, and the recruitment of leaders from business and the military to run schools. Such proposals assume that leadership preparation is fairly generic across the business, industrial, and military sectors and that current licensure requirements are artificial barriers that block schools from being run by "proven" leaders from other sectors. The actual record of success where this solution has been tried is spotty at best (see Anderson & Piny, 2005).

Cell B—The "Real World" Scenario: Universities Are Too Removed From Reality to Prepare Educational Leaders Well

This analysis proffers that leadership preparation is not adequate because university programs are too far removed from the day-to-day operations of the schools.

Schools are essentially adequate as they exist if the leaders in them know what the "real world" of administration requires. To accomplish this, university programs must retool to become more "relevant," partner with school districts, use "research-based practices . . . that will have the greatest impact on student achievement" (Southern Regional Education Board, 2006, p. 24). By improving achievement is meant raising standardized test scores within existing state accountability systems. This approach considers leadership preparation to be essentially acquiring the necessary "craft knowledge" (see Blumberg, 1989).

Cell C—Some Schools Are "Broken" Scenario: Leaders Need Incentives/Competition to "Fix" Them

In this analysis some schools are considered "broken." They are not "working" for all children. Leadership preparation is considered adequate, however. The way "broken schools" are "fixed" is by providing them with leaders who are sufficiently motivated to "take charge" and by holding them accountable for "results." The "inadequacy" of schools is not due to any inherent defects in their basic structure or design. These go unchallenged. School inadequacy is entirely a human problem with the lack of insufficient focus and unmotivated faculty. In this scenario teacher unions are a problem because they "block" attempts to make teachers work harder. The diagnosis of issues here boils down to the lack of commitment to "make schools work" for all kids. One of the antidotes is to create competition for the resources that accrue to the public schools. The so-called "monopoly" public schools enjoy is considered "the problem" (Friedman, 1962; Friedman & Friedman, 1998). The logic is, "if only the schools had to compete for their resources, they would work harder and find more efficient ways to educate everyone." The idea of treating education as "markets" is appealing because it leaves intact nearly everything else. No serious reconsideration of leadership preparation or school operations is required with this antidote (House, 1998). Essentially, the bottom line is that public schools have to be starved into efficiency. Supporting that scenario is the assumption that everything required to become successful with all children is known. Leaders simply have to have the proper motivation to forcefully apply them.

Cell D—The Social Justice Scenario: Leadership Is a Distributed Function

This analysis of the problems with schooling is the most radical. First, it posits that the structure and function of schooling are inadequate in a variety of ways. The most obvious is that schools work to reproduce the existing social order with all of its built-in social inequalities and inequities (see Brantlinger, 2003). Children from privileged families will always do well. Children from less privileged families will always do worse. Schools are not socially neutral places. They embody a culturally specific set of values that are not universal and not available to all children (Franklin & Savage, 2004). The "inadequacy" of schools is not because they don't work as they currently exist, because they were never intended to work for some families and children anyway. The "achievement gap" is "built in" to existing schooling operations (English, 2002). It will not be removed by making schools more efficient and no amount of accountability for "results" will change that. Schools have to be remade and reworked to fundamentally alter what they do. Without such "reworking," schools cannot become successful with all children.

Leadership preparation has to involve preparing principals and superintendents to engage in changing a set of internal operations that reinforce larger social inequalities. The concept of "social justice" is one that is being employed to serve as the lever for such changes (see Marshall & Oliva, 2006). Leadership in this cell is expanded to include the notion of *leadership practice,* that is, the function of leadership is distributed across a whole range of people and operations. Leadership is not simply embodied in one person, but in a whole range of people engaged in a leadership activity (Spillane, Halvorson, & Diamond, 2001).

The quality of a nation's system of public education represents an index to its economic health and its capability to ensure a prosperous future. At the vortex of the quality issue is the presence of well-prepared school leaders at the school and school district levels. Schools and school system leaders represent a critical linchpin to the continued vitality and viability of an educated citizenry and a well-educated work force as the engine of economic growth.

What this chapter should have made clear is that the issues surrounding the preparation of educational leaders are complex, are multifaceted, and involve an array of actors and agencies. No university or college preparatory program operates in isolation from these actors and agencies. Preparation curricula and experiences are subject to a variety of review and regulation from both state and national agencies, and innovation and change are often sacrificed to these forces with a vested interest in maintaining the status quo, that is, schools operating as they always have.

Calls for changing schools or changing leadership preparation can be separate as this discussion has shown, or they can be connected. Conservative think tank writers want a change in educational leadership preparation because they want to privatize the educational function, believing that by doing so they will accomplish two purposes: (a) bring the lever of the free market into play to "force" schools to become more efficient, and (b) break the "liberal" hold of thinking that they believe dominates the field and in particular schools or colleges of education on many university campuses. Transporting leadership preparation out of schools and colleges of education into either schools of business or off the university campus altogether becomes a tactic for accomplishing both of these objectives. Liberals, on the other hand, want future educational leaders to become *transformative,* that is, push for broader social changes to reduce social inequities relating to poverty, racism, sexism, and homophobia, which exist in the larger society. Liberals want a more just society. Conservatives want a more efficient society. It is not surprising that the agendas of both groups sometimes intersect. For example, take the issue of standardized testing. Some liberals see testing as a way to see if educational gaps are being reduced. Conservatives see testing as means to indicate that the schools are failing and need to be privatized. So both groups embrace testing, but for different reasons.

The debate behind national educational leadership standards is intensified by the passion that both groups bring to the subject of the nation's system of public education and their beliefs about how it can be improved.

Pursuing Learning Extensions of the Chapter

The learning extensions of the chapter involve some of the films now listed. They are intended to illustrate some of the ideas about leadership standards and leadership preparation that were part of this chapter.

Lawrence of Arabia (1962), Color, VHS, Columbia Pictures, 3 Hours 36 Minutes

Described as "a man of complex character, Lawrence was something of a self-made misfit" (Bongard, 1992, p. 428). Traditional military preparation was not the way Lawrence of Arabia (Thomas Edward Lawrence, 1888–1935) conducted his war in the desert with Arab irregulars, which brought him everlasting fame during World War I. Lawrence's education was unconventional for a military leader. He studied Crusader castles and was an honors student in history at Oxford. He worked on archaeological excavations on the Euphrates and northern Sinai and with the outbreak of the war he was assigned to British intelligence. He was sent to work as a political and liaison officer with Arab irregulars, where he won his spurs and several promotions. His leadership was described as possessing "manic energy and splendid strategic vision" (Bongard, p. 428). The film captures much of the Lawrence of Arabia of history and won seven academy awards.

The Last Emperor of China (1987), Color, VHS, Hemdale Film Corporation, 2 Hours 44 Minutes

This is the epic story of Aisin Gioro Pu Yi, the Last Emperor of China (1906–1967), based on his two-volume autobiography *From Emperor to Citizen*. The film shows the careful preparation of a very young boy to assume the role of emperor at some future point in his life. He had to abdicate his throne in 1911, however, and later became a puppet emperor under the Japanese Empire in Manchukuo. At the end of World War II he was captured by the Russians and returned to China, where he stood trial as a war criminal. The film is illustrative of how a leader is ostensibly prepared to lead, but the times overtake the entire system in which his position was embedded. One of the good objectives of this film as it pertains to leadership preparation is that if a person is groomed or trained for leadership based on tradition and stability, social stability is necessary, that is, holding the requirements of leadership constant requires a similar fixation on the context in which they function. In the case of Pu Yi (1983), society changed and he tried desperately to bring his entourage around to these changes. However, the entire system of emperors tottered and fell because it was unable to similarly change. The film also shows how absolute power can corrupt one's values, despite one's best efforts.

The Eleanor Roosevelt Story (1965), Black and White, DVD, King Video, 1 Hour 30 Minutes

Winning the academy award for best documentary, this film is about Eleanor Roosevelt (1884–1962), who came into a world of privilege as a shy, insecure, often inarticulate young woman and through tremendous energy and willpower, transformed herself into a spokesperson for many causes. Eleanor Roosevelt endured a dominating mother-in-law who ran her life and took a mild interest in politics, but it hadn't occurred to her to be in favor of female suffrage until her husband endorsed it. She was a dutiful wife in the very traditional sense until one day, handling her husband's mail, she discovered he had been having an affair with her social secretary, Lucy Mercer. The bottom dropped out of her world. While the pair reconciled, she vowed to strike out on her own and become independent in many ways. Franklin Delano Roosevelt's attack of polio also enabled her to become more independent, at the same continuing to help her husband in politics. She learned to become an accomplished public speaker. She became an independent writer and lecturer. She became a close political friend of African Americans, including Mary McLeod Bethune and Walter White of the National Association for the Advancement of Colored People. When the Daughters of the American Revolution refused to let the famed African American singer Marian Anderson perform in Constitution Hall, Eleanor Roosevelt resigned from the organization and moved the concert to the steps of the Lincoln Memorial. She wrote a best-selling autobiography. She became a tireless worker for racial equality, national health insurance, civil liberties, subsidized housing for the poor, and federal aid to education (Boller, 1988, p. 301). In her latter years she was appointed by President Truman as a delegate to the United Nations, where she won the respect of that international body for her hard work and plain speaking style. The film of Eleanor Roosevelt is about a woman's self-taught education to become a leader and to do something important with her life. She left an indelible record of accomplishment.

Writing in Your Personal Reflective Journal

This is an excellent time to reflect critically about your preparation to become an effective educational leader. Think over your program so far. What are the most important things you've learned about leadership? Have you grown in your self-confidence? Do you write better? Has your knowledge expanded? Do you feel competent or at least more competent than you began? Remember that a formal program cannot possibly include every aspect of what you will face as an educational leader in the future. What it should have done, however, is to point you in the right direction, introduce you to key ideas and ways to work with people, give you confidence to continue your own learning, which should never cease. More than anything, your graduate program should have helped you become more independent as a thinker and professional. You should have developed a healthy kind of skepticism about almost everything without becoming cynical. One of the best examples of how an educational leader can grow and engage in critical practice is that of Deborah Meier, founding principal of Central Park Elementary in Harlem, New York. Her book, *The Power of Their Ideas* (1995), is full of reflective and deeply critical analysis of her work at this pioneering school. It is a wonderful model to examine and consider.

A Review of Key Chapter Concepts

craft knowledge—There is a difference between a profession and a craft. Academic Arthur Blumberg of Syracuse coined the term "craft knowledge" to describe how school administration was actually learned. The idea of "know-how" in producing something or doing something like singing, for example, or making a cabinet involves learning "how" to do it. Blumberg (1989) rejected the idea that there was any such thing as a "science of administration" (p. 15). "Craft knowledge" is defined as knowing "how to produce a specific result be it a physical product or performing ability through the development of skills built up through practice" (Blumberg, p. 28). Much of the emphasis on the internship for graduate students, especially at the master's level, is based on assertions that school administration is a craft. Knowledge stems from a continual adjustment of means and ends within specific contexts. It is not produced by scientific research.

core technology—Sometimes referred to as an organization's "technical core," this idea seeks to explain that the central function of an organization constitutes its "core." As defined by Thompson (1967), "the technology of education rests on abstract systems of belief about relationships among teachers, teaching materials, and pupils; but learning theories assume the presence of these variables and proceed from that point" (p. 19). Mintzberg (1979) indicates that "the more sophisticated the technical system, the more elaborate the administrative structure, specifically the larger and more professional the support staff, the greater the selective decentralization to that staff and the greater the use of liaison devices to coordinate the work of that staff" (p. 262). We see the growth of central office educational staff as a direct consequence of (a) greater specialization in roles at the school site level, and (b) exponential growth in the external accountability legislation and regulations that impact the technical core.

ISLLC Standards—The ISLLC was created in early 1994 and 1995. Beginning with 23 state departments of education, representatives, and 10 national school leader associations or organizations, the group developed national leadership standards for school leaders under the umbrella of the CCSSO and the NPBEA. The standards are accompanied by about 200 indicators. The standards have been implemented by 43 states and three extraterritorial jurisdictions. These standards form the basis for the licensure exams in many of the states using them (see Shipman, 2006).

market theory of educational leadership—This is a metanarrative that transposes most situations into economic exchanges in which labor and materials become profits. In this transposition students become "products" and parents become "customers." School administrators are urged to become more efficient (perform at lower costs) by standardizing tasks and roles, thus lowering costs to maximize profits (and lower taxes). Training costs are decreased because the jobs are simplified (de-skilled). When the jobs are routinized, replacement is much easier and also cheaper (English, 2005).

transformative leadership—This is a distinction in leadership that is aimed at connecting changes within schools to changes between schools and the larger society, or schooling interiorities and school exteriorities (see Shields, 2004). Transformative leadership goes beyond institutional boundaries and thus involves reform of more than the "technical core" of schools. Only when schools become transformative can social justice be obtained.

References

Ackerman, R., & Maslin-Ostrowski, P. (2002). *The wounded leader: How real leadership emerges in times of crisis.* San Francisco: Jossey-Bass.

Alcantara, I., & Egnolff, S. (n.d.). *Frida Kahlo and Diego Rivera.* Munich, Germany: Prestel.

Alinsky, S. (1969). *Reveille for radicals.* New York: Vintage Books. (Original work published 1946)

Alinsky, S. (1971). *Rules for radicals.* New York: Vintage.

Allison, D. (1999). Saussure, Ferdinand de. In R. Audi (Ed.), *The Cambridge dictionary of philosophy* (2nd ed., pp. 815-816). Cambridge, UK: Cambridge University Press.

Anderson, G. (2001, September). Disciplining leaders: A critical discourse analysis of the ISLLC national examination and performance standards in educational administration. *International Journal of Leadership in Education Theory and Practice, 4*(3), 199–216.

Anderson, G., & Piny, M. (2005). Educational leadership and the new economy: Keeping the 'public' in public schools. In F. English (Ed.), *The Sage handbook of educational leadership* (pp. 216–236). Thousand Oaks, CA: Sage.

Apple, M. (1991). Regulating the text: The socio-historical roots of state control. In P. Altbach, G. Kelly, H. Petrie, & L. Weis (Eds.), *Textbooks in American society* (pp. 7–26). Albany: State University of New York Press.

Appleton's American higher geography. (1881). New York: D. Appleton and Company.

Argyris, C. (1962). *Interpersonal competence and organizational effectiveness.* Homewood, IL: The Dorsey Press.

Argyris, C. (1970). *Intervention theory & method: A behavioral science view.* Reading, MA: Addison-Wesley.

Argyris, C. (1972). *The applicability of organizational sociology.* Cambridge, MA: Harvard University Press.

Armstrong, K. (1992). *Muhammad: A biography of the prophet.* San Francisco: HarperCollins.

Asante, M. (1990). *Kemet, afrocentricity and knowledge.* Trenton, NJ: Africa World Press.

Ashton, J. (2001). *De-constructing heterosexism and homophobia in schools: Case study of a hate crime by an adolescent offender.* Unpublished doctoral dissertation, Texas A&M University, College Station.

Associated Press. (1992, July 25). Tires recalled so they don't tread on Allah. *Lexington Herald-Leader,* p. A3.

Attenborough, R. (1982a). *In search of Gandhi.* Piscataway, NJ: New Century Books.

Attenborough, R. (1982b). *The words of Gandhi.* New York: Newmarket Press.

Ayer, A. (1988). *Thomas Paine.* New York: Atheneum.

Ayer, R. (1973). *The moral and political thought of Mahatma Gandhi.* New York: Oxford University Press.

Ayers, W., & Klonsky, M. (2006, February). Chicago's renaissance 2010: The small schools movement meets the ownership society. *Phi Delta Kappan, 86*(6), 453–461.

Bailyn, B. (1992). *The ideological origins of the American revolution.* Cambridge, MA: The Belknap Press of Harvard University Press.

Ball, S. (1991). Management as moral technology: A Luddite analysis. In S. Ball (Ed.), *Foucault and education: Disciplines and knowledge* (pp. 153–166). London: Routledge.

Barber, J. (1985). *The presidential character: Predicting performance in the White House.* Englewood Cliffs, NJ: Prentice Hall.

Barbour, J. (2006). Critical theory. In F. English (Ed.), *Encyclopedia of educational leadership and administration* (pp. 237–240). Thousand Oaks, CA: Sage.

Baringer, P. (2000, August 15). Fundamental disagreement. Letter to the Editor. *Wall Street Journal,* p. A27.

Barnard, C. (1938). *The functions of the executive.* Cambridge, MA: Harvard University Press.

Basler, R. (1953). *The collected works of Abraham Lincoln* (Vol. 2). New Brunswick, NJ: Rutgers University Press.

Bauman, Z. (1992). *Intimations of postmodernity.* London: Routledge.

Becker, S., & Neuhauser, D. (1975). *The efficient organization.* New York: Elsevier.

Bell, T. (1988). *The thirteenth man: A Reagan cabinet memoir.* New York: Free Press.

Bem, S. (1993). *The lenses of gender.* New Haven, CT: Yale University Press.

Bennis, W. (1989). *On becoming a leader.* Cambridge, MA: Perseus Books.

Bergman, I. (1990). *Images: My life in film* (M. Ruuth, Trans.). New York: Arcade Publishing. (Original work published 1944).

Berlin, I. (1995). Chaim Weizmann's leadership. In H. Hardy (Ed.), *The power of ideas.* Princeton, NJ: Princeton University Press.

Bertalanffy, L. (1968). *General system theory.* New York: George Braziller.

Best, S., & Kellner, D. (1991). *Postmodern theories.* New York: Guilford.

Blackbourn, J. (2006). Behaviorism. In F. English (Ed.), *Encyclopedia of educational leadership and administration* (pp. 70–75). Thousand Oaks, CA: Sage.

Blasé, J., & Blasé, J. (2003). *Breaking the silence: Overcoming the problem of principal mistreatment of teachers.* Thousand Oaks, CA: Corwin Press.

Blau, P. , & Scott, R. (1962). *Formal organizations: A comparative approach.* San Francisco: Chandler.

Bloom, H. (1998). *Shakespeare: The invention of the human.* New York: Riverhead Books.

Blount, J. (1998). *Destined to rule the schools: Women and the superintendency, 1873-1995.* Albany: State University of New York Press.

Blount, J. (1999). Manliness and the gendered construction of school administration in the USA. *International Journal of Leadership in Education: Theory and Practice, 2*(2), 55–68.

Blount, J. (2003, January). Homosexuality and school superintendents: A brief history. *Journal of School Leadership, 13*(1), 7–26.

Blount, J. (2006). Lesbian/gay/bisexual/transgender issues in education. In F. English (Ed.), *Encyclopedia of educational leadership and administration* (pp. 609–612). Thousand Oaks, CA: Sage.

Blumberg, A. (1989). *School administration as a craft: Foundations of practice.* Boston: Allyn & Bacon.

Bobbitt, F. (1971). *The curriculum.* New York: New York Times. (Original work published 1918)

Bohman, J. (1999). Critical theory. In R. Audi (Ed.), *The Cambridge dictionary of philosophy* (p. 195). Cambridge, UK: Cambridge University Press.

Bolman, L., & Deal, T. (1991). *Reframing organizations.* San Francisco: Jossey-Bass.

Bongard, D. (1992). Lawrence, Thomas Edward. In T. Dupuy, C. Johnson, & D. Bongard (Eds.), *The Harper encyclopedia of military biography* (pp. 427–428). New York: HarperCollins.

Bottery, M. (2004). *The challenges of educational leadership.* London: Paul Chapman.

Brantlinger, E. (2003). *Dividing classes: How the middle class negotiates and rationalizes school advantage.* New York: RoutledgeFalmer.

Broad Foundation & Thomas B. Fordham Institute. (2003). *Better leaders for America's schools: A manifesto.* Retrieved February 11, 2004, from http://www.edexcellence.net/doc/Manifesto

Burns, J. (1978). *Leadership.* New York: Harper & Row.

Burns, J., & Dunn, S. (2004). *George Washington.* New York: Henry Holt Company.

Callahan, R. (1962). *Education and the cult of efficiency.* Chicago: University of Chicago Press.

Campbell, J. (1973). *The hero with a thousand faces.* Princeton, NJ: Princeton University Press.

Campbell, J. (1987). *The masks of god: Primitive mythology.* New York: Viking Penguin.

Campbell, J. (1990). *Transformations of myth through time.* New York: Harper & Row.

Callen, A. (1995). *The spectacular body.* New Haven, CT: Yale University Press.

Capper, C. (1995). An otherist poststructural perspectives of the knowledge base in educational administration. In R. Donmoyer, M. Imber, & J. Scheurich (Eds.), *The knowledge base in educational administration: Multiple perspectives* (pp. 285–299). Albany: State University of New York Press.

Caro, R. (1974). *The power broker: Robert Moses and the fall of New York.* New York: Random House.

Caro, R. (1986). Lyndon Johnson and the roots of power. In W. Zinsser (Ed.), *Extraordinary lives: The art and craft of American biography* (pp. 197–232). Boston: Houghton Mifflin.

Caro, R. (1990). *The years of Lyndon Johnson: Means of ascent.* New York: Knopf.

Caro, R. (2002). *The years of Lyndon Johnson: Master of the senate.* New York: Knopf.

Carr, D. (1985). Life and the narrator's art. In H. Silverman & D. Ihde (Eds.), *Hermeneutics and deconstruction* (pp. 120–130). Albany: State University of New York Press.

Carter, P., & Jackson, N. (2000). An-aesthetics. In S. Linstead & H. Hopfl (Eds.), *The aesthetics of organization.* Thousand Oaks, CA: Sage.

Caryl, C. (2005, September 22). Why they do it. *New York Review of Books,* pp. 28–32.

Cava, M. (2003, March 4). Ugly sentiments sting American tourists as Europeans cite frustrations with U.S. policy. *USA Today,* A1–2.

Cherryholmes, C. (1988). *Power and criticism.* New York: Teachers College Press.

Christensen, C., & Raynor, M. (2003, September). Why hard-nosed executives should care about management theory. *Harvard Business Review, 81*(9), 66–75.

Church, E. (2002, February 11). Tempered radicals aim to rock the boat—and stay in. *Globe and Mail,* Section C, p. 1.

Churchland, P. (1985). The ontological status of observables: In praise of the super-empirical values. In P. Churchland & C. Hooker (Eds.), *Images of science: Essays on realism and empiricism* (pp. 35–47). Chicago: University of Chicago Press.

Clark, S. (1986). *Ready from within..* Navarro, CA: Wild Trees Press.

Cleary, T. (1992). *The Japanese art of war: Understanding the culture and strategy.* Boston: Shambhala.

Clemens, J., & Wolff, M. (1999). *Movies to manage by.* Chicago: Contemporary Books.

Clifford, G., & Guthrie, J. (1988). *Ed school.* Chicago: University of Chicago Press.

Cohen, M., & March, J. (1974). *Leadership and ambiguity.* New York: McGraw-Hill.

Collins, J. (2001). *Good to great: Why some companies make the leap . . . and others don't.* New York: HarperCollins.

Collins, J. (2005). *Good to great and the social sectors.* Boulder, CO: Collins.

Collins, P. (1990). *Black feminist thought. Volume 2.* New York: Routledge.

Collins, R. (1986). *Max Weber: A skeleton key.* Beverly Hills, CA: Sage.

Collinson, D. (1998). *Fifty major philosophers: A reference guide.* London: Routledge.

Cookson, P. , & Persell, C. (1985). *Preparing for power: America's elite schools.* New York: Basic Books.

Copeland, L. (Ed.). (1942). *The world's great speeches.* New York: Garden City Publishing Company.

Corwin, R. (1975). Models of educational organizations. *Review of Research in Education, 2,* 247–295.

Covey, S. (1990). *The seven habits of highly effective people.* New York: Simon & Schuster.

Cranston, M. (2003). Some thoughts on dealing with cultural bias against women. In D. Rhode (Ed.), *The difference "difference" makes* (pp. 176–177). Stanford, CA: Stanford University Press.

Crawford, D. (1971). Mary Parker Follett. In E. James, J. James, & P. Boyer (Eds.), *Notable American women: A biographical dictionary* (pp. 639–641). Cambridge, MA: Harvard University Press.

Crawford, J. (1992, September 30). Hold your tongue: Bilingualism and the politics of English only (excerpt). *The Chronicle of Higher Education,* p. B5.

Critchley, S. (1992). *The ethics of de-construction.* Oxford, UK: Blackwell.

Crossan, J. (1975). *The dark interval: Towards a theology of story.* Niles, IL: Argus Communications.

Crossan, J. (1992). *The historical Jesus: The life of a Mediterranean Jewish peasant.* San Francisco: HarperCollins.

Crossan, J. (1994). *Jesus: A revolutionary biography.* San Francisco: HarperCollins.

Crossan, J. (1995). *Who killed Jesus? Exposing the roots of anti-semitism in the gospel story of the death of Jesus.* San Francisco: HarperCollins.

Crow, G., & Grogan, M. (2005). The development of leadership thought and practice in the United States. In F. English (Ed.), *The Sage handbook of educational leadership* (pp. 362–379). Thousand Oaks, CA: Sage.

Creswell, J. (2003). *Research design.* Thousand Oaks, CA: Sage.

Cuban, L. (1976). *Urban school chiefs under fire.* Chicago: University of Chicago Press.

Culbertson, J. (1995). *Building bridges: UCEA's first two decades.* University Park, PA: University Council for Educational Administration.

Culbertson, J. (1988). A century's quest for a knowledge base. In N. J. Boyan (Ed.), *Handbook of research on educational administration* (pp. 3–26). New York: Longman.

Cunningham, W., & Cordeiro, P. (2000). *Educational administration: A problem based approach.* Boston: Allyn & Bacon.

Curti, M. (1959/1935). The black man's place: Booker T. Washington. In M. Curti (Ed.), *The social ideas of American educators* (pp. 288–309). Totowa, NJ: Littlefield, Adams & Company.

Cyert, R., & March, J. (1963). *A behavioral theory of the firm.* Englewood Cliffs, NJ: Prentice Hall.

Dantley, M. (2005). Moral leadership: Shifting the management paradigm. In F. English (Ed.), *The Sage handbook of educational leadership* (pp. 34–46). Thousand Oaks, CA: Sage.

Dantley, M., & Rogers, J. (2001, January). Including a spiritual voice in the educational leadership and school reform discourse. *International Journal of Educational Reform, 10*(1), 87–101.

Darwin, C. (1859). *On the origin of species by natural selection.* London: Murray.

Darrow, C. (1932). *The story of my life.* New York: Grosset & Dunlap.

Davenport, N., Distler-Schwartz, R., & Pursell-Elliott, G. (1999). *Mobbing: Emotional abuse in the American workplace.* Ames, IA: Civil Society.

Dawidowicz, L. (1975). *The war against the Jews, 1933–1945.* New York: Bantam.

Deal, T., & Peterson, K. (1994). *The leadership paradox: Balancing logic and artistry in schools.* San Francisco: Jossey-Bass.

Deal, T., & Peterson, K. (1999). *Shaping school culture.* San Francisco: Jossey-Bass.

Dean, S. (2000). *Hearts and minds: A public school miracle.* New York: Viking.

De Bono, E. (1972). *Po: Beyond yes and no.* New York: Penguin Books.

De Bono, E. (1980). *Po: Beyond yes and no.* New York: Penguin Books.

De Bono, E. (1992). *Serious creativity.* New York: HarperCollins.

DeCamp, L. (1968). *The great monkey trial.* New York: Doubleday.

Delgado, R. (Ed.). (1995). *Critical race theory: The cutting edge.* Philadelphia: Temple University Press.

Deming, W. (1986). *Out of the crisis.* Cambridge: MIT Press.

Dentith, A. M., Brady, J. F., & Hammett, R. F. (2006). Feminisms and leadership in education. In F. English (Ed.), *Encyclopedia of educational leadership and administration* (pp. 384-388). Thousand Oaks, CA: Sage.

D'Este, C. (1995). *Patton: A genius for war.* New York: HarperCollins.

Devitt, M., & Sterelny, K. (1987). *Language and reality.* Cambridge: MIT Press.

Dewey, J. (1929). *The sources of a science of education.* New York: Horace Liveright.

Dewey, J. (1938). *Logic, the theory of inquiry.* New York: Holt.

Diggins, J. (1996). *Max Weber: Politics and the spirit of tragedy.* New York: HarperCollins.

Dissent over Iraq hints Europe–America schism. (2003, February 18). *Florida Times Union,* p. A–8.

Donald, D. (1995). *Lincoln.* New York: Simon & Schuster.

Donald, D. (1996). *Lincoln.* New York: A Touchstone Book.

Donmoyer, D. (1999). The continuing quest for a knowledge base: 1976–1998. In J. Murphy & K. Louis (Eds.), *Handbook of research on educational administration* (2nd ed., pp. 25–44). San Francisco: Jossey-Bass.

Donmoyer, R., Imber, M., & Scheurich, J. (1995). *The knowledge base in educational administration: Multiple perspectives.* Albany: State University of New York Press.

Dover, G. (2002, December 20). The baffling existence of the male. *London Times Literary Supplement, No. 5202,* p. 28.

Drucker, P. (1974). *Management: Tasks, responsibilities, practices.* New York: Harper & Row.

Duffy, J. (1979). *The healers: A history of American medicine.* Urbana: University of Illinois Press.

Duke, D. (1998, April). The normative context of organizational leadership. *Educational Administration Quarterly, 34*(2), 165–195.

Duncan, P., & Seguin, C. (2002, November). The perfect match: A case study of a first-year woman principal. *Journal of School Leadership, 12*(6), 608–639.

Dunham, B. (1964). *Heroes and heretics: A social history of dissent.* New York: Knopf.

Eco, U. (1990). *The limits of interpretation.* Bloomington: Indiana University Press.

Edelman, M. (1985). *The symbolic uses of politics.* Urbana: University of Illinois Press.

Eiselen, F., Lewis, F., & Downey, D. (1957). *The Abingdon Bible commentary.* Garden City, NY: Doubleday.

Eisner, E. (2003, January 3). The naked truth about strip clubs; the legacy of art. *The Chronicle Review,* p. B4.

Elmore, R. (2000). *Building a new structure for school leadership.* Washington, DC: The Albert Shanker Institute.

English, F. (1994). *Theory in educational administration.* New York: HarperCollins.

English, F. (2000). Pssst! What does one call a set of non-empirical beliefs required to be accepted on faith and enforced by authority? [Answer: a religion, aka the ISLLC standards]. *International Journal of Leadership in Education, 3*(2), 159–168.

English, F. (2002a). On the intractability of the achievement gap in urban schools and the discursive practice of continuing racial discrimination. *Education and Urban Society, 34*(3), 298–311.

English, F. (2002b). The point of scientificity, the fall of the epistemological dominos, and the end of the field of educational administration. *Studies in Philosophy and Education, 21,* 109–136.

English, F. (2003a). *The postmodern challenge to the theory and practice of educational administration.* Springfield, IL: Charles C Thomas.

English, F. (2003b). 'Functional foremanship' and the virtue of historical amnesia: The AASA, the ELCC standards, and the reincarnation of scientific management in educational preparation programs for profit (TEA-SIG, Division A). *AERA Newsletter, 10,* 1, 5–6.

English, F. (2003c). The ISLLC standards: The deskilling and deprofessionalization of educational administrators. In F. English (Ed.), *The postmodern challenge to the theory and practice of educational administration* (pp. 102–131). Springfield, IL: Charles C Thomas.

English, F. (2003d, Spring). About the policing functions of ELCC/NCATE and the standardization of university preparation programs in educational administration. *School Leadership News. AERA Division A Newsletter,* 5–8.

English, F. (2003e, March). Cookie-cutter leaders for cookie-cutter schools: The teleology of standardization and the de-legitimization of the university in educational leadership preparation. *Leadership and Policy in Schools, 2*(1), 27–46.

English, F. (2005). Educational leadership for sale: Social justice, the ISLLC standards, and the corporate assault on public schools. In T. Creighton, S. Harris, & J. Coleman (Eds.), *Crediting the past, challenging the present, creating the future* (pp. 83–106). Sam Houston State University: National Council of Professors of Educational Administration.

English, F. (2006). The unintended consequences of a standardized knowledge base in advancing educational leadership preparation. *Educational Administration Quarterly, 42*(3), 461–472.

English, F. (2007). The NRC's scientific research in education: It isn't even wrong. In F. English & G. Furman (Eds.), *Research and educational leadership: Navigating the new national research council guidelines* (pp. 1–38). Lanham, MD: Rowman & Littlefield Education and UCEA.

English, F., & Zirkel, P. (1989). The great monkey trial: Scopes in perspective. *National Forum of Applied Educational Research Journal, 2,* 4–17.

Erben, M. (Ed.). (1998). *Biography and education.* London: Falmer.

Erickson, E. (1969). *Gandhi's truth: On the origins of militant nonviolence.* New York: Norton.

Estes, C. (1992). *Women who run with the wolves: Myths and stories of the wild woman archetype.* New York: Ballantine Books.

Etchemendy, J. (1999). Semantic paradoxes. In R. Audi (Ed.), *The Cambridge dictionary of philosophy* (2nd ed., pp. 830–832). Cambridge, UK: Cambridge University Press.

Evers, C., & Lakomski, G. (1991). *Knowing educational administration.* Oxford, England: Pergamon Press.

Fairclough, N. (1992). *Discourse and social change.* Cambridge, UK: Polity Press.

Farah, C. (1994). *Islam.* Hauppauge, NY: Barrons.

Felperin, H. (1988). *Beyond deconstruction.* Oxford, UK: Clarendon Press.

Ferguson, K. (1984). *The feminist case against bureaucracy.* Philadelphia: Temple University Press.

Feyerabend, P. (1991). *Three dialogues of knowledge.* Oxford, UK: Basil Blackwell.

Fiedler, F. (1967). *A theory of leadership.* New York: McGraw-Hill.

Firestone, W., & Riehl, C. (Eds.). (2005). *A new agenda for research in educational leadership.* New York: Teachers College Press.

Fischer, L. (1950). *The life of Mahatma Gandhi.* New York: Harper & Brothers.

Flexner, E. (1971). Ida Bell Wells-Barnett. In E. T. James, J. W. James, & P. S. Boyer (Eds.), *Notable American women: A biographical dictionary* (pp. 565–567). Cambridge, MA: Belknap Press of Harvard University Press.

Follett, M. (1924). *Creative experience.* London: Longmans, Green & Company.

Foucault, M. (1972). *The archaeology of knowledge and the discourse on language.* New York: Pantheon Books.

Foucault, M. (1979). *Discipline and punish. The birth of the prison.* New York: Random House.

Foucault, M. (1990). *The history of sexuality: Volume 1: Introduction* (R. Hurley, Trans.). New York: Vintage Books.

Franklin, V., & Savage, C. (2004). *Cultural capital and black education.* Greenwich, CT: Information Age Publishing.

Franklyn, M. (1974). *My brilliant career.* Sydney, Australia: Angus and Robinson.

Fraynd, D., & Capper, C. (2003). 'Do you have any idea who you just hired?!' A study of open and closeted sexual minority K-12 administrators. *Journal of School Leadership, 13*(1), 86–124.

French, W., & Bell, C. Jr. (1973). *Organization development.* Englewood Cliffs, NJ: Prentice Hall.

Freud, S. (1964). *Leonardo da Vinci and a memory of his childhood.* New York: Norton.

Frick, D. (2004). *Robert K. Greenleaf: A life of servant leadership.* San Francisco: Berrett-Koehler.

Friedan, B. (1963). *The feminist mystique.* New York: Simon.

Friedman, M. (1962). *Capitalism & freedom.* Chicago: University of Chicago Press.

Friedman, M., & Friedman, R. (1998). *Two lucky people: Memoirs.* Chicago: University of Chicago Press.

Friedson, E. (1986). *Professional powers.* Chicago: University of Chicago Press.

Fukuyama, F. (2006). *America at the crossroads: Democracy, power, and the neoconservative legacy.* New Haven, CT: Yale University Press.

Fullan, M. (2001). *Leading in a culture of change.* San Francisco: Jossey-Bass.

Fullan, M. (2002). Leadership and sustainability. *Principal Leadership, 3*(4), 1–7.

Fumerton, R. (1999). Logical positivism. In. R. Audit (Ed.), *The Cambridge dictionary of philosophy* (pp. 514–516). Cambridge, UK: Cambridge University Press.

Funk, R., Hoover, R., & the Jesus Seminar (1993). *The five gospels: What did Jesus really say?* New York: Macmillan

Furman, G., & English, F. (2002, September). Can leadership be legislated? *Journal of School Leadership, 12*(5), 476–479.

Gabor, A. (1990). *The man who discovered quality.* New York: Penguin Books.

Gadet, F. (1986). *Saussure and contemporary culture.* London: Hutchinson Radius.

Giroux, H. (1997). *Pedagogy and the politics of hope: Theory, culture and schooling.* Boulder, CO: Westview.

Gardner, H. (1995). *Leading minds: An anatomy of leadership.* New York: HarperCollins.

Gardner, J. (1961). *Excellence: Can we be equal and excellent too?* New York: Harper & Row.

Gardner, J. (1963). *Self-renewal.* New York: Harper & Row.

Gardner, J. (1968). *No easy victories.* New York: Harper & Row.

Gardner, J. W. (1991). *On leadership.* New York: Free Press.

Gert, B. (1999). Morality. In R. Audit (Ed.), *The Cambridge dictionary of philosophy* (2nd ed., pp. 586–587). Cambridge, UK: Cambridge University Press.

Gerth, H., & Mills, C. (1970). *From Max Weber: Essays in sociology.* New York: Oxford University Press.

Gewertz, C. (2006, February 22). Race, gender, and the superintendency. *Education Week,* pp. 1, 22.

Gitlin, T. (2004). Richard Nixon. In J. Newfield & M. Jacobson (Eds.), *American monsters.* New York: Thunder's Mouth Press.

Giroux, H. (1997). *Pedagogy and the politics of hope: Theory, culture and schooling.* Boulder, CO: Westview Press.

Goggin, J. (1993). *Carter G. Woodson.* Baton Rouge: Louisiana University Press.

Goleman, D., Boyatzis, R., & McKee, A. (2002). *Primal leadership.* Boston: Harvard Business Review Press.

Golembiewski, R. (1972). *Renewing organizations.* Itasca, IL: Peacock.

Gordon, C. (Ed.). (1980). *Power-knowledge: Selected interviews and other writings 1972–1977 by Michel Foucault.* New York: Pantheon.

Gorn, E. (2001). *Mother Jones: The most dangerous woman in America.* New York: Hill and Wang.

Gould, S. (1977). *Ontogeny and phylogeny.* Cambridge, MA: The Belknap Press.

Gould, S. (1981). *The mismeasure of man.* New York: Norton.

Grant, G. (1988). *The world we created at Hamilton High.* Cambridge, MA: Harvard University Press.

Greenblatt, S. (2004, October 21). The death of Hamnet and the making of Hamlet. *New York Review of Books, 51*(16), 42–47.

Greenfield, T., & Ribbons, P. (1993). *Greenfield on educational administration: Towards a humane science.* London: Routledge.

Greenleaf, R. (1977). *Servant leadership.* New York: Paulist Press.

Greenleaf, R. (1978). *Servant: Leader and follower.* New York: Paulist Press.

Gronn, P. (1986). The boyhood, schooling and early career of J. R. Darling. *Journal of Australian Studies, 19*(1), 30–42.

Gronn, P. (1993). Psychobiography on the couch: Character, biography and the comparative study of leaders. *Journal of Applied Behavioral Science, 29*(3).

Gronn, P. (2002, September). Designer leadership: The emerging global adoption of preparation standards. *Journal of School Leadership, 12*(2), 552–578.

Gronn, P., & Ribbins, P. (1996). Leaders in context. *Educational Administration Quarterly, 32*(2), 452–473.

Gsell, P. (1983). *Rodin on art and artists* (R. Fedden, Trans.). New York: Dover Publications.

Guelzo, A. (2004). *Lincoln's emancipation proclamation: The end of slavery in America.* New York: Simon & Schuster.

Gulick, L. (1948). *Administrative reflections on World War II.* Tuscaloosa: University of Alabama Press.

Haack, S. (1988). *Philosophy of logics.* Cambridge, UK: Cambridge University Press.

Habermas, J. (1990). *Moral consciousness and communicative action.* Cambridge: MIT Press.

Hall, D. (2003). *Queer theories.* New York: Palgrave Macmillan.

Hall, E. T. (1981). *Beyond culture.* New York: Doubleday.

Hall, R. (1972). *Organizations: Structure and process.* Englewood Cliffs, NJ: Prentice Hall.

Halpin, A. (1966). *Theory and research in administration.* New York: Macmillan.

Hamburg, E. (1995). *Nixon: An Oliver Stone film.* New York: Hyperion.

Heady, T. (2003, Winter). Her kind of science. *Endeavors: Research and Creative Activity, 2,* 7–10.

Heck, R., & Hallinger, P. (1999). Next generation methods for the study of leadership and school improvement. In J. Murphy & K. Louis (Eds.), *Handbook of research on educational administration* (2nd ed., pp. 141–162). San Francisco: Jossey-Bass.

Heilbrunn, J. (1996). Can leadership be studied? In P. Temes (Ed.), *Teaching leadership: Essays in theory and practice* (pp. 1–12). New York: Peter Lang.

Hernstein, R., & Murray, C. (1994). *The bell curve.* New York: Basic Books.

Hess, F. (2003, July 9). A license to lead? Ending the 'ghettoization' of educational leaders. *Education Week, 22*(42), 39–40.

Hess, F., & Kelly, A. (2005, May 18). Learning to lead? In preparing principals, content matters. *Education Week, 24*(37), 32, 44.

Hess, G. (1991). *School restructuring Chicago style.* Newbury Park, CA: Corwin Press.

Hessel, K., & Holloway, J. (2002). *A framework for school leaders: Linking the ISLLC standards to practice.* Princeton, NJ: Educational Testing Service.

Highwater, J. (1990). *Myth and sexuality.* New York: New American Library.

Hill, F., & Awde, N. (2003). *A history of the Islamic world.* New York: Hippocrene Book, Inc.

Hills, R. (1968). *Toward a science of organization.* Eugene, OR: Center for Advanced Study of Educational Administration.

Hodgetts, R., & Kuratiko, D. (1988). *Management.* San Diego, CA: Harcourt, Brace Jovanovich.

Hodgkinson, C. (1991). *Educational leadership: The moral art.* Albany: State University of New York Press.

Hoffman, D. (1998). *Visual intelligence: How we create what we see.* New York: Norton.

Holton, G. (2003, April 25). An insider's view of 'a nation at risk' and why it still matters. *The Chronicle of Higher Education,* pp. B13–15.

Horwitt, S. (1989). *Let them call me rebel: Saul Alinsky, his life and legacy.* New York: Knopf.

House, E. (1991, August-September). Realism in research. *Educational Researcher, 20,* 20.

House, E. (1998). *Schools for sale: Why free market policies won't improve America's schools and what will.* New York: Teachers College Press.

Howe, ex-education official. (2002, December 5). *News and Observer,* p. 9B.

Howland, G. (1896). *Practical hints for the teachers of public schools.* New York: D. Appleton and Company.

Hunter, R., & Bartee, R. (2003, February). The achievement gap: Issues of competition, class, and race. *Education and Urban Society, 35*(2), 151–160.

Hymowitz, C. (2006, March 27). Mind your language: To do business today, consider delayering. *The Wall Street Journal,* p. B1.

Ide, H. (1999). Sophists. In R. Audi (Ed.), *The Cambridge dictionary of philosophy* (2nd ed., pp. 862–864). Cambridge, UK: Cambridge University Press.

Iyer, R. (1973). *The moral and political thought of Mahatma Gandhi.* New York: University Press.

James, W. (1991). *Pragmatism.* Buffalo, NY: Prometheus Books.

Jencks, C., & Phillips, M. (1998). *The black–white test score gap.* Washington, DC: Brookings Institution Press.

Jenkins, H. (2006, February 11). Preacher man: The weekend interview with Jack Welch. *The Wall Street Journal,* p. A8.

Jensen, H. (1969). *Signs, symbol and script.* New York: G. P. Putnam's Sons.

Jentz, B. (2006). Making our own minds the object of our learning: Three reasons to seek self-knowledge. In P. Kelleher & R. van der Bogert (Eds.), *Voices for democracy: Struggles and celebrations of transformational leaders* (pp. 230–238). Malden, MA: Blackwell.

Jewett, R., & Lawrence, J. (1988). *The American monomyth.* Lanham, MD: University Press of America.

Johnson, P. (1996). Antipodes: Plato, Nietzsche, and the moral dimensions of leadership. In P. Temes (Ed.), *Teaching leadership: Essays in theory and practice* (pp. 83–104). New York: Peter Lang.

Judt, T. (2003, May 1). Anti-Americans abroad. *New York Review of Books, 50*(7), 24–27.

Jung, C. (1958) *The undiscovered self* (R. F. Hull, Trans.). New York: A Mentor Book.

Jung, C. (1960). *The stages of life. The structure and dynamics of the psyche: Including 'synchronicit'y: An acausal connecting principle* (92nd ed., Vol. 8 of The Collected Works of C. G. Jung, Bollingen Series 20; R. F. C. Hull, Trans.). Princeton, NJ: Princeton University Press.

Kagan, D. (2003). *The Peloponnesian war.* New York: Penguin Books.

Kanigel, R. (1997). *The one best way: Frederick Winslow Taylor and the enigma of efficiency.* New York: Viking.

Katz, D., & Kahn, R. (1966). *The social psychology of organizations.* New York: John Wiley & Sons.

Keegan, J. (1987). *The mask of command.* New York: Viking.

Keegan, J. (2002). *Winston Churchill.* New York: Penguin Books.

Kelleher, P., & Van Der Bogert, R. (2006). Introduction: The landscape of the superintendency: From despair to hope. In P. Kelleher & R. Van Der Bogert (Eds.), *Voices for democracy: Struggles and celebrations of transformational leaders* (pp. 10–28). Malden, MA: Blackwell.

Keller, H. (1990). *The story of my life.* New York: Bantam.

Kellerman, B. (2004). *Bad leadership.* Cambridge, MA: Harvard Business School.

Kellner, D. (1992). *Critical theory, Marxism and modernity.* Baltimore: Johns Hopkins University Press.

Kenally, T. (2003). *Abraham Lincoln.* New York: Viking.

Kevles, D. J. (1999). *In the name of eugenics.* Cambridge, MA: Harvard University Press.

Keyes, M., Hanley-Maxwell, C., & Capper, C. (1999). 'Spirituality? It's the core of my leadership': Empowering leadership in an inclusive elementary school. *Educational Administration Quarterly, 35,* 203–237.

Keyes, R. (1995). *The wit and wisdom of Harry Truman.* New York: Gramercy Books.

Kincheloe, J., & Steinberg, S. (1997). Who said it can't happen here? In. J. Kincheloe, S. Steinberg, & A. Gresson (Eds.), *Measured lies: The bell curve examined* (pp. 3–50). New York: St. Martin's Press.

Klass, P. (1987). *A not entirely benign procedure: Four years as a medical student.* New York: Penguin.

Kochan, F., Jackson, B., & Duke, D. (1999). *A thousand voices from the firing line.* Columbia, MO: University Council for Educational Administration.

Koschoreck, J. (2003, January). Easing the violence: Transgressing heteronormativity in educational administration. *Journal of School Leadership, 13*(1), 27–50.

Koschoreck, J. (2006). Queer theory. In F. English (Ed.), *Encyclopedia of educational leadership and administration* (pp. 841–842).Thousand Oaks, CA: Sage.

Koschoreck, J., & Slattery, P. (2006). Meeting all students' needs: Transforming the unjust normativity of heterosexism. In C. Marshall & M. Oliva (Eds.), *Leadership for social justice: Making revolutions in education* (pp. 145–165). Boston: Pearson.

Kotter, J. (1990). *A force for change: How leadership differs from management.* New York: Free Press.

Kouzes, J., & Posner, B. (2002). *The leadership challenge.* San Francisco: Jossey-Bass.

Kridel, C., Bullough, R., & Shaker, P. (Eds.). (1996). *Teachers and mentors: Profiles of distinguished twentieth-century professors of education.* New York: Garland.

Kronholz, J. (2003, August 19). Trying to close the stubborn learning gap. *The Wall Street Journal,* p. B1–5.

Krupp, S. (1961). *Pattern in organization analysis.* New York: Holt, Rinehart & Winston.

Kuhn, T. (1996). *The structure of scientific revolutions.* Chicago: University of Chicago Press.

Kytle, C. (1982). *Gandhi, solider of nonviolence.* Cabin John, MD: Seven Locks Press.

Labaree, D. (1988). *The making of an American high school.* New Haven, CT: University Press.

Lacan, J. (1977). *Ecrits.* New York: Norton.

Ladson-Billings, G., & Tate, W. (1995). Toward a critical race theory of education. *Teachers College Record, 97,* 47–68.

Lakatos, I. (1999). *The methodology of scientific research programmes.* Cambridge, UK: Cambridge University Press.

Lakoff, G., & Johnson, M. (1980). *Metaphors we live by.* Chicago: University of Chicago Press.

Lakomski, G. (2005). *Managing without leadership: Towards a theory of organizational functioning.* Amsterdam: Elsevier.

Lanker, B. (1989). *I dream a world: Portraits of Black women who changed America.* New York: Stewart, Tabori & Chang.

Larsen, S., & Larsen, R. (1991). *A fire in the mind: The life of Joseph Campbell.* New York: Doubleday.

Larson, C., & Murtadha, K. (2002). Leadership for social justice: In J. Murphy (Ed.), *The educational leadership challenge: Redefining leadership for the 21st century* (pp. 134–161). Chicago: University of Chicago Press.

Larson, K. (2004). *Bound for the promised land: Harriet Tubman portrait of an American hero.* New York: Ballantine.

Larue, G. (1975). *Ancient myth and modern man.* Englewood Cliffs, NJ: Prentice Hall.

Lash, J. (1980). *Helen teacher: The story of Helen Keller and Anne Sullivan Macy.* New York: Delacorte Press.

Lawrence-Lightfoot, S. (1983). *The good high school: Portraits of character and culture.* New York: Basic Books.

Lawrence-Lightfoot, S., & Hoffman Davis, J. (1997). *The art and science of portraiture.* San Francisco: Jossey-Bass.

LeFanu, J. (1999). *The rise and fall of modern medicine.* New York: Carroll & Graf Publishers.

Lefkovitz, L. (1989). Creating the world: Structuralism and semiotics. In G. Douglas Atkins & L. Morrow (Eds.), *Contemporary literary theory.* Amherst: University of Massachusetts Press.

Leidecker, K. (1946). *Yankee teacher: The life of William Torrey Harris.* New York: The Philosophical Library.

Levy, J. (1975). *Cesar Chavez: Autobiography of la causa.* New York: Norton.

Lewis, C. (1929). *Mind and the world order.* New York: Dover.

Lieberman, D. (2001, November 19). Author: Data on successful firms 'faked' but still valid. *USA Today,* p. A.1.

Likert, R. (1961). *New patterns of management.* New York: McGraw-Hill.

Likert, R. (1967). *The human organization: Its management value.* New York: McGraw-Hill.

Linde, C. (2003). Narrative in institutions. In D. Schiffrin, D. Tannen, & H. Hamilton (Eds.), *The handbook of discourse analysis* (pp. 518–536). Malden, MA: Blackwell.

Lindle, J. (2006). Role theory. In F. English (Ed.), *Encyclopedia of educational leadership and administration* (p. 885). Thousand Oaks, CA: Sage.

Lipham, J. (1988). Getzel's models in educational administration. In J. Boyan (Ed.), *Handbook of research on educational administration* (pp. 171–184). New York: Longman.

Lipman-Blumen, J. (2005). *The allure of toxic leaders.* Oxford, UK: Oxford University Press.

Lippitt, G. (1982). *Organizational renewal.* Englewood Cliffs, NJ: Prentice Hall.

Littrell, J., & Foster, W. (1995). The myth of a knowledge base in educational administration. In R. Donmoyer, M. Imber, & J. Scheurich (Eds.), *The knowledge base in educational administration: Multiple perspectives* (pp. 32-46). Albany: State University of New York Press.

Lorber, J. (1996). Reflections on gender, work and leadership. In P. Temes (Ed.), *Teaching leadership: Essays in theory and practice* (pp. 147–162). New York: Peter Lang.

Lord, C. (2003). *The modern prince: What leaders need to know.* New Haven, CT: Yale University Press.

Lucas, S. (1999). *Tracking inequality: Stratification and mobility in American high schools.* New York: Teachers College Press.

Lugg, C. (2003, January). Our straitlaced administrators: The law, lesbian, gay, bisexual, and transgendered educational administrators, and the assimilationist imperative. *Journal of School Leadership, 13*(1), 51–85.

Lyotard, J. (1997). *The postmodern condition: A report on knowledge.* Minneapolis: University of Minnesota Press.

Maier, P. (1997). *American scripture: Making the Declaration of Independence.* New York: Knopf.

Manatt, R. (1995). *When right is wrong: Fundamentalists and the public schools.* Lancaster, PA: Technomic.

Mandel, R. (2003). A question about women and the leadership option. In D. Rhode (Ed.), *The difference "difference" makes* (pp. 66–75). Stanford, CA: Stanford University Press.

Mandela, N. (2006). *A prisoner in the garden.* New York: Penguin.

Mann, M. (2003). *The sources of social power: A history of power from the beginning to A.D. 1760.* Cambridge, UK: Cambridge University Press.

March, J., & Simon, H. (1958). *Organizations.* New York: John Wiley & Sons.

March, J., & Simon, H. (1966). *Organizations.* New York: John Wiley & Sons.

Marshall, C., & McCarthy, M. (2002, September). School leadership reforms: Filtering social justice through dominant discourses. *Journal of School Leadership, 12*(5), 480–502.

Marshall, C., & Oliva, M. (2006). *Leadership for social justice: Making revolutions in education.* Boston: Pearson.

Martin, R. (Ed.). (1991). *Bullfinch's mythology.* New York: HarperCollins.

Massie, J. (1965). Management theory. In J. March (Ed.), *Handbook of organizations* (pp. 387–422). Chicago: Rand McNally.

Massie, R. (2003). *Castles of steel: Britain, Germany and the winning of the great war at sea.* New York: Random House.

Matthews, G. (1965). *Hidatsa syntax.* The Hague, Netherlands: Mouton.

Maxcy, S. (1995) *Democracy, chaos, and the new school order.* Thousand Oaks, CA: Corwin Press.

Maxwell, J. (1998). *The 21 irrefutable laws.* Nashville, TN: Thomas Nelson.

Mayer, H. (1998). *All on fire: William Lloyd Garrison and the abolition of slavery.* New York: St. Martin's Griffin.

Mayo, E. (1945). *The social problems of an industrial civilization.* Boston: Harvard Business School.

McCullough, D. (1986). The unexpected Harry Truman. In W. Zinsser (Ed.), *Extraordinary lives: The art and craft of American biography* (pp. 23–62). Boston: Houghton Mifflin.

McCullough, D. (1992). *Truman.* New York: Simon & Schuster.

McCullough, D. (2001). *John Adams.* New York: Simon & Schuster.

McDonald, K. (1991, August 14). Biologist discovers that survival of common orchid challenges Darwin's natural-selection theory. *The Chronicle of Higher Education,* pp. A6–A8.

McGrayne, S. B. (1993). *Nobel prize women in science.* New York: Birch Lane Press Book.

McGregor, D. (1960). *The human side of enterprise.* New York: McGraw-Hill.

McLaren, P. (1994). *Life in schools.* New York: Longman.

Meier, D. (1995). *The power of their ideas: Lessons for America from a small school in Harlem.* Boston: Beacon.

Messerli, J. (1972). *Horace Mann.* New York: Knopf.

Miller, W. (2002). *Lincoln's virtues: An ethical biography.* New York: Knopf.

Mintzberg, H. (1979). *The structuring of organizations: A synthesis of research.* Englewood Cliffs, NJ: Prentice Hall.

Mintzberg, H. (1983). *Structure in fives: Designing effective organizations.* Englewood Cliffs, NJ: Prentice Hall.

Mises, R. (1956). *Positivism.* New York: George Braziller.

Mohawk, J. (2000). *Utopian legacies: A history of conquest and oppression in the western world.* Santa Fe, NM: Clear Light Publishers.

Montessori, M. (1965). *Spontaneous activity in education.* New York: Schocken.

Morgan, G. (1986). *Images of organizations.* Beverly Hills, CA: Sage.

Murphy, J. (1999). *The quest for a center: Notes on the state of the profession of educational leadership.* Columbia, MO: University Council for Educational Administration.

Murphy, J. (2000). Notes from the cell: A response to English's "interrogation." *Journal of School Leadership, 10*(5), 464–469.

Murphy, J. (2005). Unpacking the foundations of ISLLC standards and addressing concerns in the academic community. *Educational Administration Quarterly, 41*(1), 154–191.

Murphy, J. (2006). *Preparing school leaders: Defining a research and action agenda.* Lanham, MD: Rowman & Littlefield Education and UCEA.

Murphy, J., & Shipman, N. (2002). The interstate school leaders licensure consortium: A standards based approach to strengthening educational leadership. In K. Hessel & J. Holloway (Eds.), *A framework for school leaders: Linking the ISLLC 'standards for school leaders' to practice* (pp. 4–9). Princeton, NJ: Educational Testing Service.

Murphy, J., Yff, J., & Shipman, N. (2000, January-March). Implementation of the interstate school leaders licensure consortium standards. *The International Journal of Leadership in Education, 3*(1), 17–39.

Murtadha, K. (2006). Septima Clark. In F. English (Ed.), *The encyclopedia of educational leadership & administration* (pp. 141–142). Thousand Oaks, CA: Sage.

Murtadha, K., & Larson, C. (1999, April). *Toward a socially critical, womanist, theory of leadership in urban schools.* Paper presented at the annual meeting of the American Education Research Association, Montreal, Canada.

Nadler, D., & Tushman, M. (1988). *Strategic organization design.* Glenview, IL: Scott, Foresman.

National Commission on Excellence in Education. (1983, April). *A nation at risk: The imperative for educational reform.* Washington, DC: U.S. Government Printing Office.

National Policy Board for Educational Administration. (2002). *Instructions to implement standards for advanced programs in educational leadership.* Arlington, VA: Author.

National Research Council. (2002). *Scientific research in education.* Washington, DC: National Academy Press.

Nelson Mandela Foundation. (2005). *A prisoner in the garden.* New York: Viking.

Nelson, S. (2006). Satisficing theory. In F. English (Ed.), *The encyclopedia of educational leadership and administration* (p. 897). Thousand Oaks, CA: Sage.

Nelson, V. (2005, July 14). Arthur Fletcher, 80; Former federal official known as father of affirmative action. Obituary. *Los Angeles Times,* p. B9.

Nesbit, R. (1970). *History of the idea of progress.* New York: Basic Books.

Numbers, R. (1992). *The creationists: The evolution of scientific creationism.* Berkeley: University of California Press.

O'Boyle, T. (1998). *At any cost: Jack Welch, General Electric, and the pursuit of profit.* New York: Vintage.

Ogawa, R. (2005). Leadership as social construct: The expression of human agency within organizational constraint. In F. English (Ed.), *The Sage handbook of educational leadership* (pp. 89–108). Thousand Oaks, CA: Sage.

Ogawa, R., & Bossert, S. (1995). Leadership as an organizational quality. *Educational Administration Quarterly, 31*(2), 224–243.

Omi, M., & Winant, H. (2005). The theoretical status of the concept of race. In C. McCarthy, W. Crichlow, G. Dimitriadis, & N. Dolby (Eds.), *Race, identity, and representation in education.* (2nd ed., pp. 3–12). New York: Routledge.

Ortiz, F. (2001, February). Using social capital in interpreting the careers of three Latina superintendents. *Educational Administration Quarterly, 37*(1), 58–85.

O'Shea, J., & Madigan, C. (1997). *Dangerous company: Management consultants and the businesses they save and ruin.* New York: Penguin.

Palmer, F. (1986). *Semantics.* Cambridge, UK: Cambridge University Press.

Parks, R., with Haskins, J. (1992). *My story.* New York: Dial Books.

Parsons, T. (1951). *The social system.* Glencoe, IL: Free Press.

Partridge, E. (2002). *A dictionary of slang and unconventional English* (P. Beale, Ed.). New York: Routledge.

Pascal, C., & Ribbins, P. (1998). *Understanding primary headteachers.* London: Cassell.

Peirce, C. (1934-1948). *Collected papers* (4 vols.). Cambridge, MA: Harvard University Press

Peirce, C. (1955). *Philosophical writings of Peirce.* New York: Dover Publications.

Perrow, C. (1986). *Complex organizations.* New York: Random House.

Peters, T., & Waterman, R. (1982). *In search of excellence: Lessons from America's best-run companies.* New York: Harper & Row.

Petit, C. (2005, July). Report from the red planet. *National Geographic, 208*(1), 58–77.

Phillips, D. (1987). *Philosophy, science, and social inquiry.* Oxford, UK: Pergamon Press.

Pitts, G. (2002, September 23). Ex-military officer fighting new battle. *The Globe and Mail,* p. B3.

Popkewitz, T., Tabachnick, B., & Wehlage, G. (1982). *The myth of educational reform: A study of school responses to a program of change.* Madison: University of Wisconsin Press.

Popper, K. (1965). *Conjectures and refutations. The growth of scientific knowledge.* New York: Harper & Row.

Popper, K. (1968). *The logic of scientific discovery.* New York: Harper & Row.

Popper, K. (1979). *Objective knowledge.* Oxford, UK: Clarendon Press.

Popper, K. (1988). *The open universe.* London: Routledge.

Portin, B. (2003). *A practical look at school leadership.* Retrieved November, 2003, from http:// www.crpe.org

Presthus, R. (1962). *The organizational society: An analysis and a theory.* New York: Vintage Books, Inc.

Pu Yi, A-G. (1983). *From emperor to citizen: The autobiography of Aisin-Gioro Pu Yi.* Peking: Foreign Language Press.

Quine, W. (1974). *The roots of reference.* LaSalle, IL: Open Court.

Quine, W. (1980). *From a logical point of view.* Cambridge, MA: Harvard University Press.

Quine, W. (1986). *Philosophy of logic.* Cambridge, MA: Harvard University Press.

Radcliffe-Brown, A. (1933). *The andaman islanders.* London: Cambridge University Press.

Ramsey, F. (1931). *The foundations of mathematics.* London: Routledge & Kegan Paul.

Rapaport, H. (1989). *Heidegger and Derrida.* Lincoln: University of Nebraska Press.

Ratti, O., & Westbrook, A. (1999). *Secrets of the samurai: The martial arts of feudal Japan.* Edison, NJ: Castle Books.

Reilly, P. (1995). *A God who looks like me: Discovering a woman-affirming spirituality.* New York: Ballantine.

Rhode, D. (2003). The difference "difference" makes. In D. Rhode (Ed.), *The difference "difference" makes* (pp. 3–50). Stanford, CA: Stanford University Press.

Ribbins, P. (1997). *Leaders and leadership in the school, colleges and university.* London: Cassell.

Ribbins, P. (2000, April). *Researching leaders, leading and leadership: Towards a three level qualitative model for the study of headteachers.* Paper presented at the American Education Research Association, New Orleans, LA.

Ribbins, P. (2003). Biography and the study of school leader careers: Towards a humanistic approach. In M. Brundrett, N. N. Burton, & R. Smith (Eds.), *Leadership in education* (pp. 55–74). Thousand Oaks, CA: Sage.

Ribbins, P., & Marland, M. (1994). *Headship matters: Conversations with seven secondary school headteachers.* London: Longman.

Ribbins, P., & Sherratt, B. (1997). *Radical educational policies and conservative secretaries of state.* London: Cassell.

Ridpath, J. (1874). *History of the United States, prepared especially for schools.* Cincinnati, OH: Jones Brothers & Company.

Roethlisberger, F. (1941). *Management and morale.* Cambridge, MA: Harvard University Press.

Roethlisberger, F., & Dickson, W. (1939). *Management and the workers.* Cambridge, MA: Harvard University Press.

Ross, G., & Francks, R. (1996). Descartes, Spinoza and Leibniz. In N. Bunnin & E.P. Tsui-James (Eds.), *The Blackwell companion to philosophy* (pp. 509–529). Oxford, UK: Blackwell.

Rost, J. (1991). *Leadership for the twenty-first century.* New York: Praeger.

Runes, D. (1984). Scientific empiricism; unity of science movement. In D. Runes, *Dictionary of philosophy* (pp. 302–303). Totowa, NJ: Rowman & Allanheld.

Rusch, E. (2006). Mary Parker Follett. In F. English (Ed.), *Encyclopedia of educational leadership and administration* (pp. 401–403). Thousand Oaks, CA: Sage.

Ruse, M. (1979). *The Darwinian revolution.* Chicago: University of Chicago Press.

Russell, B. (1908). Mathematical logic as based on the theory of types. *American Journal of Mathematics, 30,* 222–262.

Russell, B. (1955). *History of western philosophy and its connection with political and social circumstances from the earliest times to the present day.* London: Allen & Unwin.

Russell, M. (2003, April). Leadership and followership as a relational process. *Educational Management & Administration. 31*(2) 145–157.

Safire, W. (1996). *Lend me your ears: Great speeches in history.* New York: Norton.

Samier, E. (2002, January). Weber on education and its administration: Prospects for leadership in a rationalized world. *Educational Management & Administration, 30*(1), 27–46.

Samier, E. (2005a). Toward a Weberian public administration: The infinite web of history, values, and authority in administrative mentalities. *Halduskultuur: Administrative Culture, 6,* 60–93.

Samier, E. (2005b).Toward public administration as a humanities discipline: A humanistic manifesto. *Halduskultuur: Administrative Culture, 6,* 6–59.

Sapon-Shevin, M. (1994). *Playing favorites: Gifted education and the disruption of community.* Albany: State University of New York Press.

Scheurich, J. (1995). The knowledge base in educational administration: Postpositivist reflections. In R. Donmoyer, M. Imber, & J. Scheurich (Eds.), *The knowledge base in educational administration: Multiple perspectives* (pp. 17–31). Albany: State University of New York Press.

Schiff, K. (2005). *Lighting the Way: Nine women who changed modern America.* New York: Hyperion.

Schlosser, E. (2001). *Fast food nation.* Boston: Houghton Mifflin.

Sears, J. (1950). *The nature of the administrative process.* New York: McGraw-Hill.

Sears, S. (1983). *Landscape turned red.* New Haven, CT: Ticknor & Fields.

Sedlak, M., Wheeler, C., Pullin, D. , & Cusick, P. (1986). *Selling students short: Classroom bargains and academic reform in the American high school.* New York: Teachers College Press.

Seidel, K. (2002, Spring). Pro(fessionalism) and Con(tenuous improvement): NCATE and standards in educational administration programs. *UCEA Review, 43*(2), 9–10.

Senge, P. (1990). *The fifth discipline: The art and practice of the learning organization.* New York: Doubleday

Sergiovanni, T. (1992). *Moral leadership: Getting to the heart of school improvement.* San Francisco: Jossey-Bass.

Sergiovanni, T. (1996). *Leadership for the schoolhouse.* San Francisco: Jossey-Bass.

Sergiovanni, T. (2000). *The lifeworld of leadership.* San Francisco: Jossey-Bass.

Seyffert, O. (1995). *The dictionary of classical mythology, religion, literature, and art.* New York: Portland House.

Shapiro, A. (2006a). Leadership, social dimensions of. In F. English (Ed.), *Encyclopedia of educational leadership and administration* (pp. 574–581). Thousand Oaks, CA: Sage.

Shapiro, A. (2006b). Chester Barnard. In F. English (Ed.), *Encyclopedia of educational leadership and administration* (pp. 68–69). Thousand Oaks, CA: Sage.

Shavelson, R., & Towne, L. (2003). *Scientific research in education.* Washington, DC: National Academy Press.

Shewart, W. (1986). *Statistical method from the viewpoint of quality control.* New York: Dover.

Shields, C. (2004, February). Dialogic leadership for social justice: Overcoming pathologies of silence. *Educational Administration Quarterly, 40*(1), 109–132. Thousand Oaks, CA: Sage.

Shipman, N. J. (2006). Licensure and certification. In F. English (Ed.), *Encyclopedia of educational leadership and administration* (pp. 614–615). Thousand Oaks, CA: Sage.

Silver, P. (1983). *Educational administration: Theoretical perspectives on practice and research.* New York: Harper & Row.

Simon, H. (1945). *Administrative behavior.* New York: Free Press.

Simonton, D. (1994). *Greatness: Who makes history and why.* New York: Guilford.

Simpson, C. (2001, March 23). 'Crouching tiger': The rebirth of myth. *The Chronicle of Higher Education,* p. B19.

Skidmore, M. S. (2006). Theory x, theory y. In F. English (Ed.), *Encyclopedia of educational leadership and administration* (pp. 1018–1019). Thousand Oaks, CA: Sage.

Skowronek, S. (1997). *The politics presidents make: Leadership from John Adams to Bill Clinton.* Cambridge, MA: Harvard University Press.

Smith, D. (1998). Faith, reason, and charisma: Rudolf Sohm, Max Weber, and the theology of grace. *Sociological Inquiry, 68*(1), 32–60.

Smith, G., & Smith, J. (1994). *Lives in education.* New York: St. Martin's Press. Smith, L., Kleine, P., Prunty, J., & Dwyer, D. (1986). *Educational innovators: Then and now.* London: Falmer.

Smith, L., & Smith, J. (1994). *Lives in education: A narrative of people and ideas.* New York: St. Martin's Press.

Smith, M., Miller-Kahn, L., Heinecke, W., & Jarvis, P. (2004). *Political spectacle and the fate of American schools.* New York: Routledge Falmer.

Smylie, M., Conley, S., & Marks, H. (2002). Building leadership into the roles of teachers. In J. Murphy (Ed.), *The educational leadership challenge: Redefining leadership for the 21st century* (pp. 162–188). Chicago: University of Chicago Press.

Snider, J. (2006, January 11). The superintendent as scapegoat. *Education Week,* 31, 40.

Southern Regional Education Board. (2006). *Schools can't wait: Accelerating the redesign of university principal preparation programs.* Atlanta, GA: SREB.

Spady, W. (2007, January 10). The paradigm trap. *Education Week, 26*(18), 27, 29.

Spencer, H. (1860). *Education.* New York: D. Appleton and Company.

Spillane, J., Halvorson, R., & Diamond, J. (2001). Investigating school leadership practice. *Educational Researcher, 30,* 23-28.

Spillane, J., & Louis, K. (2002). School improvement processes and practices: Professional learning for building instructional capacity. In J. Murphy (Ed.), *The educational leadership challenge: Redefining leadership for the 21st century* (pp. 83–104). Chicago: University of Chicago Press.

Spring, J. (1986). *The American school 1642–1985.* New York: Longman.

Stanton-Salazar, R. (1997, Spring). A social capital framework for understanding the socialization of racial minority children and youths. *Harvard Educational Review, 67,* 1–40.

Starratt, R. (1993). *The drama of leadership.* London: Falmer.

Sternberg, R. (2005, October-December). A model of educational leadership: Wisdom, intelligence, and creativity, synthesized. *International Journal of Leadership in Education: Theory and Practice, 8*(4), 347–364.

Strachey, J. (1961), Editor's note. Eine Kindheitserinnerung des Leonardo da Vinci. In S. Freud (Ed.), *Leonardo da Vinci and a memory of his childhood* (p. xxiii). New York: Norton.

Strauss, L. (2001). *On Plato's symposium.* Chicago: University of Chicago Press.

Stuart, J. (1987). *To teach, to love.* Ashland, KY: Jesse Stuart Foundation.

Tarski, A. (1956). *Logic, semantics, and metamathematics.* Oxford, UK: University Press.

Tatsuoka, M., & Silver, P. (1988). Quantitative research methods in educational administration. In N. Boyan (Ed.), *Handbook of research on educational administration* (pp. 677–702). New York: Longman.

Taylor, F. (1967). *The principles of scientific management.* New York: Norton.

Thompson, J. (1958). Modern approaches to theory in administration. In A. Halpin (Ed.), *Administrative theory in education* (pp. 20–39). New York: Macmillan.

Thompson, J. (1967). *Organizations in action: Social science bases of administrative theory.* New York: McGraw-Hill.

Tierney, W. (1997). *Academic outlaws: Queer theory and cultural studies in the academy.* Thousand Oaks, CA: Sage.

Tomlinson, H., Gunter, H., & Smith, P. (Eds.). (1999). *Living headship: Voices, values and visions.* London: Paul Chapman.

Tonn, J. (2003). *Mary Parker Follett: Creating democracy, transforming management.* New Haven, CT: Yale University Press.

Trier, J. (2003, Spring). School film 'videocompilations' as pedagogical texts in preservice education. *Journal of Curriculum Theorizing, 10,* 125–147.

Tschanz, D. (1992, January-February). The fate of the wounded in the American civil war. *Command, 14,* 34–7.

Turnbull, S. (1996). *Samurai warfare.* London: Wellington House.

Tyack, D. (1974). *The one best system: A history of American urban education.* Cambridge, MA: Harvard University Press.

Tyack, D. (1975). *The one best system: A history of American urban education.* Cambridge, MA: Harvard University Press.

Urwick, L. (1943). *The elements of administration.* New York: Harper & Row.

Usher, R., & Edwards, R. (1996). *Postmodernism and education.* London: Routledge.

Villalpando, O. (2006). Critical race theory. In F. English (Ed.), *Encyclopedia of educational leadership and administration* (pp. 236–237). Thousand Oaks, CA: Sage.

Walker, B. (1983). *The woman's encyclopedia of myths and secrets.* San Francisco: HarperCollins.

Watson, J. (1996). *The double helix: A personal account of the discovery of the structure of the DNA.* New York: Simon & Schuster.

Weber, M. (1968a). *On charisma and institution building.* Chicago: University of Chicago Press.

Weber, M. (1968b). *Economy and society: An outline of the interpretive sociology.* Berkeley: University of California Press.

Weber, M. (1991). *The sociology of religion.* Boston: Beacon.

Weinberg, A., & Weinberg, L. (1980). *Clarence Darrow: A sentimental rebel.* New York: G. P. Putnam's Sons.

Wells, I. (1970). *Crusade for justice.* Chicago: University of Chicago Press.

West, C. (1999). *The Cornell West reader.* New York: Perseus Books Group.

What's news world wide. (2003, April 17). *The Wall Street Journal,* p. A1.

Wheeler, S. (1999). De-construction. In R. Audi (Ed.), *The Cambridge dictionary of philosophy* (2nd ed., pp. 209–210). Cambridge, UK: Cambridge University Press.

White, A. (1955). *A history of the warfare of science with theology in Christendom* (Vol. 2). New York: Braziller.

White, R. (2002). *Lincoln's greatest speech: The second inaugural address.* New York: Simon & Schuster.

White, R. (2005). *The eloquent president.* New York: Random House.

Whorf, B. (1956). *Language, thought and reality: Selected writings of Benjamin Lee Whorf.* Cambridge: MIT Press.

Wiens, J. (2006). Educational leadership as civic humanism. In P. Kelleher & R. van der Bogert (Eds.), *Voices for democracy: Struggles and celebrations of transformational leaders* (pp. 199–225). Malden, MA: Blackwell.

Williams, F., Ricciardi, D., & Blackbourn, R. (2006). Leadership, theories of. In F. English (Ed.), *Encyclopedia of educational leadership and administration* (pp. 586–592). Thousand Oaks, CA: Sage.

Willower, D., & Licata, J. (1997). *Values and valuation in the practice of educational administration.* Thousand Oaks, CA: Corwin Press.

Wills, G. (1992). *Lincoln at Gettysburg: The words that remade America.* New York: Simon & Schuster.

Wills, G. (1994). *Certain trumpets: The nature of leadership.* New York: Simon & Schuster.

Winetrout, K. (1996). Boyd H. Bode: The professor and social responsibility. In C. Kridel, R. Bullough, Jr., & P. Shaker (Eds.), *Teachers and mentors: Profiles of distinguished twentieth-century professors of education* (pp. 71–79). New York: Garland.

Wise, A. (1979). *Legislated learning: The bureaucratization of the American classroom.* Berkeley: University of California Press.

Wittgenstein, L. (1961). *Tractatus Logico-Philosophicus.* London: Routledge & Kegan Paul.

Wolcott, H. (1973). *The man in the principal's office: An ethnography.* Prospect Heights, IL: Waveland.

Wollstonecraft, M. (1989). *A vindication of the rights of women.* New York: Prometheus Books.

Women barred from reading Torah at wall. (2003, April 7). *USA Today,* p. 7A.

Woodcock, G. (1971). *Mohandas Gandhi.* New York: Viking.

Yoshikawa, E. (1995). *Musashi* (C. S. Terry, Trans.). Tokyo: Kodansha International.

Young, M., & Lopez, G. (2005). The nature of inquiry in educational leadership. In F. English (Ed.), *The Sage handbook of educational leadership* (pp. 337–361). Thousand Oaks, CA: Sage.

Zaleznik, A. (1966). *Human dilemmas of leadership.* New York: Harper & Row.

Index

About the Author

Fenwick W. English is the R. Wendell Eaves Senior Distinguished Professor of Educational Leadership at the University of North Carolina at Chapel Hill. He has been both a practitioner and a professor and served in leadership positions in kindergarten through 12th-grade education and higher education. Dr. English served as a middle school principal in California, a project director in Arizona, an assistant superintendent in Florida, and a superintendent of schools in New York. In higher education, he has served as a department chair, program coordinator, dean, and vice-chancellor of academic affairs. Not only has he written about leadership in education, but he has been an educational leader in the public and private sectors. He was the elementary/secondary education practice director for KPMG Peat Marwick in the firm's Washington, DC, office for 3 years. Dr. English also was an associate director of the American Association of School Administrators (the AASA). He is the author or co-author of over 20 books in education, and served as the general editor of the 2005 *Sage Handbook of Educational Leadership* and the 2006 *Encyclopedia of Educational Leadership and Administration*. He has been a symposium presenter at Divisions A&L of the American Education Research Association and served as president of the University Council for Educational Administration from 2006 to 2007.